Costa Rican Spanish

The

Costa Rican Spanish phrasebook
2nd edition – September 2006

Published by
Lonely Planet Publications Pty Ltd ABN 36 005 607 983
90 Maribyrnong St, Footscray, Victoria 3011, Australia

Lonely Planet Offices
Australia Locked Bag 1, Footscray, Victoria 3011
USA 150 Linden St, Oakland CA 94607
UK 72-82 Rosebery Ave, London, EC1R 4RW

Cover illustration
Volando con los pajaritos by Nathan Davis

ISBN 1 74059 119 4

10 9 8 7 6 5 4 3 2

Printed through Colorcraft Ltd, Hong Kong
Printed in China

acknowledgments

Editor Francesca Coles would like to acknowledge the following people for their contributions to this phrasebook:

Thomas Kohnstamm for the translations and for his cooperation throughout the project.

Born and raised in Seattle, Thomas has an MA from Stanford and works as a freelance writer. He first worked as a guide in Costa Rica over a decade ago and now splits his time between Seattle and Latin America. He has been a contributing author to a number of Lonely Planet guidebooks to Latin America and the Caribbean.

Thomas has also authored the first edition of Lonely Planet's Costa Rican Spanish phrasebook and recognises the contribution of the late Sally Steward for having faith in the title and for making it a reality. He also wishes to thank Francesca Coles, Adriana Troyo, Yens Jimenez-Stellar, Karin Vidstrup Monk, Ben Handicott, Branislava Vladisavljevic and Jodie Martire, without whom this second edition wouldn't have been possible. Also thanks to JCK, Dr Miguel and Juanito Azucar.

The editor dedicates her work on this book to the memory of her father, Gervase Coles, diplomat, refugee lawyer and fond father (1936–2005).

Lonely Planet Language Products

Publishing Manager: Chris Rennie
Commissioning Editors: Karin Vidstrup Monk & Ben Handicott
Cartographer: Wayne Murphy
Editors: Francesca Coles & Branislava Vladisavljevic
Assisting Editors: Jodie Martire & Vanessa Battersby
Layout Designer: Michael Ruff

Managing Editor: Annelies Mertens
Managing Layout Designer: Celia Wood
Layout Manager: Adriana Mammarella
Series Designer: Yukiyoshi Kamimura
Production Manager: Jennifer Bilos

make the most of this phrasebook ...

Anyone can speak another language! It's all about confidence. Don't worry if you can't remember your school language lessons or if you've never learnt a language before. Even if you learn the very basics (on the inside covers of this book), your travel experience will be the better for it. You have nothing to lose and everything to gain when the locals hear you making an effort.

finding things in this book

For easy navigation, this book is in sections. The Tools chapters are the ones you'll thumb through time and again. The Practical section covers basic travel situations like catching transport and finding a bed. The Social section gives you conversational phrases, pick-up lines, the ability to express opinions – so you can get to know people. Food has a section all of its own: gourmets and vegetarians are covered and local dishes feature. Safe Travel equips you with health and police phrases, just in case. Remember the colours of each section and you'll find everything easily; or use the comprehensive Index. Otherwise, check the two-way traveller's Dictionary for the word you need.

being understood

Throughout this book you'll see coloured phrases on each page. They're phonetic guides to help you pronounce the language. You don't even need to look at the language itself, but you'll get used to the way we've represented particular sounds. The pronunciation chapter in Tools will explain more, but you can feel confident that if you read the coloured phrase slowly, you'll be understood.

communication tips

Body language, ways of doing things, sense of humour – all have a role to play in every culture. 'Local talk' boxes show you common ways of saying things, or everyday language to drop into conversation. 'Listen for ...' boxes supply the phrases you may hear. They start with the language (so local people can point out what they want to say to you) and then lead in to the pronunciation guide and the English translation.

food 153

safe travel 179

dictionaries 195

index 247

finder 253

costa rican spanish

official language

For more details, see the **introduction**.

Costa Rican Spanish lounges under the beach umbrella of Latin American Spanish – the term given to the many varieties of Spanish that have evolved in the Americas after the Spanish conquests in the 16th century. The language that originally emerged as one of the branches of vulgar Latin successfully took root and spread in the New World and now has official status in 20 countries of Latin America.

Not only did the Spanish language successfully transplant itself, it also hybridised with the indigenous languages and became a colourful array of different varieties of Spanish. Among them, Costa Rican stands out as a unique linguistic entity with its own intriguing quirks of both grammar and vocabulary.

The main grammatical peculiarity is *voseo* vo·se·o – the use of *vos* (meaning 'you') as the second-person singular pronoun, which is considered an archaism in Spain. This is a feature that Costa Rican shares with varieties of Spanish found in other Latin American countries, particularly Argentina, Uruguay, Paraguay, Guatemala, Honduras, Nicaragua and El Salvador. In vocabulary, the abundance of diminutives formed by adding -*tico* ·tee·ko and -*tica* ·tee·ka to the ends of masculine and feminine words respectively – a cutesy way of saying 'small' or expressing affection – has earned Costa Ricans the nickname *Ticos*.

Perhaps what gives Costa Rican Spanish its most distinctive flavour is the rich store of slang expressions commonly known as *tiquismos* tee·*kees*·mos.

at a glance ...

language name:
Costa Rican Spanish

name in language:
español (costarricense) es·pa·*nyol* (kos·ta·ree·*sen*·se), *castellano* kas·te·*ya*·no

language family: Romance

approximate number of speakers: over 3 million

close relatives:
Castilian Spanish, Latin American Spanish, Italian, French, Portuguese

introduction

This phrasebook contains many of these unique turns of phrase to get you talking like a Tico or a Tica and blending in with the crowd. Take it with you and you'll learn exactly why the expression *pura vida* poo·ra vee·da embodies the friendly, unhurried approach to life in Costa Rica. You'll also learn a lot about other key elements of Costa Rican culture expressed in the language.

Though it's a distinct variety of Spanish, Costa Rican does share many similarities with its Latin American siblings which set it apart from the mother language, Castilian Spanish. Costa Rican was influenced by the southern Spanish dialect of Andalucia, from where the first Spanish conquistadors sailed to the New World. The most noticeable trait that sets Costa Rican pronunciation apart from Castilian Spanish is common for the entire continent – *seseo* se·se·o, or the absence of the lisping consonants *c* and *z*, as in *cerveza* ser·ve·sa (beer).

By learning some Costa Rican Spanish, you're opening the door to a world of over 350 million speakers – and be reassured, while it's a distinct variety with its own beautiful individualities, Costa Rican Spanish will be understood by speakers all over Latin America – and even in Spain.

This book gives you the practical phrases you need to get by, as well as the fun, social phrases that lead to a better understanding of Costa Rica and its people. It will also ensure that you can pronounce them like a true *Tico* or *Tica*. To help you get the most out of your travels in beautiful Costa Rica with its many natural wonders, this phrasebook also provides you with an ecotourism section listing the names of flora, fauna and natural features in both Spanish and English.

The contacts you make through speaking Costa Rican Spanish will make your travel experience unique. Local knowledge, new relationships and a sense of satisfaction are on the tip of your tongue – so don't just stand there, say something!

abbreviations used in this book

a	adjective	n	noun
adv	adverb	pl	plural
f	feminine	pol	polite
inf	informal	sg	singular
m	masculine	v	verb

TOOLS > pronunciation

Costa Rican Spanish pronunciation isn't hard, as most of the sounds are also found in English. The best way to learn the correct pronunciation is to listen to the people around you.

Costa Rican Spanish pronunciation differs from the Castilian Spanish spoken in Spain. The most obvious difference is the lack of the lisping 'th' sound. With a little practice you'll soon get the basics and even if you can't roll your *r*'s or hiss out your *j*'s like a Tico or a Tica, your efforts are certain to be rewarded.

vowel sounds

Vowels are generally short and clear. In a number of cases, however, two vowels can be very closely combined (so-called 'diphthongs').

symbol	english equivalent	spanish example	transliteration
a	run	*agua*	*a*·gwa
ai	aisle	*baile*	*bai*·le
ay	say	*seis*	says
e	bed	*edad*	e·*dad*
ee	bee	*idioma, y*	ee·*dyo*·ma, ee
o	not	*ojo*	*o*·kho
oo	good	*uva*	*oo*·va
ow	cow	*autobús*	ow·to·*boos*
oy	boy	*hoy*	oy
ya	yard	*viaje*	*vya*·khe
ye	yes	*tiempo*	*tyem*·po

pronunciation

11

consonant sounds

symbol	english equivalent	spanish example	transliteration
b	big	*barco*	*bar*·ko
ch	chat	*chico*	*chee*·ko
d	dog	*dedo*	*de*·do
f	friend	*falso*	*fal*·so
g	get	*gato*	*ga*·to
k	kick	*cabeza, quitar*	ka·*be*·sa, kee·*tar*
kh	as in the Scottish 'loch' (a harsh, breathy sound from the back of your throat)	*gente, jamón*	*khen*·te, kha·*mon*
l	let	*lado*	*la*·do
m	man	*manto*	*man*·to
n	not	*nada*	*na*·da
ny	canyon	*riñón*	ree·*nyon*
p	pig	*padre*	*pa*·dre
r	right (lightly rolled, but at the start of a word and in words with *rr* strongly rolled)	*pero, roto, carro*	*pe*·ro, *ro*·to, *ka*·ro
s	so	*celos, sábado, zeta*	*se*·los, *sa*·ba·do, *se*·ta
t	top	*tiempo*	*tyem*·po
v	a soft 'b', half way between a 'v' and a 'b'	*vago*	*va*·go
w	wet	*puedo*	*pwe*·do
y	yes	*ya, llamada*	ya, ya·*ma*·da

word stress

Words in Spanish have stress, which means that you emphasise one syllable over another. Rule of thumb: when a word ends in -n, -s or a vowel, the stress falls on the second-last syllable. Otherwise, the last syllable is stressed. If you see an accent mark over a syllable, it cancels out these rules and you just stress that syllable instead. Don't worry if you can't remember these rules – in our coloured pronunciation guides, the stressed syllable is always in italics.

reading & writing

The Spanish alphabet is presented in the following table. For spelling purposes (eg when you need to spell your name to book into a hotel), the pronunciation of each letter is provided. The order shown below is used in the **culinary reader** and the **costa rican spanish–english dictionary**.

spanish alphabet				
A, a a	B, b be *lar*·ga	C, c se	Ch, ch* che	D, d de
E, e e	F, f e·fe	G, g khe	H, h *a*·che	I, i ee
J, j kho·ta	K, k ka	L, l e·le	Ll, ll* *do*·ble e·le	M, m e·me
N, n e·ne	Ñ, ñ e·nye	O, o o	P, p pe	Q, q koo
R, r er	Rr, rr* e·re	S, s e·se	T, t te	U, u oo
V, v be *kor*·ta	W, w *do*·ble be	X, x e·kees	Y, y ee *grye*·ga	Z, z se·ta

* The letters *ch*, *ll* and *rr* are no longer officially considered separate letters, but they're still sounds in their own right.

pronunciation

13

The relationship between Spanish sounds and their spelling is quite straightforward and consistent. The rules given in the table below will help you read any written Costa Rican Spanish that you may come across outside this phrasebook.

letter	pronunciation	example	transliteration
c	before e or i pronounced as an 's'	*cerveza, cinco*	ser·*ve*·sa, *seen*·ko
	before a, o and u pronounced as a 'k'	*carro, corto, cubo*	*ka*·ro, *kor*·to, *koo*·bo
g	before e or i pronounced as the 'ch' in 'loch'	*gente, gigante*	*khen*·te, khee·*gan*·te
	before a, o and u pronounced as the 'g' in 'go'	*gato, gordo, guante*	*ga*·to, *gor*·do, *gwan*·te
gu	pronounced as the 'g' in 'go' (the u is not pronounced unless there are two dots over the u)	*guerra, güiski*	*ge*·ra, *gwees*·kee
h	never pronounced (silent)	*haber, huevo*	a·*ber*, *we*·vo
j	as the 'ch' in 'loch'	*jardín*	khar·*deen*
ll	pronounced as the 'y' in 'yes'	*llave*	*ya*·ve
ñ	pronounced as the 'ny' in 'canyon'	*niño*	*nee*·nyo
qu	pronounced as a 'k' (the u is not pronounced)	*quince*	*keen*·se
z	pronounced as an 's'	*zorro*	*so*·ro

a–z phrasebuilder
construyendo frases

contents

The index below shows which grammatical structures you can use to say what you want. Look under each function – listed in alphabetical order – for information on how to build your own sentences. For example, to tell the taxi driver where your hotel is, look for **giving instructions** and you'll be directed to information on **demonstratives** and **prepositions**. A **glossary** of grammatical terms is included at the end of this chapter to help you.

making statements

naming people/things

negating

pointing things out

possessing

TOOLS

16

adjectives & adverbs

When using an adjective to describe a noun, you need to use the appropriate ending depending on whether the noun is masculine or feminine, and singular or plural (see **gender** and **plurals**). Most adjectives have four forms and the endings are easy to remember:

masculine	sg	*un sombrero blanco* oon som·*bre*·ro *blan*·ko	a white hat
	pl	*unos sombreros blancos* oo·nos som·*bre*·ros *blan*·kos	some white hats
feminine	sg	*una camisa blanca* oo·na ka·*mee*·sa *blan*·ka	a white shirt
	pl	*unas camisas blancas* oo·nas ka·*mee*·sas *blan*·kas	some white shirts

As you can see above, unlike English adjectives, Spanish adjectives almost always come after the noun. However, 'adjectives' of quantity (such as 'much', 'a lot', 'a little/a few', 'too much'), numbers, and words expressing possession ('my' and 'your') always precede the noun.

many cars	*muchos carros* m pl (lit: many cars)	moo·chos *ka*·ros
first class	*primera clase* f sg (lit: first class)	pree·*me*·ra *kla*·se
my passport	*mi pasaporte* m sg (lit: my passport)	mee pa·sa·*por*·te

Adverbs are formed by adding the ending *-mente* to the singular form of an adjective (in the feminine form if there is one). If the adjective has an accent marked in writing, the stress remains on that syllable with the additional stress in pronunciation on *-mente*. Adverbs generally follow the verb they modify.

a–z phrasebuilder

She has a fantastic voice.
> *Ella tiene una voz*
> *fantástica.*
> (lit: she has a voice fantastic)

e·ya tye·ne oo·na vos
fan·tas·tee·ka

She sings fantastically.
> *Ella canta*
> *fantásticamente.*
> (lit: she sings fantastically)

e·ya kan·ta
fan·tas·tee·ka·men·te

articles

describing people/things • naming people/things • pointing things out

The articles *el* and *la* both mean 'the'. Whether you use *el* or *la* depends on the gender of the noun talked about, which in Spanish will always be either masculine or feminine. *El* is used with masculine nouns while *la* is used with feminine nouns. When talking about plural nouns you use *los* instead of *el* and *las* instead of *la*. See also **gender** and **plurals**.

	singular		**plural**	
masculine	*el carro* el ka·ro	the car	*los carros* los ka·ros	the cars
feminine	*la tienda* la tyen·da	the shop	*las tiendas* las tyen·das	the shops

Spanish also has masculine and feminine articles meaning 'a/an': *un* and *una*. Again, the gender of the noun determines which one you use. *Un* and *una* also have plural forms: *unos* and *unas*, meaning 'some'.

	singular		**plural**	
masculine	*un huevo* oon we·vo	an egg	*unos huevos* oo·nos we·vos	some eggs
feminine	*una tortuga* oo·na tor·too·ga	a turtle	*unas tortugas* oo·nas tor·too·gas	some turtles

be

doing things • making statements • negating

Spanish has two words for the verb 'be' – *ser* and *estar*. These two verbs have slightly different functions which are outlined below:

use *ser* to express	examples	
permanent characteristics of people/things	*Ángel es muy amable.* an·khel es mooy a·ma·ble	Ángel is very nice.
occupations or nationalities	*Pablo es de Costa Rica.* pa·blo es de kos·ta ree·ka	Pablo is from Costa Rica.
the time & location of events	*Son las tres.* son las tres	It's 3 o'clock.
possession	*¿De quién es esta mochila?* de kyen es es·ta mo·chee·la	Whose backpack is this?

use *estar* to express	examples	
temporary characteristics of people/things	*La comida está fría.* la ko·mee·da es·ta free·a	The meal is cold.
the time & location of people/things	*Estamos en San José.* es·ta·mos en san kho·se	We're in San José.
the mood of a person	*Estoy contento/a.* m/f es·toy kon·ten·to/a	I'm happy.

The forms of both verbs are given on the next page.

forms of ser

I	am	yo	yo	soy	soy
you sg inf	are	tú/vos *	too/vos	eres/sos *	e·res/sos
you sg pol	are	usted	oos·ted	es	es
he/she	is	él/ella	el/e·ya	es	es
we	are	nosotros/ as m/f	no·so·tros/ as	somos	so·mos
you pl	are	ustedes	oos·te·des	son	son
they	are	ellos/as m/f	e·yos/as	son	son

forms of estar

I	am	yo	yo	estoy	es·toy
you sg inf	are	tú/vos *	too/vos	estás	es·tas
you sg pol	are	usted	oos·ted	está	es·ta
he/she	is	él/ella	el/e·ya	está	es·ta
we	are	nosotros/ as m/f	no·so·tros/ as	estamos	es·ta·mos
you pl	are	ustedes	oos·te·des	estan	es·tan
they	are	ellos/as m/f	e·yos/as	estan	es·tan

TOOLS

* For an explanation on the alternate forms, see **personal pronouns**.

demonstratives

**giving instructions • indicating location •
naming people/things • pointing things out**

To refer to or point at a person or thing, use one of the words
from the table below, depending on whether someone or
something is close (this/these), away from you (that/those) or
even further away in time or distance (that/those over there).

Demonstratives can be used on their own or with a noun.
They go before the noun they accompany and agree in gender
and number with it (see **gender** and **plurals**). They're written
without an accent mark when used with a noun. If they're used
on their own, an accent mark is added in writing.

masculine	singular		plural	
close (this/these)	*éste*	es·te	*éstos*	es·tos
away (that/those)	*ése*	e·se	*ésos*	e·sos
further away (that/those over there)	*aquél*	a·kel	*aquéllos*	a·ke·yos
feminine	singular		plural	
close (this/these)	*ésta*	es·ta	*éstas*	es·tas
away (that/those)	*ésa*	e·sa	*ésas*	e·sas
further away (that/those over there)	*aquélla*	a·ke·ya	*aquéllas*	a·ke·yas

this plant	*esta mata* f sg	es·ta *ma*·ta
	(lit: this plant)	
those animals	*esos animales* m pl	e·sos a·nee·*ma*·les
	(lit: those animals)	

gender

In Spanish, all nouns are either masculine or feminine. The gender of a noun is not really concerned with the sex of something – the word for turtle, *tortuga* tor·*too*·ga, is a feminine noun, even if the animal is male! There's no rule as to why, say, the sun (*el sol* el sol) is masculine but a cloud (*la nube* la *noo*·be) is feminine. The gender is often arbitrary, but here are some handy tips to help you determine gender:

- gender is masculine when talking about a man and feminine when talking about a woman
- words ending in -*o* are usually masculine
- words ending in -*a* are usually feminine
- words ending in -*d*, -*z* or -*ión* are usually feminine

All nouns in the **dictionaries**, the **culinary reader** and the word lists in this phrasebook have their gender marked with the abbreviations m and f for masculine and feminine respectively. For more information, see the box **masculine or feminine?** in **feelings & opinions**, page 115.

Remember that the gender of nouns also determines the endings on any articles, adjectives and demonstratives you use to describe them. See also **articles**, **adjectives & adverbs**, **demonstratives**, **plurals** and **possessives**.

have

The easiest way of expressing possession in Spanish is by using the verb *tener* (have). The present tense forms of this verb are shown in the table on the following page.

I have two brothers.

Tengo dos hermanos.   ten·go dos er·*ma*·nos
(lit: I-have two brothers)

forms of *tener*					
I	have	*yo*	yo	*tengo*	*ten*·go
you sg inf	have	*tú/vos* *	too/vos	*tienes/ tenés* *	*tye*·nes/ te·*nes*
you sg pol	have	*usted*	oos·*ted*	*tiene*	*tye*·ne
he/she	has	*él/ella*	el/e·ya	*tiene*	*tye*·ne
we	have	*nosotros/ as* m/f	no·*so*·tros/ as	*tenemos*	te·*ne*·mos
you pl	have	*ustedes*	oos·*te*·des	*tienen*	*tye*·nen
they	have	*ellos/as* m/f	e·yos/as	*tienen*	*tye*·nen

* For an explanation on the alternate forms, see **personal pronouns**.

Ownership can also be expressed with possessive pronouns – for more information, see **possessives**.

negatives

negating

To make a sentence negative, just add the word *no* (no) before the main verb:

I (don't) live with my family.
  (No) Vivo con mi familia.   (no) *vee*·vo kon mee fa·*mee*·ya
  (lit: (no) I-live with my family)

personal pronouns

making statements • naming people/things

Costa Rican Spanish has three forms for the singular 'you'. The polite form of 'you' singular (*usted*) is used when you're meeting someone for the first time, talking to someone older than you or when you're in a formal situation (eg talking to the police, customs officers etc). When talking to someone familiar to you or younger than you, use the informal forms *tú* or *vos*, rather than the polite form *usted*. *Tú* and *vos* are used more or less interchangeably though *vos* is more common.

All phrases in this book use the form of 'you' that's appropriate for the situation. Where you see the symbols pol (polite) and inf (informal) you're given a choice as either form might be appropriate depending upon the situation. For 'you' plural there's no informal/formal distinction – you just use *ustedes*.

I	yo	yo
you sg inf	tú/vos	too/vos
you sg pol	usted	oos·ted
he	él	el
she	ella	e·ya
it	ello	e·yo
we	nosotros/as m/f	no·so·tros/as
you pl	ustedes	oos·te·des
they	ellos/as m/f	e·yos/as

Personal pronouns are often left out in Spanish because the endings on verbs tell you who is the doer of the action (subject) – you only need to use them if you want to emphasise who or what is doing the action. You may also notice that *tú* verb forms differ slightly from *vos* verb forms – eg *tienes* ('you have' – *tú* form) versus *tenés* ('you have' – *vos* form).

You don't need to worry about this feature of Costa Rican Spanish because all phrases in this book use the appropriate verb forms. If you do want to try your hand at concocting your own phrases, Costa Ricans will understand if you just stick to *tú* rather than trying your hand at the relatively idiosyncratic *vos*. This feature is called *voseo* vo·se·o and is limited to only a few varieties of Central American Spanish and the Spanish spoken in Argentina, Paraguay and Uruguay.

See also **be**, **have**, **verbs** and **word order**.

plurals

describing people/things • naming people/things

In general, if the noun ends in a vowel, you add *-s* for plural. If the noun ends in a consonant, you add *-es*:

singular			plural		
bed	*cama*	ka·ma	beds	*camas*	ka·mas
woman	*mujer*	moo·kher	women	*mujeres*	moo·khe·res

See also **articles**, **adjectives & adverbs**, **demonstratives**, **gender** and **possessives**.

possessives

naming people/things • possessing

There are a number of words for 'my', 'your' etc in Spanish. Choose the correct form according to the gender and number of the noun – ie the thing owned, not the owner.

	with singular noun		with plural noun	
my	*mi*	mee	*mis*	mees
your sg inf	*tu*	too	*tus*	toos
your sg pol	*su*	soo	*sus*	soos
his/her/its	*su*	soo	*sus*	soos
our	*nuestro/a* m/f	nwes·tro/a	*nuestros/as* m/f	nwes·tros/as
your pl	*su*	soo	*sus*	soos
their	*su*	soo	*sus*	soos

Ownership can also be expressed with the word *de* (of) or by using the verb *tener* (have).

This is my friend's tent.
Esta es la carpa de mi   es·ta es la *kar*·pa de mee
amiga.   a·*mee*·ga
(lit: this is the tent of my friend)

We have two dogs.
Tenemos dos perros.   te·*ne*·mos dos *pe*·ros
(lit: we-have two dogs)

See also **gender**, **have** and **plurals**.

prepositions

giving instructions • indicating location

Prepositions are used to show the relationship between words in a sentence, just like in English. They're placed before the word they accompany. These are the most useful ones:

at (place)	*en*	en	on (place)	*en*	en
at (time)	*a*	a	on (time)	*a*	a
for (purpose)	*para*	pa·ra	outside	*fuera de*	fwe·ra de
for (time)	*durante*	doo·*ran*·te	since	*desde*	des·de
from (time)	*desde*	des·de	to (place)	*a*	a
in (place)	*en*	en	until	*hasta*	as·ta
in (time)	*en*	en	with	*con*	kon
inside	*dentro de*	den·tro de	without	*sin*	seen

Let's meet at eight o'clock at the entrance.
Veámonos a las ocho   ve·*a*·mo·nos a las *o*·cho
en la entrada.   en la en·*tra*·da
(lit: let-see-us at the eight at the entrance)

questions

To ask a question, simply make a statement, but raise your intonation towards the end of the sentence, as you would in English. The inverted question mark written at the start of a sentence prompts you to do this.

Do you have a car?
   ¿Tienes un carro?   *tye·nes oon ka·ro*
   (lit: you-have a car)

You can also place the following question words at the beginning of a phrase:

How?	*¿Cómo?*	*ko·mo*
How many?	*¿Cuántos/as?* m/f pl	*kwan·tos/as*
How much?	*¿Cuánto?*	*kwan·to*
What?	*¿Qué?*	ke
When?	*¿Cuándo?*	*kwan·do*
Where?	*¿Dónde?*	*don·de*
Which?	*¿Cuál/Cuáles?* sg/pl	kwal/*kwa·les*
Who?	*¿Quién/Quiénes?* sg/pl	kyen/*kye·nes*
Why?	*¿Por qué?*	por ke

When does the bus arrive?
   ¿Cuándo llega   *kwan·do ye·ga*
   el autobús?   el ow·to·*boos*
   (lit: when arrives the bus)

Where can I buy tickets?
   ¿Dónde puedo   *don·de pwe·do*
   comprar tiquetes?   kom·*prar* tee·*ke*·tes
   (lit: where I-can buy tickets)

It's not impolite to answer questions with a simple *sí* (yes) or *no* (no) in Spanish. Unlike in English, there's no direct way in Spanish to say 'Yes, it is/does', or 'No, it isn't/doesn't'.

requests

A polite and easy way to make a request is by starting with the word ¿Podría …? (equivalent to 'Could you …?') followed by the infinitive (dictionary form) of the main verb:

Please help me.
¿Podría ayudarme?   po·*dree*·a a·yoo·*dar*·me
(lit: could-you help-me)

See also **questions** and **verbs**.

there is/are

To say 'there is/are' in Spanish, use the word hay (lit: it-has). Add no before it to say 'there isn't/aren't'.

Do you have any rooms?
¿Hay habitaciones?   ai a·bee·ta·*syo*·nes
(lit: it-has rooms)

There aren't any.
No hay.   no ai
(lit: no it-has)

See also **negatives**.

verbs

There are three groups of verbs in Spanish – those ending in -ar (eg hablar 'speak'), -er (eg comer 'eat') and -ir (eg vivir 'live'). Tenses are formed by adding different endings for each person to the verb stem (part of the verb that remains after you take off -ar, -er and -ir). These endings vary according to which one of the three groups the verb belongs to. The present tense endings for each person are given in the table below.

present tense						
	hablar		*comer*		*vivir*	
I	-o	-o	-o	-o	-o	-o
you sg inf (*tú*)	-as	-as	-es	-es	-es	-es
you sg inf (*vos*)	-ás	-as	-és	-es	-ís	-ees
you sg pol	-a	-a	-e	-e	-e	-e
he/she	-a	-a	-e	-e	-e	-e
we	-amos	-a·mos	-emos	-e·mos	-imos	-ee·mos
you pl	-an	-an	-en	-en	-en	-en
they	-an	-an	-en	-en	-en	-en

As in any language, some verbs are irregular. The most important ones are *ser* (be), *estar* (be) and *tener* (have). For more details, see **be** and **have**.

word order

asking questions • making statements • negating

Sentences in Spanish have a basic word order of subject–verb–object, just as English does.

I study business.
   Yo estudio comercio.   yo es·*too*·dyo ko·*mer*·syo
   (lit: I study-I business)

However, the subject pronoun is often omitted – 'Estudio comercio' is enough. Generally, you only use a subject pronoun if you wish to emphasise who is the 'doer' of an action. See also **negatives** and **questions**.

glossary

adjective	word that describes something – '**active** volcanoes are widespread'
adverb	word that explains how an action is done – 'jaguars are **rarely** seen'
article	the words 'a', 'an' and 'the'
demonstrative	word that means 'this' or 'that'
direct object	thing or person in the sentence that has the action directed to it – 'national parks protect the **wildlife**'
gender	grouping of *nouns* into classes (like masculine and feminine), requiring other words (eg *adjectives*) to belong to the same class
indirect object	person or thing in the sentence that is the recipient of the action – 'birds are the main attraction for **nature lovers**'
infinitive	dictionary form of a *verb* – 'monkeys are the easiest to **observe** in the wild'
noun	thing, person or idea – 'the **environment**'
number	whether a word is singular or plural – 'there are deadly poisonous **snakes**'
personal pronoun	word that means 'I', 'you', etc
possessive pronoun	word that means 'mine', 'yours', etc
preposition	word like 'for' or 'before' in English
subject	person or thing in the sentence that does the action – '**sea turtles** are dying out'
tense	form of a *verb* that tells you whether the action is in the present, past or future – eg 'eat' (present), 'ate' (past), 'will eat' (future)
verb	word that tells you what action happened – 'ecotourism **is growing**'
verb ending	ending added to the *verb stem* to indicate the *tense* and/or the *subject* in the sentence
verb stem	part of a *verb* which does not change – '**surf**' in '**surf**ing' and '**surf**ed'

Do you speak (English)?
¿Habla (inglés)? · a·bla (een·gles)

Does anyone speak (English)?
¿Alguien habla (inglés)? · al·gyen a·bla (een·gles)

Do you understand (me)?
¿(Me) Entiende? · (me) en·tyen·de

Yes, I understand.
Sí, entiendo. · see en·tyen·do

No, I don't understand.
No, no entiendo. · no no en·tyen·do

talking like a *tico*

If you know any Spanish at all, you're bound to expand your repertoire of slang expressions no end while in Costa Rica. The following colourful turns of phrase are typical Costa Rican slang and colloquialisms (known as *tiquismos* tee·*kees*·mos).

agüevado/a m/f	a·gwe·*va*·do/a	bored/boring
buena nota f	*bwe*·na *no*·ta	all right
chapulín m	cha·poo·*leen*	young thief
chunche m	*choon*·che	thingumajig
guavero/a m/f	gwa·*ve*·ro/a	lucky
macho/a m/f	*ma*·cho/a	blonde person
sabanero m	sa·ba·*ne*·ro	cowboy
salado m	sa·*la*·do	bad luck

For other *tiquismos*, see the box **talking *tiquismos***, page 134.

I speak (English).
Hablo (inglés). a·blo (een·*gles*)

I don't speak (Spanish).
No hablo (español). no a·blo (es·pa·*nyol*)

I speak a little.
Hablo un poquito. a·blo oon po·*kee*·to

I'd like to practise (Spanish).
Quisiera practicar (español). kee·*sye*·ra prak·tee·*kar* (es·pa·*nyol*)

Let's speak (Spanish).
Hablemos (español). a·*ble*·mos (es·pa·*nyol*)

Pardon?
¿Perdón? per·*don*

What does (*pura vida*) mean?
¿Que significa (pura vida)? ke seeg·nee·*fee*·ka (*poo*·ra *vee*·da)

How do you ...?	*¿Cómo ...?*	*ko*·mo ...
pronounce	*se pronuncia*	se pro·*noon*·sya
this	*esto*	*es*·to
write	*se escribe*	se es·*kree*·be
(*pura vida*)	*(pura vida)*	(*poo*·ra *vee*·da)

Could you please ...?	*¿Podría ...?*	po·*dree*·a ...
repeat that	*repetir eso*	re·pe·*teer e*·so
speak more	*hablar más*	a·*blar* mas
slowly	*despacio*	des·*pa*·syo
write it down	*escribirlo*	es·kree·*beer*·lo

---

rev it up

When you see the letter *r* at the beginning of a Spanish word, or when you see a double *rr*, remember to trill the 'r' sound. It's a case of blowing air past your tongue so that it produces a sound like a cat purring. It may help to visualise yourself sitting astride a powerful motorbike revving on the throttle as you do so. Try practising on the word *Costarricense(s)* sg/pl kos·ta·ree·*sen*·se(s), the official name for the Costa Rican people.

cardinal numbers

números cardinales

0	cero	se·ro	6	seis	says
1	uno	oo·no	7	siete	sye·te
2	dos	dos	8	ocho	o·cho
3	tres	tres	9	nueve	nwe·ve
4	cuatro	kwa·tro	10	diez	dyes
5	cinco	seen·ko			

11	once	on·se
12	doce	do·se
13	trece	tre·se
14	catorce	ka·tor·se
15	quince	keen·se
16	dieciséis	dye·see·says
17	diecisiete	dye·see·sye·te
18	dieciocho	dye·see·o·cho
19	diecinueve	dye·see·nwe·ve
20	veinte	vayn·te
21	veintiuno	vayn·tee·oo·no
22	veintidós	vayn·tee·dos
30	treinta	trayn·ta
40	cuarenta	kwa·ren·ta
50	cincuenta	seen·kwen·ta
60	sesenta	se·sen·ta
70	setenta	se·ten·ta
80	ochenta	o·chen·ta
90	noventa	no·ven·ta
100	cien	syen
200	doscientos	do·syen·tos
1000	mil	meel
2000	dos mil	dos meel
1,000,000	un millón	oon mee·yon

ordinal numbers

números ordinales

Ordinal numbers are written with a degree sign – 1st is written '1º', 2nd is '2º', and so on.

1st	*primero/a* m/f	pree·*me*·ro/a
2nd	*segundo/a* m/f	se·*goon*·do/a
3rd	*tercero/a* m/f	ter·*se*·ro/a
4th	*cuarto/a* m/f	*kwar*·to/a
5th	*quinto/a* m/f	*keen*·to/a

fractions

fracciones

a quarter	*un cuarto*	oon *kwar*·to
a third	*un tercio*	oon *ter*·syo
a half	*un medio*	oon *me*·dyo
three-quarters	*tres cuartos*	tres *kwar*·tos
all	*todos/as* m/f pl	*to*·dos/as
none	*ninguno/a* m/f	neen·*goo*·no/a

useful amounts

cantidades útiles

How much?	*¿Cuánto/a?* m/f	*kwan*·to/a
How many?	*¿Cuántos/as?* m/f pl	*kwan*·tos/as
Please give me ...	*Por favor deme ...*	por fa·*vor de*·me ...
(just) a little	*un poquitito*	oon po·kee·*tee*·to
a lot	*mucho/a* m/f	*moo*·cho/a
many	*muchos/as* m/f pl	*moo*·chos/as
some	*unos/as* m/f pl	*oo*·nos/as

For more amounts, see **self-catering**, page 165.

TOOLS

telling the time

Time is expressed by the phrase *Son las …* (It is …) followed by a number. Times past the hour are expressed using *y* (and) while times before the hour take *para* (to). The words *medianoche* me·dya·*no*·che (midnight) and *mediodía* me·dyo·*dee*·a (midday) are used instead of 12am and 12pm.

Costa Ricans refer to a 12-hour clock. The terms 'am' and 'pm', however, are used only in writing. When speaking, time is designated by the part of the day. The day is roughly broken up into four time periods. To specify whether a time is am or pm, just state the hour and link it to the time of the day using the phrase *de la* (lit: of the).

What time is it?	¿Qué hora es?	ke *o*·ra es
It's one o'clock.	Es la una.	es la *oo*·na
It's (ten) o'clock.	Son las (diez).	son las (dyes)
Five past (ten).	(Diez) y cinco.	(dyes) ee *seen*·ko
Quarter past (ten).	(Diez) y cuarto.	(dyes) ee *kwar*·to
Half past (ten).	(Diez) y media.	(dyes) ee *me*·dya
Quarter to (eleven).	Cuarto para las (once).	*kwar*·to *pa*·ra las (*on*·se)

am (dawn)	de la madrugada	de la ma·droo·*ga*·da
am (morning)	de la mañana	de la ma·*nya*·na
pm (afternoon)	de la tarde	de la *tar*·de
pm (evening)	de la noche	de la *no*·che

At what time …?	¿A qué hora …?	a ke *o*·ra …
At (five).	A las (cinco).	a las (*seen*·ko)
At (7.57pm).	A las (siete y cincuenta y siete de la noche).	a las (*sye*·te ee seen·*kwen*·ta ee *sye*·te de la *no*·che)

the calendar

days

Monday	*lunes*	*loo*·nes
Tuesday	*martes*	*mar*·tes
Wednesday	*miércoles*	*myer*·ko·les
Thursday	*jueves*	*hwe*·ves
Friday	*viernes*	*vyer*·nes
Saturday	*sábado*	*sa*·ba·do
Sunday	*domingo*	do·*meen*·go

months

January	*enero*	e·*ne*·ro
February	*febrero*	fe·*bre*·ro
March	*marzo*	*mar*·so
April	*abril*	a·*breel*
May	*mayo*	*ma*·yo
June	*junio*	*khoo*·nyo
July	*julio*	*khoo*·lyo
August	*agosto*	a·*gos*·to
September	*septiembre*	se·*tyem*·bre
October	*octubre*	ok·*too*·bre
November	*noviembre*	no·*vyem*·bre
December	*diciembre*	dee·*syem*·bre

dates

Dates are expressed using cardinal numbers. The exception to this rule is the first day of the month which uses the ordinal number – eg *el primero de octubre* el pree·*me*·ro de ok·*too*·bre (lit: the first of October).

What date is it today?
    ¿Qué fecha es hoy?   ke *fe*·cha es oy

It's (18 October).
    Es (el dieciocho   es (el dye·see·*o*·cho
    de octubre).   de ok·*too*·bre)

seasons

dry season	*estación seca* f	es·ta·*syon se*·ka
wet season	*estación lluviosa* f	es·ta·*syon* yoo·*vyo*·sa
spring	*primavera* f	pree·ma·*ve*·ra
summer	*verano* m	ve·*ra*·no
autumn	*otoño* m	o·*to*·nyo
winter	*invierno* m	een·*vyer*·no

present

el presente

now	*ahora*	a·*o*·ra
today	*hoy*	oy
tonight	*hoy en la noche*	oy en la *no*·che
this morning	*hoy en la mañana*	oy en la ma·*nya*·na
this afternoon	*hoy en la tarde*	oy en la *tar*·de
this week	*esta semana*	*es*·ta se·*ma*·na
this month	*este mes*	*es*·te mes
this year	*este año*	*es*·te *a*·nyo

past

el pasado

yesterday	*ayer*	a·*yer*
day before yesterday	*anteayer*	an·te·a·*yer*
(three days) ago	*hace (tres días)*	*a*·se (tres *dee*·as)
since (May)	*desde (mayo)*	*des*·de (*ma*·yo)
last night	*anoche*	a·*no*·che
last week	*la semana pasada*	la se·*ma*·na pa·*sa*·da
last month	*el mes pasado*	el mes pa·*sa*·do
last year	*el año pasado*	el *a*·nyo pa·*sa*·do

yesterday ...	ayer ...	a·yer ...
morning	en la mañana	en la ma·nya·na
afternoon	en la tarde	en la tar·de
evening	en la noche	en la no·che

future

el futuro

tomorrow	mañana	ma·nya·na
day after tomorrow	pasado mañana	pa·sa·do ma·nya·na
in (two days)	dentro de (dos días)	den·tro de (dos dee·as)
until (June)	hasta (junio)	as·ta (khoo·nyo)
next ...	... entrante	... en·tran·te
week	la semana	la se·ma·na
month	el mes	el mes
year	el año	el a·nyo
tomorrow ...	mañana ...	ma·nya·na ...
morning	en la mañana	en la ma·nya·na
afternoon	en la tarde	en la tar·de
evening	en la noche	en la no·che

during the day

durante el día

afternoon	tarde f	tar·de
dawn	madrugada f	ma·droo·ga·da
day	día m	dee·a
evening	noche f	no·che
midday	mediodía m	me·dyo·dee·a
midnight	medianoche f	me·dya·no·che
morning	mañana f	ma·nya·na
night	noche f	no·che
sunrise	amanecer m	a·ma·ne·ser
sunset	atardecer m	a·tar·de·ser

money
dinero

How much is it?
¿Cuánto es? — kwan·to es

Can you write down the price?
¿Podría escribir el precio? — po·dree·a es·kree·beer el pre·syo

What's the exchange rate?
¿A cómo está el tipo de cambio? — a ko·mo es·ta el tee·po de kam·byo

What's the charge?
¿Cuánto me cobras? — kwan·to me ko·bras

I'd like to ...	Quiero ...	kye·ro ...
cash a cheque	cambiar un cheque	kam·byar oon che·ke
change a travellers cheque	cambiar un cheque de viajero	kam·byar oon che·ke de vya·khe·ro
change money into *colones*	cambiar dinero a colones	kam·byar dee·ne·ro a ko·lo·nes
change money/ dollars	cambiar plata/ dólares	kam·byar pla·ta/ do·la·res
get a cash advance	que me den un adelanto en efectivo	ke me den oon a·de·lan·to en e·fek·tee·vo
withdraw money	sacar plata	sa·kar pla·ta

Do you accept ...?	¿Acepta ...?	a·sep·ta ...
credit cards	tarjetas de crédito	tar·khe·tas de kre·dee·to
debit cards	tarjetas de débito	tar·khe·tas de de·bee·to
travellers cheques	cheques de viajero	che·kes de vya·khe·ro

I'd like …, please.	Quiero …, por favor.	kye·ro … por fa·vor
a receipt	un recibo	oon re·see·bo
a refund	un reintegro	oon re·een·te·gro
my change	mi vuelto	mee vwel·to
to return this	devolver ésto	de·vol·ver es·to

Where's a/an …?	¿Dónde hay …?	don·de ai …
automated teller machine	un cajero automático	oon ka·khe·ro ow·to·ma·tee·ko
foreign exchange office	una casa de cambio	oo·na ka·sa de kam·byo

How much is it per …?	¿Cuánto es por …?	kwan·to es por …
day	día	dee·a
hour	hora	o·ra
night	noche	no·che
person	persona	per·so·na
visit	visita	vee·see·ta

the colour of money

The Costa Rican currency is the *colón* ko·lon, named after the explorer Christopher Columbus (whose name in Spanish is *Cristóbal Colón* krees·to·bal ko·lon). One *colón* comprises 100 *centavos* sen·ta·vos (cents). The plural of *colón* is *colones* ko·lo·nes. In practice though, *pesos* pe·sos – the slang term for money – is often used. In addition, you may come across the following colourful terms for individual notes:

media teja f — me·dya te·kha — 50 *colón* bill
(lit: half tile)

teja f — te·kha — 100 *colón* bill
(lit: tile)

rojo m — ro·kho — 1000 *colón* bill
'red' – refers to the red colour of the bill. Also known as *pargo* par·go 'red snapper' (type of fish).

tucán m — too·kan — 5000 *colón* bill
'toucan' – depicts one of Costa Rica's avian emblems

getting around

para transportarse

Which ... goes to (Quepos)?	¿Cuál ... va para (Quepos)?	kwal ... va pa·ra (ke·pos)
4WD	cuatro por cuatro	kwa·tro por kwa·tro
boat	barco	bar·ko
bus	bus	boos
jeep	jeep	yeep
train	tren	tren

Is this the ... to (Limón)?	Este es el ... que va para (Limón)?	es·te es el ... ke va pa·ra (lee·mon)
boat	barco	bar·ko
bus	bus	boos
train	tren	tren

When's the ... (bus)?	¿A qué hora sale el ... (bus)?	a ke o·ra sa·le el ... (boos)
first	primer	pree·mer
last	último	ool·tee·mo
next	próximo	prok·see·mo

What time does it leave?
¿A qué hora sale?   a ke o·ra sa·le

What time does it get to (San José)?
¿A qué hora llega a (San José)?   a ke o·ra ye·ga a (san kho·se)

How long will it be delayed?
¿Cuánto se va a atrasar?   kwan·to se va a a·tra·sar

Is this seat taken?
   ¿Está ocupado?   es·*ta* o·koo·*pa*·do

That's my seat.
   Este es mi asiento.   es·te es mee a·*syen*·to

Please tell me when we get to (Alajuela).
   Por favor, avíseme cuando   por fa·*vor* a·*vee*·se·me *kwan*·do
   lleguemos a (Alajuela).   ye·*ge*·mos a (a·la·*khwe*·la)

Please stop here.
   Puede parar aquí, por favor.   pwe·de pa·*rar* a·*kee* por fa·*vor*

How long do we stop here?
   ¿Cuánto tiempo vamos   *kwan*·to *tyem*·po *va*·mos
   a parar aquí?   a pa·*rar* a·*kee*

tickets

Transportation in Costa Rica is mainly on cheap and cheerful (and often crowded) buses. Seating on buses isn't divided up into separate classes. The only time you may need to specify which class you wish to travel is on international flights in and out of San José.

Where do I buy a ticket?
   ¿Adónde puedo comprar   a·*don*·de *pwe*·do kom·*prar*
   un pasaje?   oon pa·*sa*·khe

Do I need to book (well in advance)?
   ¿Necesito reservar el   ne·se·*see*·to re·ser·*var* el
   tiquete (muy por   tee·*ke*·te (mooy por
   adelantado)?   a·de·lan·*ta*·do)

A ... ticket	*Un pasaje ...*	oon pa·*sa*·khe ...
(to Monteverde).	*para (Monteverde).*	*pa*·ra (mon·te·*ver*·de)
child's	*para niño*	*pa*·ra *nee*·nyo
one-way	*solo de ida*	*so*·lo de *ee*·da
return	*de ida y vuelta*	de *ee*·da ee *vwel*·ta
student	*de estudiante*	de es·too·*dyan*·te

PRACTICAL

42

I'd like	Quiero un	kye·ro oon
a/an … seat.	asiento en …	a·syen·to en …
aisle	el pasillo	el pa·see·yo
nonsmoking	el área de	el a·re·a de
	no fumado	no foo·ma·do
smoking	el área de	el a·re·a de
	fumado	foo·ma·do
window	la ventana	la ven·ta·na
Is there a …?	¿Tiene …?	tye·ne …
blanket	una cobija	oo·na ko·bee·kha
sick bag	una bolsa para	oo·na bol·sa pa·ra
	vomitar	vo·mee·tar
toilet	un baño	oon ba·nyo

Is there air conditioning?
¿Tiene aire acondicionado? tye·ne ai·re a·kon·dee·syo·na·do

How long does the trip take?
¿Cuánto dura el viaje? kwan·to doo·ra el vya·khe

Is it a direct route?
¿Es un viaje directo? es oon vya·khe dee·rek·to

How much is it?
¿Cuánto cuesta? kwan·to kwes·ta

Can I get a stand-by ticket?
¿Puedo comprar un pwe·do kom·prar oon
tiquete de stand-by? tee·ke·te de sten·bai

What time should I check in?
¿A qué hora debo a ke o·ra de·bo
hacer el chequeo? a·ser el che·ke·o

I'd like to … my	Quisiera … mi	kee·sye·ra … mee
ticket, please.	tiquete, por favor.	tee·ke·te por fa·vor
cancel	cancelar	kan·se·lar
change	cambiar	kam·byar
confirm	confirmar	kon·feer·mar

agente de viajes m&f	a·*khen*·te de vee·*a*·khes	travel agent
atrasado/a m/f	a·tra·*sa*·do/a	delayed
cancelado/a m/f	kan·se·*la*·do/a	cancelled
huelga f	*wel*·ga	strike n
itinerario m	ee·tee·ne·*ra*·ryo	timetable
lleno/a m/f	*ye*·no/a	full
plataforma f	pla·ta·*for*·ma	platform
ventanilla f	ven·ta·*nee*·ya	ticket window

luggage

equipaje

Where's (a/the) ...?	¿Adónde está el ...?	a·*don*·de es·*ta* el ...
baggage claim	reclamo de equipaje	re·*kla*·mo de e·kee·*pa*·khe
left-luggage office	cuarto para guardar equipaje	*kwar*·to *pa*·ra gwar·*dar* e·kee·*pa*·khe
luggage locker	lócker para equipaje	*lo*·ker *pa*·ra e·kee·*pa*·khe
trolley	carrito para equipaje	ka·*ree*·to *pa*·ra e·kee·*pa*·khe

Can I have some coins/tokens?
¿Me puede dar monedas/fichas? — me *pwe*·de dar mo·*ne*·das/*fee*·chas

My luggage has been damaged.
Me dañaron el equipaje. — me da·*nya*·ron el e·kee·*pa*·khe

My luggage has been lost.
Se perdieron mis maletas. — se per·*dye*·ron mees ma·*le*·tas

My luggage has been stolen.
Se robaron mis maletas. — se ro·*ba*·ron mees ma·*le*·tas

That's (not) mine.
Eso (no) es mío. — *e*·so (no) es *mee*·o

plane

Where does flight (CO52) arrive/depart?
¿Adónde llega/sale   a·*don*·de *ye*·ga/*sa*·le
el vuelo (CO52)?   el *vwe*·lo (se o seen·*kwen*·ta dos)

A (1st-class) ticket to (New York).
Un pasaje (en primera   oon pa·*sa*·khe (en pree·*me*·ra
clase) para (Nueva York).   *kla*·se) *pa*·ra (*nwe*·va york)

Where's (the) ...?	*¿Dónde está ...?*	*don*·de es·*ta* ...
airport shuttle	*la buseta del aeropuerto*	la boo·*se*·ta del a·e·ro·*pwer*·to
arrivals hall	*el área de llegadas*	el *a*·re·a de ye·*ga*·das
departures hall	*el área de salidas*	el *a*·re·a de sa·*lee*·das
duty-free shop	*el duty-free*	el *dyoo*·tee·free
gate (7)	*la puerta (siete)*	la *pwer*·ta (*sye*·te)

---

listen for ...

cambio m	*kam*·byo	**transfer**
pasaporte m	pa·sa·*por*·te	**passport**
tiquete de	tee·*ke*·te	**boarding pass**
abordaje m	de a·bor·*da*·khe	
tránsito m	*tran*·see·to	**transit**

---

bus

There are two main types of buses in Costa Rica – *directos* dee·*rek*·tos and *colectivos* ko·lek·*tee*·vos. The term *directos* is a bit of a misnomer because they still stop frequently. Not as frequently, however, as the *colectivos*, which require a Latin American patience to endure. *Buses de turistas* boo·ses de too·*rees*·tas are privately owned and used only for tours.

Is this a bus stop?
¿Esta es una parada de bus?   es·ta es *oo*·na pa·*ra*·da de boos

How often do buses come?
¿Cada cuánto pasa el bus?   *ka*·da *kwan*·to *pa*·sa el boos

Does it stop at (Puerto Viejo)?
¿Hace parada en   *a*·se pa·*ra*·da en
(Puerto Viejo)?   (*pwer*·to *vye*·kho)

What's the next stop?
¿Cuál es la próxima   kwal es la *prok*·see·ma
parada?   pa·*ra*·da

I'd like to get off at (San Pedro).
Quiero bajarme en   *kye*·ro ba·*khar*·me en
(San Pedro).   (san *pe*·dro)

bus station	*estación de buses* f	es·ta·*syon* de *boo*·ses
bus terminal	*terminal de buses* f	ter·mee·*nal* de *boo*·ses
departure bay	*área de salida* m	*a*·re·a de sa·*lee*·da
local bus station	*estación de buses locales* f	es·ta·*syon* de *boo*·ses lo·*ka*·les
minibus	*microbús* m	mee·kro·*boos*
shuttle bus	*buseta* f	boo·*se*·ta
timetable display	*pizarra con itinerario* f	pee·*sa*·ra kon ee·tee·ne·*ra*·ryo

---

listen for ...

equipaje de mano m	e·ke·*pa*·khe de *ma*·no	carry-on baggage
exceso de equipaje m	ek·*se*·so de e·kee·*pa*·khe	excess baggage
ficha f	*fee*·cha	token

Travelling by bus can be a chaotic affair in Costa Rica. In San José there's no central terminal of the kind that you might be used to – just an area called 'the Coca Cola' in honour of a bottling plant that used to occupy the site. Other terminals and offices are scattered all over the city.

Brightly painted timetables on station walls may not have been updated … ever. Always ask at the ticket office about departure times. If there isn't one, try your luck with the women who clean the restrooms. These phrases might help:

Where's the bus terminal?
   ¿Adónde está la   a·*don*·de es·*ta* la
   terminal de buses?   ter·mee·*nal* de *boo*·ses

What time does bus number (five) leave?
   ¿A qué hora sale el   a ke *o*·ra *sa*·le el
   bus número (cinco)?   boos *noo*·me·ro (*seen*·ko)

boat

barco

What's the lake/sea like today?
   ¿Cómo está el lago/   *ko*·mo es·*ta* el *la*·go/
   mar hoy?   mar oy

What island/beach is this?
   ¿Cuál isla/playa es esta?   kwa *ees*·la/*pla*·ya es *es*·ta

I feel seasick.
   Me siento mareado/a. m/f   me *syen*·to ma·re·*a*·do/a

Are there life jackets?
   ¿Hay chalecos salvavidas?   ai cha·*le*·kos sal·va·*vee*·das

Can I dine at the captain's table?
   ¿Podría cenar con   po·*dree*·a se·*nar* kon
   el capitán?   el ka·pee·*tan*

boat (general)	*barco* m	*bar*·ko
boat (small)	*bote* m	*bo*·te
cabin	*cabina* f	ka·*bee*·na
captain	*capitán* m	ka·pee·*tan*
car deck	*plataforma para*	pla·ta·*for*·ma *pa*·ra
	carros f	*ka*·ros
deck	*cubierta* f	koo·*byer*·ta
ferry	*ferry* m	*fe*·ree
hammock	*hamaca* f	a·*ma*·ka
lifeboat	*bote*	*bo*·te
	salvavidas m	sal·va·*vee*·das
life jacket	*chaleco*	cha·*le*·ko
	salvavidas m	sal·va·*vee*·das
yacht	*yate* m	*ya*·te

taxi

I'd like a	*Quiero un taxi*	*kye*·ro oon *tak*·see
(shared) taxi …	*(compartido)* …	(kom·par·*tee*·do) …
at (9am)	*para las (nueve*	*pa*·ra las (*nwe*·ve
	de la mañana)	de la ma·*nya*·na)
for a full day	*para un*	*pa*·ra oon
	día entero	*dee*·a en·*te*·ro
for a half day	*para medio*	*pa*·ra *me*·dyo
	día	*dee*·a
for (two) hours	*para (dos) horas*	*pa*·ra (dos) *o*·ras
now	*para ahora*	*pa*·ra a·*o*·ra
tomorrow	*para mañana*	*pa*·ra ma·*nya*·na

PRACTICAL

Where's the taxi stand?
¿Adónde está la   a·*don*·de es·*ta* la
parada de taxis?   pa·*ra*·da de *tak*·sees

Is there a taxi available?
¿Hay un taxi disponible?   ai oon *tak*·see dees·po·*nee*·ble

Please take me to (this address).
Por favor, lléveme a   por fa·*vor ye*·ve·me a
(esta dirección).   (*es*·ta dee·rek·*syon*)

How much is it to (San Isidro)?
¿Cuánto es hasta   *kwan*·to es *as*·ta
(San Isidro)?   (san ee·*see*·dro)

How much is the (initial) charge?
¿Cuánto es la tarifa   *kwan*·to es la ta·*ree*·fa
(básica)?   (*ba*·see·ka)

Please put the meter on.
Por favor, ponga la maría. por fa·*vor pon*·ga la ma·*ree*·a

I don't want to pay a flat fare.
No quiero pagar   no *kye*·ro pa·*gar*
una tarifa fija.   *oo*·na ta·*ree*·fa *fee*·kha

Please …	*Por favor, …*	por fa·*vor* …
come back at	*vuelva a las*	*vwel*·va a las
(10pm)	*(diez de la noche)*	(dyes de la *no*·che)
slow down	*baje la*	*ba*·khe la
	velocidad	ve·lo·see·*dad*
stop here	*pare aquí*	*pa*·re a·*kee*
wait here	*espéreme aquí*	es·*pe*·re·me a·*kee*

For other useful phrases, see **directions**, page 57, and **money**, page 39.

---

all the way to Chepe

Both the man's name *José* kho·*se* and the capital city *San José* san kho·*se* carry the nickname *Chepe che*·pe. Rumour has it that if you ask a taxi driver to take you from the airport to *Chepe*, rather than to *San José*, you'll get a better deal on the taxi fare.

car & motorbike

car & motorbike hire

I'd like to hire a/an …	*Quiero alquilar …*	*kye·*ro al·kee·*lar* …
4WD	*un cuatro por cuatro*	oon *kwa·*tro por *kwa·*tro
automatic	*un carro automático*	oon *ka·*ro ow·to·*ma·*tee·ko
car	*un carro*	oon *ka·*ro
manual	*un carro de marchas*	oon *ka·*ro de *mar·*chas
motorbike	*una motocicleta*	*oo·*na mo·to·see·*kle·*ta

with …	*con …*	kon …
air conditioning	*aire acondicionado*	*ai·*re a·kon·dee·syo·*na·*do
a driver	*un chofer*	oon cho·*fer*

How much for daily/weekly hire?
¿Cuánto cuesta el alquiler por día/semana?
*kwan·*to *kwes·*ta el al·kee·*ler* por *dee·*a/se·*ma·*na

Does that include insurance/mileage?
¿Incluye seguro/ kilometraje?
een·*kloo·*ye se·*goo·*ro/ kee·lo·me·*tra·*khe

Do you have a guide to the road rules (in English)?
¿Tiene un manual de tránsito (en inglés)?
*tye·*ne oon ma·*nwal* de *tran·*see·to (en een·*gles*)

Do you have a road map?
¿Tiene un mapa de carreteras?
*tye·*ne oon *ma·*pa de ka·re·*te·*ras

on the road

What's the speed limit?
*¿Cuál es el límite
de velocidad?*
kwal es el *lee*·mee·te
de ve·lo·see·*dad*

Is this the road to (Tamarindo)?
*¿Por aquí se va a
(Tamarindo)?*
por a·*kee* se va a
(ta·ma·*reen*·do)

Where's a petrol station?
¿Adónde hay una bomba?
a·*don*·de ai *oo*·na *bom*·ba

Please fill it up.
Lleno, por favor.
ye·no por fa·*vor*

I'd like (25) litres.
*Échele (veinticinco) litros,
por favor.*
e·che·le (*vayn*·tee·*seen*·ko)
lee·tros por fa·*vor*

diesel	*diesel* m	dee·*sel*
premium	*súper* m	*soo*·per
regular	*regular* m	re·goo·*lar*

Can you	*¿Le revisa …,*	le ree·*vee*·sa …
check the …?	*por favor?*	por fa·*vor*
oil	*el aceite*	el a·*say*·te
tyre pressure	*las llantas*	las *yan*·tas
water	*el agua*	el *a*·gwa

(How long) Can I park here?
    ¿(Cuánto tiempo)   (*kwan*·to *tyem*·po)
    Puedo parquear aquí?   *pwe*·do par·ke·*ar* a·*kee*

Do I have to pay?
    ¿Tengo que pagar?   *ten*·go ke pa·*gar*

signs

Alto	*al*·to	**Stop**
Ceda	*se*·da	**Give Way**
Desvío	des·*vee*·o	**Detour**
Entrada	en·*tra*·da	**Entrance**
No Hay Paso	no ai *pa*·so	**No Entry**
Peaje	pe·*a*·khe	**Toll**
Peligro	pe·*lee*·gro	**Danger**
Salida	sa·*lee*·da	**Exit**
Una Vía	*oo*·na *vee*·a	**One Way**

problems

I need a mechanic.
    Necesito un mecánico.   ne·se·*see*·to oon me·*ka*·nee·ko

I've had an accident.
    Tuve un accidente.   *too*·ve oon ak·see·*den*·te

The car has broken down (at Golfito).
    El carro se varó (en Golfito).   el *ka*·ro se va·*ro* (en gol·*fee*·to)

The motorbike has broken down (at Golfito).
    La moto se varó (en Golfito).   la *mo*·to se va·*ro* (en gol·*fee*·to)

The car won't start.
El carro no arranca.   el *ka*·ro no a·*ran*·ka

The motorbike won't start.
La moto no arranca.   la *mo*·to no a·*ran*·ka

I have a flat tyre.
Se me estalló una llanta.   se me es·ta·*yo* oo·na *yan*·ta

I've lost my car keys.
Se me perdieron   se me per·*dye*·ron
las llaves del carro.   las *ya*·ves del *ka*·ro

I've locked the keys inside.
Dejé las llaves adentro.   de·*khe* las *ya*·ves a·*den*·tro

I've run out of petrol.
Me quedé sin gasolina.   me ke·*de* seen ga·so·*lee*·na

Can you fix it (today)?
¿Lo puede arreglar (hoy)?   lo *pwe*·de a·reg·*lar* (oy)

How long will it take?
¿Cuánto va a durar?   *kwan*·to va a doo·*rar*

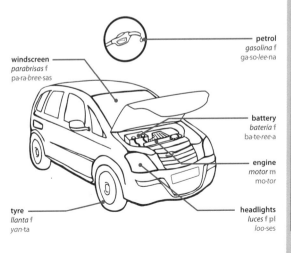

windscreen
parabrisas f
pa·ra·*bree*·sas

petrol
gasolina f
ga·so·*lee*·na

battery
batería f
ba·te·*ree*·a

engine
motor m
mo·*tor*

tyre
llanta f
yan·ta

headlights
luces f pl
loo·ses

bicycle

I'd like …	Quiero …	kye·ro …
my bicycle repaired	que me arreglen la bicicleta	ke me a·re·glen la bee·see·kle·ta
to buy	comprar	kom·prar
a bicycle	una bicicleta	oo·na bee·see·kle·ta
to hire a bicycle	alquilar una bicicleta	al·kee·lar oo·na bee·see·kle·ta

I'd like a … bike.	Quiero una bicicleta …	kye·ro oo·na bee·see·kle·ta …
mountain	montañera	mon·ta·nye·ra
racing	de carreras	de ka·re·ras
second-hand	de segunda mano	de se·goon·da ma·no

How much is it per day/hour?

¿Cuánto cuesta por día/hora?
kwan·to kwes·ta por dee·a/o·ra

Do you have a better bicycle?

¿Tiene una bici mejor?
tye·ne oo·na bee·see me·khor

Do I need a helmet?

¿Necesito un casco?
ne·se·see·to oon kas·ko

I have a puncture.

Se me estalló una llanta.
se me es·ta·yo oo·na yan·ta

Can you recommend a bike tour?

¿Me podría recomendar un tur de bici?
me po·dree·a re·ko·men·dar oon toor de bee·see

---

costa rican place names

Alajuela	a·la·khwe·la	**Puerto**	pwer·to
Cartago	kar·ta·go	**Limón**	lee·mon
Heredia	e·re·dya	**Puntarenas**	poon·ta·re·nas
Montezuma	mon·te·soo·ma	**San José**	san kho·se

border crossing

cruzando la frontera

I'm ...	Estoy ...	es·toy ...
in transit	de paso	de pa·so
on business	de negocios	de ne·go·syos
on holiday	de vacaciones	de va·ka·syo·nes

I'm here for ...	Voy a estar aquí por ...	voy a es·tar a·kee por ...
(10) days	(diez) días	(dyes) dee·as
(three) weeks	(tres) semanas	(tres) se·ma·nas
(two) months	(dos) meses	(dos) me·ses

I'm going to (Jacó).
Voy para (Jacó). voy pa·ra (kha·ko)

I'm staying at (the Hotel Tropical).
Estoy hospedado en (el Hotel Tropical). es·toy o·spe·da·do en (el o·tel tro·pee·kal)

listen for ...

familia f	fa·mee·lya	family
grupo m	groo·po	group
impuesto de salida m	eem·pwes·to de sa·lee·da	departure tax
pasaporte m	pa·sa·por·te	passport
solo/a m/f	so·lo/a	alone
visa f	vee·sa	visa

at customs

I have nothing to declare.

No tengo nada que
declarar.

no *ten*·go *na*·da ke
de·kla·*rar*

I have something to declare.

Tengo algo para
declarar.

ten·go *al*·go *pa*·ra
de·kla·*rar*

Do I have to declare this?

¿Tengo que declarar esto?

ten·go ke de·kla·*rar es*·to

That's (not) mine.

Eso (no) es mío.

e·so (no) es *mee*·o

I didn't know I had to declare it.

Yo no sabía que
tenía que declararlo.

yo no sa·*bee*·a ke
te·*nee*·a ke de·kla·*rar*·lo

Do you have this form in (English)?

¿Tiene este formulario
en (inglés)?

tye·ne *es*·te for·moo·*la*·ryo
en (een·*gles*)

Could I please have an (English) interpreter?

¿Podría conseguirme
un intérprete (en inglés),
por favor?

po·*dree*·a kon·se·*geer*·me
oon een·*ter*·pre·te (en een·*gles*)
por fa·*vor*

For phrases on payments and receipts, see **money**, page 39.

signs		
Aduana	a·*dwa*·na	**Customs**
Control de	kon·*trol* de	**Passport Control**
Pasaporte	pa·sa·*por*·te	
Cuarentena	kwa·ren·*te*·na	**Quarantine**
Duty-Free	*dyoo*·tee·free	**Duty-Free**
Migración	mee·gra·*syon*	**Immigration**

PRACTICAL

Where's (the bank)?
¿Adónde está (el banco)?   a·*don*·de es·*ta* (el *ban*·ko)

What's the address?
¿Cuál es la dirección?   kwal es la dee·rek·*syon*

How do I get there?
¿Cómo llego ahí?   ko·mo *ye*·go a·*ee*

How far is it?
¿Qué tan largo está?   ke tan *lar*·go es·*ta*

Can you show me (on the map)?
¿Me puede enseñar   me *pwe*·de en·se·*nyar*
(en el mapa)?   (en el *ma*·pa)

What ... is this?	*¿Cuál ... es este/a?* m/f	kwal ... es *es*·te/a
square	*plaza* f	*pla*·sa
street	*calle* f	*ka*·ye
village	*pueblo* m	*pwe*·blo

It's ...	*Está ...*	es·*ta* ...
behind ...	*detrás de ...*	de·*tras* de ...
close	*cerrado*	se·*ra*·do
here	*aquí*	a·*kee*
in front of ...	*en frente de ...*	en *fren*·te de ...
near ...	*cerca de ...*	*ser*·ka de...
next to ...	*a la par de ...*	a la par de ...
opposite ...	*opuesto a ...*	o·*pwes*·to a ...
straight ahead	*aquí directo*	a·*kee* dee·*rek*·to
there	*ahí*	a·*ee*

---

just around the corner

Costa Ricans will often give directions using the phrase *cien metros* syen *me*·tros (100 metres). This is really shorthand for 'one city block', known locally as *una cuadra* oo·na *kwa*·dra.

Turn ...	Doble ...	do·ble ...
at the corner	en la esquina	en la es·kee·na
at the traffic lights	en el semáforo	en el se·ma·fo·ro
left	a la izquierda	a la ees·kyer·da
right	a la derecha	a la de·re·cha
north	norte	nor·te
south	sur	soor
east	este	es·te
west	oeste	o·es·te
by bus	por bus	por boos
by taxi	por taxi	por tak·see
by train	por tren	por tren
on foot	por a pie	a pye

For information on Costa Rican addresses, see the box **return to sender**, page 82.

traffic lights
semáforo m
se·ma·fo·ro

shop
tienda f
tyen·da

pedestrian crossing
cruce peatonal m
kroo·se pe·a·to·nal

bus
bus m
boos

intersection
intersección f
een·ter·sek·syon

corner
esquina f
es·kee·na

taxi
taxi m
tak·see

accommodation

hospedaje

finding accommodation

encontrando un lugar para hospedarse

An *apartotel* is basically a hotel room equipped with a kitchen to allow for self-catering. The word *cabina* is loosely used to cover cheap to mid-range accommodation. Both the words *pensión* pen·*syon* and *casa de huéspedes* are used for 'guesthouse'. Bed and breakfasts are an increasingly popular accommodation option and the English term is used.

Where's a/an …?	¿Adónde hay …?	a·*don*·de ai …
apartotel	un apartotel	oon a·par·to·*tel*
cabina	una cabina	oo·na ka·*bee*·na
camping ground	una área para acampar	oo·na *a*·re·a *pa*·ra a·kam·*par*
ecolodge	un ecolodge	oon e·ko·loj
guesthouse	una casa de huéspedes	oo·na *ka*·sa de wes·pe·des
hostel	un hospedaje	oon os·pe·*da*·khe
hotel	un hotel	oon o·*tel*
youth hostel	un albergue juvenil	oon al·*ber*·ge khoo·ve·*neel*

Can you recommend somewhere …?	¿Me podría recomendar algún lugar …?	me po·*dree*·a re·ko·men·*dar* al·*goon* loo·*gar* …
cheap	barato	ba·*ra*·to
good	bueno	*bwe*·no
luxurious	lujoso	loo·*kho*·so
nearby	cerca de aquí	ser·ka de a·*kee*
romantic	romántico	ro·*man*·tee·ko
safe for women travellers	que sea seguro para mujeres	ke *se*·a se·*goo*·ro *pa*·ra moo·*khe*·res

accommodation

59

I want something near the ...	Quiero algo que esté cerca ...	kye·ro al·go ke es·te ser·ka ...
beach	de la playa	de la pla·ya
bus stop	de la parada de buses	de la pa·ra·da de boo·ses
city centre	del centro	del sen·tro
shops	de las tiendas	de las tyen·das
What's the address?	¿Cuál es la dirección?	kwal es la dee·rek·syon

For responses, see **directions**, page 57.

For responses, see **directions**, page 57.

local talk		
dive n	chinchorro m	cheen·cho·ro
roach motel	cucarachero m	koo·ka·ra·che·ro
top spot	lugar pura vida m	loo·gar poo·ra vee·da

booking ahead & checking in

haciendo una reservación y llegando

I'd like to book a room, please.
| Quiero reservar una habitación, por favor. | kye·ro re·ser·var oo·na a·bee·ta·syon por fa·vor |

I have a reservation.
| Tengo una reservación. | ten·go oo·na re·ser·va·syon |

My name's ...
| Mi nombre es ... | mee nom·bre es ... |

For (three) nights/weeks.
| Por (tres) noches/semanas. | por (tres) no·ches/se·ma·nas |

From (2 July) to (6 July).
| Del (dos de julio) al (seis de julio). | del (dos de khoo·lyo) al (says de khoo·lyo) |

Do I need to pay upfront?
| ¿Necesito pagar por adelantado? | ne·se·see·to pa·gar por a·de·lan·ta·do |

PRACTICAL

60

¿Cuántas noches?	kwan·tas no·ches	**How many nights?**
llave f	ya·ve	**key**
lleno/a m/f	ye·no/a	**full**
pasaporte m	pa·sa·por·te	**passport**
recepción f	re·sep·syon	**reception**

Do you have a ... room?	¿Tiene una habitación ...?	tye·ne oo·na a·bee·ta·syon ...
single	sencilla	sen·see·ya
double	doble	do·ble
twin	con dos camas sencillas	kon dos ka·mas sen·see·yas
How much is it per ...?	¿Cuánto es por ...?	kwan·to es por ...
night	noche	no·che
person	persona	per·so·na
week	semana	se·ma·na
Can I pay by ...?	¿Puedo pagar con ...?	pwe·do pa·gar kon ...
credit card	tarjeta de crédito	tar·khe·ta de kre·dee·to
debit card	tarjeta de débito	tar·khe·ta de de·bee·to
travellers cheque	cheque de viajero	che·ke de vya·khe·ro
Can I see it?	¿Puedo verla?	pwe·do ver·la
I'll take it.	Sí, la quiero.	see la kye·ro

signs

Baño	ba·nyo	**Bathroom**
Espacio Disponible	es·pa·syo dees·po·nee·ble	**Vacancy**
Lavandería	la·van·de·ree·a	**Laundry**
No Hay Espacio	no ai es·pa·syo	**No Vacancy**

requests & queries

preguntas y peticiones

Is breakfast included?
¿Incluye el desayuno?   een·*kloo*·ye el de·sa·*yoo*·no

When/Where is breakfast served?
¿Cuándo/Adónde   kwan·do/a·*don*·de
sirven el desayuno?   *seer*·ven el de·sa·*yoo*·no

Is there hot water all day?
¿Hay agua caliente   ai *a*·gwa ka·*lyen*·te
todo el día?   *to*·do el *dee*·a

Please wake me at (seven).
Por favor, despiérteme   por fa·*vor* des·*pyer*·te·me
a las (siete).   a las (*sye*·te)

Do you have a/an ...?	*¿Tienen ...?*	*tye*·nen ...
elevator	*ascensor*	a·sen·*sor*
laundry service	*servicio de lavandería*	ser·*vee*·syos de la·van·de·*ree*·a
message board	*pizarra de mensajes*	pee·*sa*·ra de men·*sa*·khes
safe	*caja fuerte*	*ka*·kha *fwer*·te
swimming pool	*piscina*	pee·*see*·na

Can I use the ...?	*¿Podría usar ...?*	po·*dree*·a oo·*sar* ...
kitchen	*la cocina*	la ko·*see*·na
laundry	*la lavandería*	la la·van·de·*ree*·a
telephone	*el teléfono*	el te·*le*·fo·no

PRACTICAL

62

a knock at the door ...

Who is it?	¿Quién es?	kyen es
Just a moment.	Un momento.	oon mo·men·to
Come in.	Pase.	pa·se
Come back later, please.	Vuelva más tarde, por favor.	vwel·va mas tar·de por fa·vor

Could I have (a) ..., please?	¿Me podría dar ..., por favor?	me po·dree·a dar ... por fa·vor
mosquito net	un mosquitero	oon mos·kee·te·ro
my key	la llave	la ya·ve
receipt	una factura	oo·na fak·too·ra

Do you ... here?	¿Aquí ...?	a·kee ...
arrange tours	organizan tours	or·ga·nee·san toors
change money	cambian dinero	kam·byan dee·ne·ro

Is there a message for me?
¿Tengo algún mensaje?   ten·go al·goon men·sa·khe

Can I leave a message for someone?
¿Le puedo dejar un mensaje a alguien?   le pwe·do de·khar oon men·sa·khe a al·gyen

I'm locked out of my room.
No puedo entrar al cuarto.   no pwe·do en·trar al kwar·to

complaints

quejas

It's too ...	Está demasiado ...	es·ta de·ma·sya·do ...
bright	claro	kla·ro
cold	frío	free·o
dark	oscuro	os·koo·ro
expensive	caro	ka·ro
hot	caliente	ka·lyen·te
noisy	ruidoso	rwee·do·so
small	pequeño	pe·ke·nyo

The ... doesn't work.   *El ... no sirve.*   el ... no *seer*·ve

air conditioner	*aire acondicionado*	*ai*·re a·kon·dee·syo·*na*·do
fan	*ventilador*	ven·tee·la·*dor*
toilet	*baño*	*ba*·nyo

Can I get (another blanket)?
¿Me podría dar (otra cobija)?   me po·*dree*·a dar (*o*·tra ko·*bee*·kha)

This ... isn't clean.
Este/a ... está sucio/a. m/f   *es*·te/a ... es·*ta soo*·syo/a

There's no hot water.
No hay agua caliente.   no ai *a*·gwa ka·*lyen*·te

air conditioner
aire acondicionado m
ai·re a·kon·dee·syo·*na*·do

fan
ventilador m
ven·tee·la·*dor*

toilet
baño m
ba·nyo

key
llave f
ya·ve

bed
cama f
ka·ma

bathroom
baño m
ba·nyo

TV
televisión f
te·le·vee·*syon*

checking out

What time is checkout?
¿A qué hora es la salida?   a ke *o*·ra es la sa·*lee*·da

Can I have a late checkout?
¿Puedo salir más tarde?   *pwe*·do sa·*leer* mas *tar*·de

Can you call a taxi for me (for 11 o'clock)?
¿Usted me podría llamar   oos·*ted* me po·*dree*·a ya·*mar*
un taxi (para las once)?   oon *tak*·see (*pa*·ra las *on*·se)

I'm leaving now.
Ya me voy.   ya me voy

Can I leave my bags here?
¿Puedo dejar mis   *pwe*·do de·*khar* mees
maletas aquí?   ma·*le*·tas a·*kee*

There's a mistake in the bill.
Hay un error en la cuenta.   ai oon e·*ror* en la *kwen*·ta

I had a great stay, thanks.
La pasé muy bien,   la pa·*se* mooy byen
muchas gracias.   *moo*·chas *gra*·syas

I'll recommend it to my friends.
Voy a recomendar   voy a re·ko·men·*dar*
a mis amigos.   a mees a·*mee*·gos

Could I have my ..., please?	*¿Me puede dar ..., por favor?*	me *pwe*·de dar ... por fa·*vor*
deposit	*mi depósito*	mee de·*po*·see·to
passport	*mi pasaporte*	mee pa·sa·*por*·te
valuables	*mis valores*	mees va·*lo*·res
I'll be back ...	*Voy a volver ...*	voy a vol·*ver* ...
in (three) days	*en (tres) días*	en (tres) *dee*·as
on (Tuesday)	*el (martes)*	el (*mar*·tes)

camping

Can I ...?	¿Puedo ...?	pwe·do ...
camp here	acampar aquí	a·kam·par a·kee
park next	parquearme a la	par·ke·ar·me a la
to my tent	par de la tienda	par de la tyen·da

How much is it per ...?	¿Cuánto cuesta por ...?	kwan·to kwes·ta por ...
person	persona	per·so·na
tent	tienda de campaña	tyen·da de kam·pa·nya
vehicle	carro	ka·ro

Do you have (a) ...?	¿Tiene ...?	tye·ne ...
electricity	electricidad	e·lek·tree·see·dad
laundry service	servicio de lavandería	ser·vee·syos de la·van·de·ree·a
shower facilities	duchas	doo·chas
site	un espacio	oon es·pa·syo
tents for hire	tiendas de campaña para alquilar	tyen·das de kam·pa·nya pa·ra al·kee·lar
toilets	baños	ba·nyos

Who do I ask to stay here?
¿A quién le pregunto   a kyen le pre·goon·to
para quedarme aquí?   pa·ra ke·dar·me a·kee

Is it coin-operated?
¿Es de monedas?   es de mo·ne·das

Is the water drinkable?
¿Se puede beber el agua?   se pwe·de be·ber el a·gwa

Could I borrow ...?
¿Podría prestarme ...?   po·dree·a pres·tar·me ...

For cooking utensils, see **self-catering,** page 166.

renting

I'm here about the ... for rent.	*Vengo por el/la ... que está alquilando.* m/f	ven·go por el/la ... ke es·ta al·kee·lan·do
Do you have a/an ... for rent?	*¿Tiene un/una ... para alquilar?* m/f	tye·ne oon/oo·na ... pa·ra al·kee·lar
apartment	*apartamento* m	a·par·ta·men·to
cabina	*cabina* f	ka·bee·na
house	*casa* f	ka·sa
room	*cuarto* m	kwar·to
villa	*villa* f	vee·ya
(partly) furnished	*(parcialmente) amueblado*	(par·syal·men·te) a·mwe·bla·do
unfurnished	*sin amueblar*	seen a·mwe·blar

Is there a deposit?

¿Hay que dejar depósito?	ai ke de·khar de·po·see·to

Are utilities included?

¿Incluye los servicios de luz y agua?	een·kloo·ye los ser·vee·syos de loos ee a·gwa

staying with locals

If you're invited to stay with a local family, make sure you not only bring a small gift (such as food or a souvenir), but also offer to help with the housework. You may need to insist on helping out, as your offer will usually be declined on first attempt.

Can I stay at your place?

¿Puedo quedarme en su casa?	pwe·do ke·dar·me en soo ka·sa

I have my own …	Yo tengo mi	yo *ten*·go mee
	propio/a … m/f	*pro*·pyo/a …
sleeping bag	saco de dormir m	*sa*·ko de dor·*meer*
sleeping mat	colchoneta f	kol·cho·*ne*·ta

Is there anything I can do to help?
¿En que le puedo ayudar?   en ke le *pwe*·do a·yoo·*dar*

Can I bring anything for the meal?
¿Le traigo algo   le *trai*·go *al*·go
para la comida?   *pa*·ra la ko·*mee*·da

Can I set/clear the table?
¿Pongo/Quito la mesa?   *pon*·go/*kee*·to la *me*·sa

Can I take out the rubbish?
¿Saco la basura?   *sa*·ko la ba·*soo*·ra

Thanks for your hospitality.
Muchas gracias   *moo*·chas *gra*·syas
por hospedarme.   por os·pe·*dar*·me

the host with the most

If you're invited to share a meal in a Costa Rican home, your solicitous hosts will ply you with food and drink. Remember that politeness is highly valued in their culture, so be sure to extoll the virtues of your hosts' cooking. This phrase should do the trick:

La comida está muy rica!
   la ko·*mee*·da es·*ta* mooy *ree*·ka   **The food is very good!**

For more dining-related phrases, see **eating out**, page 153.

PRACTICAL

looking for ...

Are shops open (on Independence Day)?
¿El comercio abre (el día de la independencia)?
el ko·*mer*·syo *a*·bre (el *dee*·a de la een·de·pen·*den*·sya)

What hours are shops open?
¿Cuál es el horario de las tiendas?
kwal es el o·*ra*·ryo de las *tyen*·das

Where can I buy (a padlock)?
¿Adónde puedo comprar (un candado)?
a·*don*·de *pwe*·do kom·*prar* (oon kan·*da*·do)

Where's (a/the) ...?	*¿Adónde hay ...?*	a·*don*·de ai ...
department store	*una tienda*	*oo*·na *tyen*·da
kiosk	*un quiosco*	oon *kyos*·ko
mall	*un mall*	oon mol
neighbourhood store	*una pulpería*	*oo*·na pool·pe·*ree*·a
market	*un mercado*	oon mer·*ka*·do

For more items and shopping locations, see the **dictionary**.

making a purchase

I'm just looking.
Sólo estoy viendo.
so·lo es·*toy* vyen·do

I'd like to buy (an adaptor plug).
Quiero (un adaptador).
kye·ro (oon a·dap·ta·*dor*)

How much is it?
¿Cuánto cuesta?   *kwan·*to kwes·ta

Can you write down the price?
¿Podría escribir el precio?   po·dree·a es·kree·*beer* el *pre·*syo

Can I look at it?
¿Lo/la puedo ver? m/f   lo/la *pwe·*do ver

Do you have any others?
¿Tiene más?   *tye·*ne mas

Is this (240) volts?
¿Éste es de (doscientos   es·te es de (do·*syen·*tos
cuarenta) voltios?   kwa·*ren·*ta) *vol·*tee·os

Do you accept …?	*¿ Acepta …?*	a·*sep·*ta …
credit cards	*tarjetas de*	tar·*khe·*tas de
	crédito	*kre·*dee·to
debit cards	*tarjetas de*	tar·*khe·*tas de
	débito	*de·*bee·to
travellers	*cheque de*	*che·*ke de
cheques	*viajero*	vya·*khe·*ro

Could I have	*¿Me da …,*	me da …
a …, please?	*por favor?*	por fa·*vor*
bag	*una bolsa*	*oo·*na *bol·*sa
receipt	*un recibo*	oon re·*see·*bo

I don't need a bag, thanks.
No necesito bolsa, gracias.   no ne·se·*see·*to *bol·*sa *gra·*syas

Could I have it wrapped?
¿Me lo puede   me lo *pwe·*de
envolver, por favor?   en·vol·*ver* por fa·*vor*

Does it have a guarantee?
¿Tiene garantía?   *tye·*ne ga·ran·*tee·*a

Can I have it sent abroad?
¿Lo puedo mandar   lo *pwe·*do man·*dar*
al extranjero?   al eks·tran·*khe·*ro

Can you order it for me?
¿Usted me lo podría pedir?   oos·*ted* me lo po·*dree·*a pe·*deer*

Can I pick it up later?
¿Puedo pasar a   pwe·do pa·sar a
recogerlo después?   re·ko·kher·lo des·pwes

The quality isn't good.
No es de buena calidad.   no es de bwe·na ka·lee·dad

It doesn't work.
No funciona.   no foon·see·o·na

It's broken/damaged.
Está roto/dañado.   es·ta ro·to/da·nya·do

It's dirty/stained.
Está sucio/manchado.   es·ta soo·syo/man·cha·do

I'd like to return this.
Quiero devolver ésto.   kye·ro de·vol·ver es·to

I'd like (a) ...,	*Me da ...,*	me da ...
please.	*por favor.*	por fa·vor
my change	*el vuelto*	el vwel·to
receipt	*un recibo*	oon re·see·bo
refund	*un reintegro*	oon re·een·te·gro

local talk		
bargain n	*ganga* f	gan·ga
rip-off	*robo* m	ro·bo
sale	*promoción* f	pro·mo·syon

bargaining

el regateo

That's too expensive.
Está muy caro.   es·ta mooy ka·ro

Can you lower the price?
¿Podría bajarle el precio?   po·dree·a ba·khar·le el pre·syo

Do you have something cheaper?
¿Tiene algo más barato?   tye·ne al·go mas ba·ra·to

What's your final price?
¿Entonces, cuál　　　　　en·*ton*·ses kwal
es el precio final?　　　　es el *pre*·syo fee·*nal*

I'll give you (1000 *colones*).
Le doy (mil colones).　　le doy (meel ko·*lo*·nes)

listen for ...		
¿Algo más?	*al*·go mas	**Anything else?**
¿Le puedo ayudar	le *pwe*·do a·yoo·*dar*	**Can I help you?**
en algo?	en *al*·go	
No tenemos.	no te·*ne*·mos	**We don't have any.**

books & reading

libros y lectura

Can you recommend a book to me?
¿Me podría　　　　　　me po·*dree*·a
recomendar un libro?　　re·ko·men·*dar* oon *lee*·bro

Do you have ...?	*¿Tiene ...?*	*tye*·ne ...
a book by	*un libro de*	oon *lee*·bro de
(Carmen Lyra)	*(Carmen Lyra)*	(*kar*·men *lee*·ra)
an entertainment	*una guía de*	*oo*·na *gee*·a de
guide	*entretenimientos*	en·tre·te·nee·*myen*·tos

Is there an English-	*¿Hay alguna ...*	ai al·*goo*·na ...
language ...?	*de (inglés)?*	de (een·*gles*)
bookshop	*librería*	lee·bre·*ree*·a
section	*sección*	sek·*syon*

I'd like a ...	*Quiero ...*	*kye*·ro ...
dictionary	*un diccionario*	oon deek·syo·*na*·ryo
newspaper	*un periódico*	oon pe·*ryo*·dee·ko
(in English)	*(en inglés)*	(en een·*gles*)

Do you have ...?	*¿Tiene ...?*	*tye*·ne ...
guidebooks	*guías*	*gee*·as
phrasebooks	*libros de frases*	*lee*·bros de *fra*·ses

clothes

My size is …	Mi talla es …	mee ta·ya es …
small	pequeño	pe·ke·nyo
medium	mediano	me·dya·no
large	grande	gran·de

Can I try it on?
¿Me lo puedo probar?   me lo pwe·do pro·bar

It doesn't fit.
No me queda.   no me ke·da

hairdressing

I'd like (a) …	Quiero …	kye·ro …
colour	un tinte	oon teen·te
my beard	que me recorten	ke me re·kor·ten
trimmed	la barba	la bar·ba
my hair	que me laven/	ke me la·ven/
washed/dried	sequen el pelo	se·ken el pe·lo
shave	que me afeiten	ke me a·fay·ten
streaks	hacerme unos	a·ser·me oo·nos
	rayitos	ra·yee·tos
trim	que me recorten	ke me re·kor·ten
	el pelo	el pe·lo

Don't cut it too short.
No me lo corte   no me lo kor·te
demasiado corto.   de·ma·sya·do kor·to

Please use a new blade.
Por favor, use   por fa·vor oo·se
una navajilla nueva.   oo·na na·va·khee·ya nwe·va

Shave it all off!
Córtemelo todo.   kor·te·me·lo to·do

music

I'd like a ... | *Quiero un ...* | *kye·ro oon ...*
blank tape | *cassette* | ka·*se*·te
  | *en blanco* | en *blan*·ko
CD/DVD | *CD/DVD* | se de/de ve de
video | *vídeo* | *vee*·de·o

I'm looking for something by (Editus).
Estoy buscando   es·*toy* boos·*kan*·do
algo de (Editus).   *al*·go de (e·*dee*·toos)

Can I listen to this?
¿Lo puedo escuchar?   lo *pwe*·do es·koo·*char*

Will this work on any DVD player?
¿Este servirá en   *es*·te ser·vee·*ra* en
cualquier DVD?   kwal·*kyer* de ve de

Is this for a (PAL/NTSC) system?
¿Es para un sistema   es *pa*·ra oon sees·*te*·ma
(PAL/NTSC)?   (pe a e·le/e·ne te e·se se)

photography

Can you ...? | *¿Puede ...?* | *pwe*·de ...
develop digital photos | *revelar fotos digitales* | re·ve·*lar fo*·tos dee·khee·*ta*·les
develop this film | *revelar este rollo* | re·ve·*lar es*·te *ro*·yo
load my film | *ponerme este rollo en la cámara* | po·*ner*·me *es*·te *ro*·yo en la *ka*·ma·ra
recharge the battery for my digital camera | *recargar la batería de mi cámara digital* | re·kar·*gar* la ba·te·*ree*·a de mee *ka*·ma·ra dee·khee·*tal*
transfer photos from my camera to CD | *pasar las fotos de mi cámara digital a un CD* | pa·*sar* las *fo*·tos de mee *ka*·ma·ra dee·khee·*tal* a oon se de

I need a/an ... film for this camera.	Necesito un rollo ... para esta cámara.	ne·se·see·to oon ro·yo ... pa·ra es·ta ka·ma·ra
APS	APS	a pe e·se
B&W	blanco y negro	blan·ko ee ne·gro
colour	a color	a ko·lor
slide	para diapositivas	pa·ra dee·a·po·see·tee·vas
(200) speed	asa (doscientos)	a·sa (do·syen·tos)

Do you have a ... for this camera?	¿Tiene un ... para esta cámara?	tye·ne oon ... pa·ra es·ta ka·ma·ra
flash	flash	flash
light meter	medidor de luz	me·dee·dor de loos
telephoto lens	teleobjetivo	te·le·ob·khe·tee·vo
zoom lens	zoom	soom

Do you have ... for this camera?	¿Tiene ... para esta cámara?	tye·ne ... pa·ra es·ta ka·ma·ra
batteries	baterías	ba·te·ree·as
memory cards	memorias	me·mo·ree·as

... camera	... cámara	... ka·ma·ra
digital	digital	dee·khee·tal
disposable	desechable	de·se·cha·ble
underwater	sumergible	soo·mer·khee·ble
video	de vídeo	de vee·de·o

I need a cable to connect my camera to a computer.

Necesito un cable para conectar mi cámara a la computadora.

ne·se·see·to oon ka·ble pa·ra ko·nek·tar mee ka·ma·ra a la kom·poo·ta·do·ra

I need a cable to recharge this battery.

Necesito un cable para recargar esta batería.

ne·se·see·to oon ka·ble pa·ra re·kar·gar es·ta ba·te·ree·a

I need a video cassette for this camera.
Necesito un cassette — ne·se·*see*·to oon ka·*se*·te
para esta cámara de vídeo. — *pa*·ra *es*·ta *ka*·ma·ra de *vee*·de·o

I need a passport photo taken.
Necesito tomarme una — ne·se·*see*·to to·*mar*·me *oo*·na
foto tamaño pasaporte. — *fo*·to ta·*ma*·nyo pa·sa·*por*·te

I'm not happy with these photos.
No me gusta la — no me *goos*·ta la
calidad de estas fotos. — ka·lee·*dad* de *es*·tas *fo*·tos

I don't want to pay the full price.
No quiero pagarle el — no *kye*·ro pa·*gar*·le el
precio completo. — *pre*·syo kom·*ple*·to

repairs

reparaciones

Can I have my	¿Me pueden	me *pwe*·den
... repaired here?	arreglar ... aquí?	a·reg·*lar* ... a·*kee*
backpack	mi mochila	mee mo·*chee*·la
bag	mi bolso	mee *bol*·so
(video) camera	mi cámara	mee *ka*·ma·ra
	(de vídeo)	(de *vee*·de·o)
(sun)glasses	mis anteojos	mees an·te·o·khos
	(oscuros)	(os·*koo*·ros)
shoes	mis zapatos	mees sa·*pa*·tos

When will it be ready?
¿Cuándo va a estar listo? — *kwan*·do va a es·*tar* *lees*·to

souvenirs		
ceramics	cerámica f	se·*ra*·mee·ka
hammock	hamaca f	a·*ma*·ka
handicraft	artesanías f pl	ar·te·sa·*nee*·as
jewellery	joyas f pl	*kho*·yas
painted miniature ox carts	carretas f pl	ka·*re*·tas

communications
comunicaciones

the internet

Where's the local Internet café?
¿Adónde hay un café internet?
a·*don*·de ai oon ka·*fe* een·ter·*net*

I'd like to …	*Quiero …*	*kye*·ro …
burn a CD	*quemar un disco*	ke·*mar* oon *dees*·ko
check my email	*revisar mi correo*	re·vee·*sar* mee ko·re·o
download my photos	*bajar mis fotos*	ba·*khar* mees *fo*·tos
get Internet access	*tener acceso al internet*	te·*ner* ak·*se*·so al een·ter·*net*
use a printer	*usar una impresora*	oo·*sar* oo·na eem·pre·*so*·ra
use a scanner	*usar un escáner*	oo·*sar* oon es·*ka*·ner

Do you have …?	*¿Tiene …?*	*tye*·ne …
PCs	*PCs*	pe ses
Macs	*Macs*	maks
a Zip drive	*unidad de Zip*	oo·nee·*dad* de seep

Can I connect my … to this computer?	*¿Puedo conectar mi … a esta computadora?*	*pwe*·do ko·nek·*tar* mee … a *es*·ta kom·poo·ta·*do*·ra
camera	*cámara*	*ka*·ma·ra
media player	*reproductor media*	re·pro·dook·*tor* *me*·dya
portable hard drive	*disco duro portátil*	*dees*·ko doo·ro por·*ta*·teel

communications

77

How much per …?	¿Cuánto es por …?	kwan·to es por …
hour	hora	o·ra
(five)	(cinco)	(seen·ko)
minutes	minutos	mee·noo·tos
page	página	pa·khee·na

How do I log on?	¿Cómo entro?	ko·mo en·tro
It's crashed.	Está caída.	es·ta ka·ee·da
I've finished.	Ya terminé.	ya ter·mee·ne

where the @!*# is it?

Spanish-language and English-language keyboard layouts differ because the two alphabets aren't quite the same. This shouldn't generally be a problem, but for one pesky – all too useful in the age of email – key.

The @ ('at') symbol – in Spanish this symbol is called *la arroa* la a·ro·a – isn't necessarily labeled on keyboards or may not be accessed by simply pressing the keys you're used to. Try the F2 key, use an ALT code – or ask for help:

Where's the @ key?
¿Dónde está la arroa?   don·de es·ta la a·ro·a

mobile/cell phone

teléfono celular

I'd like a …	Necesito …	ne·se·see·to …
charger for my phone	un cargador para mi celular	oon kar·ga·dor pa·ra mee se·loo·lar
mobile/cell phone for hire	alquilar un teléfono celular	al·kee·lar oon te·le·fo·no se·loo·lar
prepaid mobile/ cell phone	un celular prepagado	oon se·loo·lar pre·pa·ga·do
SIM card for your network	una tarjeta SIM para su red	oo·na tar·khe·ta seem pa·ra soo red

What are the call rates?
   ¿Cuánto es la tarifa?   *kwan*·to es la ta·*ree*·fa

(30) *colones* **per (30) minutes.**
   (Treinta) colones por   (*trayn*·ta) ko·*lo*·nes por
   (treinta) minutos.   (*trayn*·ta) mee·*noo*·tos

phone

el teléfono

What's your phone number?
   ¿Cuál es tu número   kwal es too *noo*·me·ro
   de teléfono?   de te·*le*·fo·no

Where's the nearest public phone?
   ¿Adónde está el teléfono   a·*don*·de es·*ta* el te·*le*·fo·no
   público más cercano?   *poo*·blee·ko mas ser·*ka*·no

Can I look at a phone book?
   ¿Puedo ver la   *pwe*·do ver la
   guía telefónica?   *gee*·a te·le·*fo*·nee·ka

What's the area/country code for (Panama)?
   ¿Cuál es el código de   kwal es el *ko*·dee·go de
   área/país para (Panamá)?   *a*·re·a/pa·*ees* pa·ra (pa·na·*ma*)

The number is …
   El número es …   el *noo*·me·ro es …

I want to …	*Quiero …*	*kye*·ro …
buy a	*comprar una*	kom·*prar* oo·na
phonecard	*tarjeta*	tar·*khe*·ta
	telefónica	te·le·*fo*·nee·ka
call (Canada)	*llamar a*	ya·*mar* a
	(Canadá)	(ka·na·*da*)
make a (local)	*hacer una*	a·*ser* oo·na
call	*llamada (local)*	ya·*ma*·da (lo·*kal*)
reverse the	*llamar de cobro*	ya·*mar* de *ko*·bro
charges	*revertido*	re·ver·*tee*·do
speak for (three)	*hablar (tres)*	a·*blar* (tres)
minutes	*minutos*	mee·*noo*·tos

communications

79

How much	¿Cuánto	*kwan·to*
does ... cost?	cuesta ...?	*kwes·ta ...*
a (three)-minute call	*una llamada de (tres) minutos*	*oo·na ya·ma·da de (tres) mee·noo·tos*
each extra minute	*cada minuto extra*	*ka·da mee·noo·to eks·tra*

It's engaged.	*Está ocupado.*	es·ta o·koo·pa·do
I've been cut off.	*Se cortó.*	se kor·to
The connection's bad.	*La conexión está muy mala.*	la ko·nek·syon es·ta mooy ma·la
Hello.	*Aló.*	a·lo
It's ...	*Es ...*	es ...

Please tell him/her I called.
¿Le podría decir que yo llamé, por favor?
le po·dree·a de·seer ke yo ya·me por fa·vor

Can I leave a message?
¿Le puedo dejar un mensaje?
le pwe·do de·khar oon men·sa·khe

I don't have a contact number.
No tengo un número dónde me pueda llamar.
no ten·go oon noo·me·ro don·de me pwe·da ya·mar

I'll call back later.
Yo llamo después.
yo ya·mo des·pwes

What time should I call?
¿A qué hora debo llamar?
a ke o·ra de·bo ya·mar

post office

I want to send a ...	Quiero mandar ...	kye·ro man·dar ...
fax	un fax	oon faks
letter	una carta	oo·na kar·ta
parcel	un paquete	oon pa·ke·te
postcard	una postal	oo·na pos·tal

I want to buy a/an ...	Quiero comprar...	kye·ro kom·prar...
(padded) envelope	un sobre (acolchonado)	oon so·bre (a·kol·cho·na·do)
stamp	una estampilla	oo·na es·tam·pee·ya

Please send it by air/surface mail to (Australia).
Por favor, envíelo por avión/tierra a (Australia).
por fa·vor en·vee·e·lo por a·vyon/tye·ra a (ow·stra·lya)

It contains (souvenirs).
Contiene (recuerdos).
kon·tye·ne (re·kwer·dos)

Is there any mail for me?
¿Me llegó algo?
me ye·go al·go

snail mail

... mail	correo ...	ko·re·o ...
air	aéreo	a·e·re·o
express	express	eks·pres
registered	certificado	ser·tee·fee·ka·do
sea	marítimo	ma·ree·tee·mo
surface	por tierra	por tye·ra

communications

81

customs declaration	declaración de aduana f	de·kla·ra·syon de a·dwa·na
domestic	local m&f	lo·kal
fragile	frágil m&f	fra·kheel
international	internacional m&f	een·ter·na·syo·nal
mail n	correo m	ko·re·o
mailbox	buzón m	boo·son
PO box	apartado m	a·par·ta·do
postcode	código postal m	ko·dee·go pos·tal

return to sender

Addresses in Costa Rica sometimes take a surprising form. For one thing, outside San José and other larger cities, numbered addresses and street names don't really exist. Instead, Costa Ricans use descriptive addresses.

People can get quite creative in their choice of landmarks, and rural addresses have even been known to make reference to natural features such as streams or trees! Most addresses include the name of the province and the name of the nearest large town or city. A house address may read something like:

Anna Fernández
2km después de la fábrica hacia el Aguila
(2km after the factory on the way to Aguila)
Pejibaye de Perez Zeledón
San Isidro el General (closest major town)
Costa Rica
Centroamérica

What times/days is the bank open?
¿A qué horas/días   a ke o·ras/*dee*·as
está abierto el banco?   es·*ta* a·*byer*·to el *ban*·ko

Where can I ...?	*¿Adónde puedo ...?*	a·*don*·de *pwe*·do ...
I'd like to ...	*Quisiera ...*	kee·*sye*·ra ...
cash a cheque	*cambiar un cheque*	kam·*byar* oon *che*·ke
change a travellers cheque	*cambiar un cheque de viajero*	kam·*byar* oon *che*·ke de vya·*khe*·ro
change money into *colones*	*cambiar dinero a colones*	kam·*byar* dee·*ne*·ro a ko·*lo*·nes
change money/ dollars	*cambiar plata/ dólares*	kam·*byar* pla·ta/ *do*·la·res
get a cash advance	*obtener un adelanto en efectivo*	ob·te·*ner* oon a·de·*lan*·to en e·fek·*tee*·vo
get change for this note	*cambiar este pagaré*	kam·*byar* es·te pa·ga·*re*
withdraw money	*sacar dinero*	sa·*kar* dee·*ne*·ro
Where's a/an ...?	*¿Adónde hay ...?*	a·*don*·de ai ...
automated teller machine	*un cajero automático*	oon ka·*khe*·ro ow·to·*ma*·tee·ko
foreign exchange office	*una casa de cambio*	*oo*·na *ka*·sa de *kam*·byo

For more information on the Costa Rican currency, the *colón*, see the box **the colour of money**, page 40.

What's the exchange rate?
¿A cómo está el   a ko·mo es·ta el
tipo de cambio?   tee·po de kam·byo

What's the charge for that?
¿Cuánto cobran por eso? kwan·to ko·bran por e·so

The automated teller machine took my card.
El cajero automático   el ka·khe·ro ow·to·ma·tee·ko
se dejó mi tarjeta.   se de·kho mee tar·khe·ta

I've forgotten my PIN.
Se me olvidó mi PIN.   se me ol·vee·do mee peen

Can I use my credit card to withdraw money?
¿Puedo usar mi tarjeta de   pwe·do oo·sar mee tar·khe·ta de
crédito para sacar plata?   kre·dee·to pa·ra sa·kar pla·ta

Has my money arrived yet?
¿Ya llegó mi plata?   ya ye·go mee pla·ta

How long will it take to arrive?
¿Cuánto va a durar   kwan·to va a doo·rar
en llegar?   en ye·gar

For other useful phrases, see **money**, page 39.

listen for ...	
Firme aquí. feer·me a·kee	Sign here.
Hay un problema. ai oon pro·ble·ma	There's a problem.
No podemos hacer eso. no po·de·mos a·ser e·so	We can't do that.
Usted no tiene fondos. oos·ted no tye·ne fon·dos	You have no funds left.
identificación f pasaporte m	ee·den·tee·fee·ka·syon pa·sa·por·te	identification passport

I'd like a …	Quisiera …	kee·sye·ra …
brochure	un panfleto	oon pan·fle·to
catalogue	un catálogo	oon ka·ta·lo·go
guide	un guía	oon gee·a
guidebook	una guía	oo·na gee·a
(in English)	turística	too·rees·tee·ka
	(en inglés)	(en een·gles)
(local) map	un mapa (local)	oon ma·pa (lo·kal)

Do you have	¿Tiene	tye·ne
information on	información sobre	een·for·ma·syon so·bre
… sights?	atracciones …?	a·trak·syo·nes …
cultural	culturales	kool·too·ra·les
historical	históricas	ees·to·ree·kas
religious	religiosas	re·lee·khyo·sas

I'd like to see …
Me gustaría ver …   me goos·ta·ree·a ver …

What's that?
¿Qué es eso?   ke es e·so

Who built/made it?
¿Quién lo construyó/hizo?   kyen lo kons·troo·yo/ee·so

How old is it?
¿Qué tan viejo es?   ke tan vye·kho es

Could you take a photo of me?
¿Podría/Podrías   po·dree·a/po·dree·as
tomarme una foto? pol/inf   to·mar·me oo·na fo·to

Can I take a photo (of you)?
¿(Le/Te) Puedo sacar   (le/te) pwe·do sa·kar
una foto? pol/inf   oo·na fo·to

I'll send you the photo.
Yo le/te mando la foto. pol/inf   yo le/te man·do la fo·to

getting in

What time does it open/close?
¿A qué hora abren/cierran?   a ke *o*·ra *a*·bren/*sye*·ran

What's the admission charge?
¿Cuánto cuesta la entrada?   kwan·to *kwes*·ta la en·*tra*·da

Is there a discount for …?	*¿Hay algún descuento para …?*	ai al·*goon* des·*kwen*·to *pa*·ra …
children	*niños*	*nee*·nyos
families	*familias*	fa·*mee*·lyas
groups	*grupos*	*groo*·pos
older people	*personas mayores*	per·*so*·nas ma·*yo*·res
pensioners	*pensionados*	pen·syo·*na*·dos
students	*estudiantes*	es·too·*dyan*·tes

tours

Can you recommend a/an ...?	¿Me podría recomendar un/una ...? m/f	me po·dree·a re·ko·men·dar oon/oo·na ...
When's the next ...?	¿Cuándo es el/la próximo/a ...? m/f	kwan·do es el/la prok·see·mo/a ...
boat trip	excursión en lancha f	eks·koor·syon en lan·cha
day trip	tour de un día m	toor de oon dee·a
ecotour	ecotour m	e·ko·toor
natural history tour	tour de historia natural m	toor de ees·to·rya na·too·ral
tour	tour m	toor
I'd like to go ...	Me gustaría ...	me goos·ta·ree·a ...
bird watching	ver pájaros	ver pa·kha·ros
canoeing	hacer canoa	a·ser ka·no·a
horse riding	hacer una cabalgata	a·ser oo·na ka·bal·ga·ta
on a guided trek	hacer trekking con guía	a·ser tre·keen kon gee·a
river rafting	ir rafting	eer raf·teen
walking on the beach	caminar en la playa	ka·mee·nar en la pla·ya
wildlife spotting	ver fauna	ver fow·na
Is ... included?	¿Incluye ...?	een·kloo·ye ...
accommodation	la dormida	la dor·mee·da
food	la comida	la ko·mee·da
transport	el transporte	el trans·por·te

I want to hire a guide.

Quiero contratar un guía.   kye·ro kon·tra·tar oon gee·a

How much for one day?

¿Cuánto cuesta por un día?   kwan·to kwes·ta por oon dee·a

How long is the tour?
   ¿Cuánto dura el tour?   kwan·to doo·ra el toor

What time should we be back?
   ¿A qué hora volvemos?   a ke o·ra vol·ve·mos

Where will we meet?
   ¿Adónde nos encontramos?   a·don·de nos en·kon·tra·mos

I'm with them.
   Yo vengo con ellos.   yo ven·go kon e·yos

I've lost my group.
   Perdí mi grupo.   per·dee mee groo·po

biological reserve	*reserva biológica* f	re·ser·va byo·lo·khee·ka
botanical garden	*jardín botánico* m	khar·deen bo·ta·nee·ko
habitat	*hábitat* m	a·bee·tat
indigenous reserve	*reserva indígena* f	re·ser·va een·dee·khe·na
national park	*parque nacional* m	par·ke na·syo·nal
wildlife refuge	*refugio de fauna silvestre* m	re·foo·khyo de fow·na seel·ves·tre

For more on habitats and wildlife, see **ecotourism**, page 149.

---

costa rican national parks

Parque Nacional Chirripó	par·ke na·syo·nal chee·ree·po	Chirripó National Park
Parque Nacional Corcovado	par·ke na·syo·nal kor·ko·va·do	Corcovado National Park
Parque Nacional Santa Rosa	par·ke na·syo·nal san·ta ro·sa	Santa Rosa National Park
Parque Nacional Tortuguero	par·ke na·syo·nal tor·too·ge·ro	Tortuguero National Park
Reserva Monteverde	re·ser·va mon·te·ver·de	Monteverde Nature Reserve

I'm attending a …	Estoy aquí para …	es·toy a·kee pa·ra …
conference	una conferencia	oo·na kon·fe·ren·sya
course	un curso	oon koor·so
meeting	una reunión	oo·na re·oo·nyon
trade fair	una feria de comercio	oo·na fe·rya de ko·mer·syo

I'm here with …	Estoy aquí con …	es·toy a·kee kon …
my colleague(s)	mi(s) colega(s)	mee(s) ko·le·ga(s)
(two) others	(dos) personas más	(dos) per·so·nas mas

I'm alone.
Estoy aquí solo/a. m/f
es·toy a·kee so·lo/a

I have an appointment with …
Tengo una cita con …
ten·go oo·na see·ta kon …

I'm staying at (the Hotel Brisamar), room (200).
*Me estoy quedando en
(el Hotel Brisamar),
habitación (doscientos).*
me es·toy ke·dan·do en
(el o·tel bree·sa·mar)
a·bee·ta·syon (do·syen·tos)

I'm here for (two) days/weeks.
*Voy a estar aquí
(dos) días/semanas.*
voy a es·tar a·kee
(dos) dee·as/se·ma·nas

Can I have your business card?
*¿Me podría dar su
tarjeta de presentación?*
me po·dree·a dar soo
tar·khe·ta de pre·sen·ta·syon

Here's my ...	*Este es mi ...*	es·te es mee ...
What's your ...?	*¿Cuál es su ...?*	kwal es soo ...
address	*dirección*	dee·rek·*syon*
email address	*correo*	ko·*re*·o
	electrónico	e·lek·*tro*·nee·ko
fax number	*número*	*noo*·me·ro
	de fax	de faks
mobile/cell	*número de*	*noo*·me·ro de
phone number	*celular*	se·loo·*lar*
pager number	*número*	*noo*·me·ro
	de beeper	de *bee*·per
work number	*número de*	*noo*·me·ro de
	teléfono del	te·*le*·fo·no del
	trabajo	tra·*ba*·kho
Where's the ...?	*¿Adónde es la ...?*	a·*don*·de es la ...
business centre	*sala*	*sa*·la
	ejecutiva	e·khe·koo·*tee*·va
conference	*conferencia*	kon·fe·*ren*·sya
meeting	*reunión*	re·oo·*nyon*
I need (a/an) ...	*Necesito ...*	ne·se·*see*·to ...
computer	*una*	*oo*·na
	computadora	kom·poo·ta·*do*·ra
Internet	*una conexión*	*oo*·na ko·nek·*syon*
connection	*de internet*	de een·ter·*net*
interpreter	*un traductor*	oon tra·dook·*tor*
who speaks	*que hable*	ke *a*·ble
(English)	*(inglés)*	(een·*gles*)
to send a fax	*mandar un fax*	man·*dar* oon faks

Thank you for your attention.
Gracias por su atención.   gra·syas por soo a·ten·*syon*

That went very well.
Estuvo muy bien.   es·*too*·vo mooy byen

Shall we go for a drink/meal?
¿Vamos a comer/tomar algo?   va·mos a ko·*mer*/to·*mar* al·go

It's on me.
Yo invito.   yo een·*vee*·to

Costa Rica is making strides to implement facilities for the elderly and people with disabilities. There are already special seats, parking spots and, in government offices, express queues reserved for people with disabilities (*filas para discapacitados* fee·las *pa*·ra dees·ka·pa·see·*ta*·dos). Wheelchair ramps are increasingly common in San José, and the country has recently established its first disabled taxi service (*taxi para discapacitados* tak·see *pa*·ra dees·ka·pa·see·*ta*·dos).

I have a disability.
Tengo una discapacidad.   ten·go *oo*·na dees·ka·pa·see·*dad*

I need assistance.
Necesito asistencia.   ne·se·*see*·to a·sees·*ten*·sya

I'm deaf.
Soy sordo/a. m/f   soy *sor*·do/a

I have a hearing aid.
Tengo un audífono.   ten·go oon ow·*dee*·fo·no

My (companion) is blind.
Mi (compañero/a)   mee (kom·pa·*nyer*·o/a)
es ciego/a. m/f   es *sye*·go/a

What services do you have for people with a disability?
¿Qué servicios tiene   ke ser·*vee*·syos *tye*·ne
para personas con   *pa*·ra per·*so*·nas kon
discapacidad?   dees·ka·pa·see·*dad*

Are guide dogs permitted?
¿Se permiten perros guías?   se per·*mee*·ten *pe*·ros *gee*·as

Are there disabled parking spaces?
¿Hay parqueo para   ai par·*ke*·o para
discapacitados?   dees·ka·pa·see·*ta*·dos

Is there wheelchair access?
¿Hay acceso para   ai ak·*se*·so *pa*·ra
silla de ruedas?   *see*·ya de *rwe*·das

How wide is the entrance?
¿Qué tan ancha   ke tan *an*·cha
es la entrada?   es la en·*tra*·da

How many steps are there?
¿Cuántas gradas hay?   *kwan*·tas *gra*·das ai

Is there an elevator?
¿Hay ascensor?   ai a·sen·*sor*

Are there disabled toilets?
¿Hay baños para   ai *ba*·nyos *pa*·ra
discapacitados?   dees·ka·pa·see·*ta*·dos

Are there rails in the bathroom?
¿Hay barras para   ai *ba*·ras *pa*·ra
sostenerse en el baño?   sos·te·*ner*·se en el *ba*·nyo

Could you call me a disabled taxi?
¿Me podría llamar   me po·*dree*·a ya·*mar*
un taxi para   oon *tak*·see *pa*·ra
discapacitados?   dees·ka·pa·see·*ta*·dos

Could you help me cross the street safely?
¿Me podría ayudar   me po·*dree*·a a·yoo·*dar*
a cruzar la calle?   a kroo·*sar* la *ka*·ye

Is there somewhere I can sit down?
¿Hay algún lugar   ai al·*goon* loo·*gar*
donde me pueda sentar?   *don*·de me *pwe*·da sen·*tar*

guide dog	*perro guía* m	*pe*·ro *gee*·a
older person	*persona mayor* f	per·*so*·na ma·*yor*
person with a disability	*discapacitado/a* m/f	dees·ka·pa·see·*ta*·do/a
ramp	*rampa* f	*ram*·pa
walking frame	*baranda* f	ba·*ran*·da
walking stick	*bastón* m	bas·*ton*
wheelchair	*silla de ruedas* f	*see*·ya de *rwe*·das

golden age

Costa Rican senior citizens are designated *ciudadanos de oro* syoo·da·*da*·nos de *o*·ro (lit: golden citizens) and have ID cards which entitle them to special privileges.

travelling with children

viajando con niños

Is there a …?	¿Tienen …?	tye·nen …
baby change room	un lugar para cambiar bebés	oon loo·gar pa·ra kam·byar be·bes
child discount	un descuento para niños	oon des·kwen·to pa·ra nee·nyos
child-minding service	una guardería	oo·na gwar·de·ree·a
children's menu	un menú para niños	oon me·noo pa·ra nee·nyos
child's portion	una porción para niños	oo·na por·syon pa·ra nee·nyos
family ticket	un tiquete familiar	oon tee·ke·te fa·mee·lyar
I need a/an …	Necesito …	ne·se·see·to …
baby seat	una silla para bebé	oo·na see·ya pa·ra be·be
(English-speaking) babysitter	una niñera (que hable inglés)	oo·na nee·nye·ra (ke a·ble een·gles)
booster seat	una silla de carro para niños	oo·na see·ya de ka·ro pa·ra nee·nyos
cot	un catre	oon ka·tre
highchair	una silla para comer	oo·na see·ya pa·ra ko·mer
plastic bag	una bolsa plástica	oo·na bol·sa plas·tee·ka
potty	una vacenilla	oo·na va·se·nee·ya
pram	un coche	oon ko·che
stroller	un coche sombrilla	oon ko·che som·bree·ya

children

93

Where's the nearest ...?	¿Adónde está el/la ... más cercano/a? m/f	a·don·de es·ta el/la ... mas ser·ka·no/a
drinking fountain	fuente de agua m	fwen·te de a·gwa
park	parque m	par·ke
playground	play m	plai
swimming pool	piscina f	pee·see·na
tap	tubo m	too·bo
toyshop	juguetería f	khoo·ge·te·ree·a

Do you sell ...?	¿Venden ...?	ven·den ...
baby wipes	pañitos desechables para bebé	pa·nyee·tos de·se·cha·bles pa·ra be·be
disposable nappies/diapers	pañales desechables	pa·nya·les de·se·cha·bles
painkillers for infants	pastillas pediátricas para el dolor	pas·tee·yas pe·dee·a·tree·kas pa·ra el do·lor
tissues	klíneks	klee·neks

Are there any good places to take children around here?

¿Hay algún lugar bonito para llevar niños por aquí? ai al·goon loo·gar bo·nee·to pa·ra ye·var nee·nyos por a·kee

Are children allowed?

¿Se permiten niños? se per·mee·ten nee·nyos

Where can I change a nappy/diaper?

¿Adónde puedo cambiar un pañal? a·don·de pwe·do kam·byar oon pa·nyal

Do you mind if I breast-feed here?

¿Le molestaría si doy de mamar aquí? le mo·les·ta·ree·a see doy de ma·mar a·kee

Could I have some paper and pencils, please?

¿Me podría dar un papel y lápices, por favor? me po·dree·a dar oon pa·pel ee la·pee·ses por fa·vor

Is this suitable for (five)-year-old children?

¿Ésto está bien para niños de (cinco) años? es·to es·ta byen pa·ra nee·nyos de (seen·ko) a·nyos

Do you know a dentist/doctor who is good with children?
¿Usted conoce algún dentista/doctor que sea bueno con los niños?	oos·*ted* ko·*no*·se al·*goon* den·*tees*·ta/dok·*tor* ke *se*·a *bwe*·no kon los *nee*·nyos

If your child is sick, see **health**, page 183.

talking with children

What's your name?
¿Cómo te llamás? — ko·mo te ya·*mas*

How old are you?
¿Cuántos años tenés? — kwan·tos *a*·nyos te·*nes*

When's your birthday?
¿Cuándo cumplís años? — kwan·do koom·*plees a*·nyos

Do you go to kindergarten?
¿Vas al kínder? — vas al *keen*·der

Do you go to school?
¿Vas a la escuela? — vas a la es·*kwe*·la

What grade are you in?
¿En qué grado estás? — en ke *gra*·do es·*tas*

Do you like (school)?
¿Te gusta (la escuela)? — te *goos*·ta (la es·*kwe*·la)

Do you learn (English)?
¿Aprendés (ingles)? — a·pren·*des* (een·*gles*)

What do you do after school?
¿Qué hacés después de la escuela? — ke a·*ses* des·*pwes* de la es·*kwe*·la

talking about children

When's the baby due?
¿Para cuándo está el bebé?   pa·ra kwan·do es·ta el be·be

What are you going to call the baby?
¿Cómo le va/vas   ko·mo le va/vas
a poner? pol/inf   a po·ner

Is this your first child?
¿Es su primer hijo/a? pol m/f   es soo pree·mer ee·kho/a
¿Es tu primer hijo/a? inf m/f   es too pree·mer ee·kho/a

How many children do you have?
¿Cuántos hijos   kwan·tos ee·khos
tiene/tenés? pol/inf   tye·ne/te·nes

What a beautiful child!
¡Qué chiquito/a   ke chee·kee·to/a
más lindo/a! m/f   mas leen·do/a

Is it a boy or a girl?
¿Es chiquito o chiquita?   es chee·kee·to o chee·kee·ta

How many months is he/she?
¿Cuántos meses tiene?   kwan·tos me·ses tye·ne

How old is he/she?
¿Cuántos años tiene?   kwan·tos a·nyos tye·ne

What's his/her name?
¿Cómo se llama?   ko·mo se ya·ma

---

who's who in the zoo?

Ever wondered how a rooster says 'cock-a-doodle-do' in Costa Rica? To break the ice with the local domestic fauna, try addressing them in their native tongue:

cat	miau	myow
chicken	pío pío	pee·o pee·o
cow	muu	moo
dog	guau guau	wow wow
rooster	ki ki ri ki	kee kee ree kee

basics

lo básico

Yes.	*Sí.*	see
No.	*No.*	no
Please.	*Por favor.*	por fa·*vor*
Thank you (very much).	*(Muchas) Gracias.*	(*moo*·chas) *gra*·syas
You're welcome.	*Con mucho gusto.*	kon *moo*·cho *goos*·to
Excuse me. (to get attention/ to get past)	*Con permiso.*	kon per·*mee*·so
Excuse me. (apology)	*Discúlpeme.*	dees·*kool*·pe·me
Sorry. (apology)	*Perdón.*	per·*don*
Sorry. (condolence)	*Lo siento.*	lo *syen*·to

greetings & goodbyes

saludos y despedidas

Costa Ricans are very conscious of civilities in their public behaviour. Never address a stranger without first extending a greeting such as *buenos días* (good morning), *buenas tardes* (good afternoon) or *buenas noches* (good evening). These may be abbreviated to simply *buenos* (for *buenos días*) and *buenas* (for *buenas tardes* and *buenas noches*).

Good ...		
day	*Buen día.*	bwen *dee*·a
morning	*Buenos (días).*	*bwe*·nos (*dee*·as)
afternoon	*Buenas (tardes).*	*bwe*·nas (*tar*·des)
evening	*Buenas (noches).*	*bwe*·nas (*no*·ches)

meeting people

97

In addition to the formal greetings on the preceding page, you can use the expressions below to greet a friend or someone you're familiar with. The expressions *pura vida* (lit: pure life) and *tuanis* (lit: too nice – from the English) are quintessential *tiquismos* tee·*kees*·mos (Costa Rican slang). If you bandy them about you might soon be taken for a *Tico* tee·ko or *Tica* tee·ka (Costa Rican man or woman) yourself. See the box **talking tiquismos**, page 134, for more on these expressions.

Hello/Hi.	*Hola.*	o·la
Hello. How's it going?	*Hola. ¿Pura vida?*	o·la poo·ra vee·da
Hello. How are things?	*Hola. ¿Todo bien?*	o·la to·do byen
Great, thanks.	*Tuanis.*	too·a·nees

How are you?
¿Cómo va/vas? sg pol/inf	ko·mo va/vas
¿Cómo van? pl	ko·mo van

Fine. And you?
Bien. ¿Y usted/vos? sg pol/inf	byen ee oos·ted/vos
Bien. ¿Y ustedes? pl	byen ee oos·te·des

What's your name?
¿Cómo se llama? pol	ko·mo se ya·ma
¿Cómo te llamás? inf	ko·mo te ya·mas

My name is …
Me llamo …	me ya·mo …

I'd like to introduce you to (Daniel).
Quiero presentarle/	kye·ro pre·sen·tar·le/
presentarte a (Daniel). pol/inf	pre·sen·tar·te a (da·nyel)

I'm pleased to meet you.
Mucho gusto.	moo·cho goos·to

knock knock …

If you're paying a visit to someone's house and can't find a doorbell, call out the following greeting to announce your presence:

¡Upe!	oo·pe	**Anyone home?**

This is my ...	*Él/Ella es mi ...* m/f	el/e·ya es mee ...
boyfriend	*novio*	*no*·vyo
child	*hijo/a* m/f	*ee*·kho/a
colleague	*colega* m&f	ko·*le*·ga
friend	*amigo/a* m/f	a·*mee*·go/a
girlfriend	*novia*	*no*·vya
husband	*esposo*	es·*po*·so
partner	*compañero/a* m/f	kom·pa·*nye*·ro/a
wife	*esposa*	es·*po*·sa

See you later.	*Nos vemos.*	nos *ve*·mos
Bye.	*Chao.*	chao
Goodbye.	*Adiós.*	a·*dyos*
Good night.	*Buenas (noches).*	*bwe*·nas (*no*·ches)
Bon voyage!	*¡Buen viaje!*	bwen *vya*·khe

addressing people

The usual nonverbal greetings are either shaking hands or kissing once on the cheek. In a formal situation or when you're meeting someone for the first time, it's probably best to shake hands. For a more informal everyday encounter, one kiss on the cheek is the usual protocol – unless it's between men, who usually just shake hands. The following titles are used in formal situations, and they're frequently abbreviated in writing:

Mr/Sir	*Señor (Sr)*	se·*nyor*
Mrs/Madam	*Señora (Sra)*	se·*nyo*·ra
Miss	*Señorita (Srta)*	se·nyo·*ree*·ta

meeting people

99

making conversation

empezando una conversación

Costa Ricans will do everything they can to *quedar bien* ke·*dar* byen (leave a good impression). To respond in kind, you should preface any conversation with enquiries about the other person's wellbeing and engage in a little small talk too.

Everything fine?
  ¿Pura vida?   poo·ra vee·da

What's going down?
  ¿Qué hay de nuevo?   ke ai de nwe·vo

Everything cool?
  ¿Qué, todo bien?   ke to·do byen

What's the news?
  ¿Qué me cuenta?   ke me kwen·ta

What a beautiful day!
  ¡Qué día más bonito!   ke dee·a mas bo·nee·to

Nice/Awful weather, isn't it?
  Qué tiempo más   ke tyem·po mas
  bonito/feo, ¿verdad?   bo·nee·to/fe·o ver·dad

Do you live here?
   ¿Vive/Vivís   vee·ve/vee·vees
   por aquí? pol/inf   por a·kee

Where are you going?
   ¿Adónde va/vas? pol/inf   a·don·de va/vas

What are you doing?
   ¿Qué está/estás   ke es·ta/es·tas
   haciendo? pol/inf   a·syen·do

Do you like it here?
   ¿Le/Te gusta aquí? pol/inf   le/te goos·ta a·kee

I love it here.
   Me encanta aquí.   me en·kan·ta a·kee

Can I take a photo of you?
   ¿Puedo tomarle/   pwe·do to·mar·le/
   tomarte una foto? pol/inf   to·mar·te oo·na fo·to

I'll send you the photo.

Yo le/te mando	yo le/te la *man*·do
la foto. pol/inf	la *fo*·to

That's (beautiful), isn't it?

Qué (bonito), ¿verdad?	ke (bo·*nee*·to) ver·*dad*

How long are you here for?

¿Cuánto tiempo va/vas	*kwan*·to *tyem*·po va/vas
a estar aquí? pol/inf	a es·*tar* a·*kee*

I'm here for (four) weeks/days.

Voy a estar aquí (cuatro)	voy a es·*tar* a·*kee* (*kwa*·tro)
semanas/días.	se·*ma*·nas/*dee*·as

Are you here on holiday?

¿Está/Estás aquí	es·*ta*/es·*tas* a·*kee*
de vacaciones? pol/inf	de va·ka·*syo*·nes

I'm here ...

	Estoy aquí ...	es·*toy* a·*kee* ...
for a holiday	*de vacaciones*	de va·ka·*syo*·nes
on business	*de negocios*	de ne·*go*·syos
to study	*estudiando*	es·too·*dyan*·do

local talk

Hey!	*¡Hey!*	khe
Great!	*¡Tuanis!*	too·*a*·nees
Just a minute.	*Dame un toque.*	da·me oon *to*·ke
Just joking.	*Estoy vacilando.*	es·*toy* va·see·*lan*·do
Maybe.	*Tal vez.*	tal ves
No problem.	*No te preocupés.*	no te pre·o·koo·*pes*
No way!	*¡Qué va!*	ke va
Sure.	*Claro.*	*kla*·ro

nationalities

Where are you from?
¿De dónde es/sos? sg pol/inf   de *don*·de es/sos

I'm from …   Soy de …   soy de …
Australia   Australia   ow·*stra*·lya
Canada   Canadá   ka·na·*da*
the USA   los Estados   los es·*ta*·dos
    Unidos   oo·*nee*·dos

---

ticomania

Costa Ricans are nicknamed *Ticos* *tee*·kos and *Ticas* *tee*·kas due to their affinity for adding endings such as *-tico/a* ·*tee*·ko/a, *-ito/a* ·*ee*·to/a or *-(c)illo/a* ·(s)ee·yo/a m/f, to the ends of words. These endings are known as diminutives. Diminutives can indicate the smallness of something – eg *gato* ga·to (cat) becomes *gatico* ga·*tee*·ko 'kitten' – but they also express how a speaker feels about something. Not surprisingly, many terms of endearment are in the form of diminutives – eg *palomita* pa·lo·*mee*·ta (darling) is a diminutive of *paloma* pa·*lo*·ma (dove). Diminutives can also give a friendly tone to a conversation. For instance, *un momentito* oon mo·men·*tee*·to (just a moment) sounds more light-hearted than *un momento* oon mo·*men*·to (one moment).

---

age

How old …?   ¿Cuantos años …?   *kwan*·tos *a*·nyos …
are you   tiene/tenés pol/inf   *tye*·ne/te·*nes*
is your   tiene su hija pol   *tye*·ne soo *ee*·kha
    daughter   tiene tu hija inf   *tye*·ne too *ee*·kha
is your son   tiene su hijo pol   *tye*·ne soo *ee*·kho
    tiene tu hijo inf   *tye*·ne too *ee*·kho

I'm … years old.
Tengo … años.   *ten*·go … *a*·nyos

He/She is … years old.
Él/Ella tiene … años.   el/*e*·ya tye·ne … *a*·nyos

Too old!
¡Demasiado viejo/a! m/f   de·ma·*sya*·do *vye*·kho/a

I'm younger than I look.
Soy menor de lo que parezco.   soy me·*nor* de lo ke pa·*res*·ko

For your age, see **numbers & amounts**, page 33.

occupations & studies

trabajo y estudio

What's your occupation?
¿Qué hace usted? pol   ke *a*·se oos·*ted*
¿Vos qué hacés? inf   vos ke a·*ses*

I'm self-employed.
Tengo mi propio negocio.   *ten*·go mee *pro*·pyo ne·*go*·syo

I'm a …	Soy …	soy …
chef	chef m&f	shef
engineer	ingeniero/a m/f	een·khe·*nye*·ro/a
journalist	periodista m&f	pe·ryo·*dees*·ta
student	estudiante m&f	es·too·*dyan*·te
teacher	profesor/	pro·fe·*sor*
	profesora m/f	pro·fe·*so*·ra

I work in …	Yo trabajo en …	yo tra·*ba*·kho en …
administration	administración	ad·mee·nees·tra·*syon*
health	salud	sa·*lood*
sales &	ventas y	*ven*·tas ee
marketing	mercadeo	mer·ka·*de*·o

I'm …	Soy …	soy …
retired	pensionado/a m/f	pen·syo·*na*·do/a
unemployed	desempleado/a m/f	de·sem·ple·*a*·do/a

What are you studying?
   ¿Qué estás estudiando?   ke es·*tas* es·too·*dyan*·do

I'm studying ...   *Estudio ...*   es·*too*·dyo ...
   humanities   *humanidades*   oo·ma·nee·*da*·des
   science   *ciencias*   *syen*·syas
   Spanish   *español*   es·pa·*nyol*

family

Family is one of the sacred pillars of Costa Rican society, so this vocabulary could well come in handy.

Do you have (a) ...?	*¿Tiene ...?* pol	*tye*·ne ...
	¿Tenés ...? inf	te·*nes* ...
I (don't) have (a) ...	*(No) Tengo ...*	(no) *ten*·go ...
boyfriend	*novio*	*no*·vyo
brother	*un hermano*	oon er·*ma*·no
children	*hijos*	*ee*·khos
daughter	*una hija*	*oo*·na *ee*·kha
girlfriend	*novia*	*no*·vya
husband	*esposo*	es·*po*·so
partner	*una pareja* m&f	*oo*·na pa·*re*·kha
sister	*una hermana*	*oo*·na er·*ma*·na
son	*un hijo*	oon *ee*·kho
wife	*esposa*	es·*po*·sa

Are you married?
   ¿Está casado/a? pol m/f   es·*ta* ka·*sa*·do/a
   ¿Estás casado/a? inf m/f   es·*tas* ka·*sa*·do/a

I live with someone.
   Vivo con alguien.   *vee*·vo kon *al*·gyen

I'm ...	*Soy ...*	soy ...
married	*casado/a* m/f	ka·*sa*·do/a
separated	*separado/a* m/f	se·pa·*ra*·do/a
single	*soltero/a* m/f	sol·*te*·ro/a

farewells

Tomorrow is my last day here.

Mañana es mi	ma·*nya*·na es mee
último día acá.	ool·*tee*·mo *dee*·a a·*ka*

If you come to (the States) you can stay with me.

Si usted venga a (los	see oos·*ted ven*·ga a (los
Estados Unidos) se puede	es·*ta*·dos oo·*nee*·dos) se *pwe*·de
quedar conmigo. pol	ke·*dar* kon·*mee*·go
Si venís a (los Estados	see ve·*nees* a (los es·*ta*·dos
Unidos) te podés	oo·*nee*·dos) te po·*des*
quedar conmigo. inf	ke·*dar* kon·*mee*·go

It's been great meeting you.

Fue un placer conocerle/	fwe oon pla·*ser* ko·no·*ser*·le/
conocerte. pol/inf	ko·no·*ser*·te

Here's my …	*Este es mi …*	es·*te* es mee …
What's your …?	*¿Cuál es*	kwal es
	su/tu …? pol/inf	soo/too …
address	*dirección*	dee·rek·*syon*
email address	*correo*	ko·*re*·o
	electrónico	e·lek·*tro*·nee·ko
phone number	*teléfono*	te·*le*·fo·no

---

well-wishing

All the best!	*¡Qué te vaya bien!*	ke te *va*·ya byen
Congratulations!	*¡Felicidades!*	fe·lee·see·*da*·des
Good luck!	*¡Buena suerte!*	*bwe*·na *swer*·te
Happy Birthday!	*¡Feliz*	fe·*lees*
	cumpleaños!	koom·ple·*a*·nyos
May God be	*¡Qué Dios te*	ke dee·*os* te
with you!	*acompañe!*	a·kom·*pa*·nye
God bless you!	*¡Qué Dios*	ke dee·*os*
	te bendiga!	te ben·*dee*·ga
Merry Christmas!	*¡Feliz Navidad!*	fe·*lees* na·vee·*dad*
Take care!	*¡Cuidate!*	*kwee*·da·te

In this chapter, phrases are given in the informal *tú* and *vos* forms. For more details on polite and informal forms, see the **phrasebuilder**, page 23.

common interests

intereses comunes

What do you do in your spare time?
¿Qué te gusta hacer en   ke te *goos*·ta a·*ser* en
el tiempo libre?   el *tyem*·po *lee*·bre

Do you like …?	*¿Te gusta …?*	te *goos*·ta …
I (don't) like …	*(No) Me gusta …*	(no) me *goos*·ta …
art	*el arte*	el *ar*·te
cooking	*cocinar*	ko·see·*nar*
dancing	*bailar*	bai·*lar*
drawing	*dibujar*	dee·boo·*khar*
gardening	*hacer el jardín*	a·*ser* el khar·*deen*
hiking	*ir a caminar*	eer a ka·mee·*nar*
listening to	*escuchar*	es·koo·*char*
music	*música*	*moo*·see·ka
painting	*pintar*	peen·*tar*
reading	*leer*	le·*er*
shopping	*ir de compras*	eer de *kom*·pras
socialising	*socializar*	so·sya·lee·*sar*
sport	*hacer deporte*	a·*ser* de·*por*·te
surfing the	*navegar el*	na·ve·*gar* el
Internet	*internet*	een·ter·*net*
travelling	*viajar*	vya·*khar*
watching films	*ver películas*	ver pe·*lee*·koo·las
watching TV	*ver tele*	ver *te*·le

For types of sports, see **sport**, page 135, and the **dictionary**.

music

música

Do you dance/sing?
¿Bailás/Cantás?   bai·*las*/kan·*tas*

Do you go to concerts?
¿Vas a conciertos?   vas a kon·*syer*·tos

Do you listen to music?
¿Escuchás música?   es·koo·*chas* moo·see·ka

Do you play an instrument?
¿Tocás algún   to·*kas* al·*goon*
instrumento?   eens·troo·*men*·to

What music do you like?
¿Qué música te gusta?   ke moo·see·ka te *goos*·ta

Which bands/singers do you like?
¿Qué grupos/cantantes   ke *groo*·pos/kan·*tan*·tes
te gustan?   te *goos*·tan

blues	*blues*	bloos
classical music	*música clásica*	moo·see·ka *kla*·see·ka
electronic music	*música electrónica*	moo·see·ka e·lek·*tro*·nee·ka
folk music	*música folklórica*	moo·see·ka fol·*klo*·ree·ka
jazz	*jazz*	shass
pop	*pop*	pop
rock	*rock*	rok
traditional music	*música tradicional*	moo·see·ka tra·dee·syo·*nal*
world music	*música internacional*	moo·see·ka een·ter·na·syo·*nal*

costa rican grooves

In Costa Rica you'll hear music from all over the world, but your ears will also become attuned to Latin American rhythms. Guanacaste province, in particular, is known for its traditional music, often based around the marimba. Here are some of the musical styles that may get you jumping:

cumbia   koom·bya
Rhythmic dance music incorporating guitars, accordions, brass, drums and percussion. It encompasses indigenous, Spanish and African influences and was originally a courtship dance among slave populations.

merengue   me·ren·ge
Lively dance music originating in the Dominican Republic, combining African and Spanish influences. Signature instruments include the tambora drum, saxophone and accordion.

reggaetón   re·ge·ton
Reggae music reborn for a new generation. It's sung in Spanish and is a hip hop and dancehall hybrid originating in Puerto Rico and New York City. Eminently danceable and wildly popular with Costa Rican youth.

salsa   sal·sa
Popular dance music originating in New York, which spread like wildfire throughout the Caribbean in the 1960s.

Planning to go to a concert? See **tickets**, page 42, and **going out**, page 119.

cinema & theatre

cine y teatro

I feel like going to a ...	Tengo ganas de ir a ...	ten·go ga·nas de eer a ...
concert	un concierto	oon kon·syer·to
film	una película	oo·na pe·lee·ko·la
play	una obra de teatro	oo·na o·bra de te·a·tro

interests

109

Did you like (the concert)?
¿Te gustó (el concierto)? te goos·to (el kon·syer·to)

What's showing at the cinema/theatre tonight?
¿Qué están dando en el ke es·tan dan·do en el
cine/teatro hoy en la noche? see·ne/te·a·tro hoy en la no·che

Is it in (English)?
¿Es en (inglés)? es en (een·gles)

Does it have (English) subtitles?
¿Tiene subtítulos en tye·ne soob·tee·too·los en
(inglés)? (een·gles)

Do you have tickets for ...?
¿Tenés entradas para ...? te·nes en·tra·das pa·ra ...

Are there any extra tickets for ...?
¿Hay más entradas para ...? ai mas en·tra·das pa·ra ...

Have you seen ...?
¿Has visto ...? as vees·to ...

Who's in it?
¿Quién tiene? kyen tye·ne

It stars ...
Protagoniza ... pro·ta·go·nee·sa ...

Is this seat taken?
¿Está ocupado? es·ta o·ko·pa·do

Is there a/an ...?	¿Hay un ...?	ai oon ...
intermission	intermedio	een·ter·me·dyo
programme	programa	pro·gra·ma
I thought it was ...	Me pareció ...	me pa·re·syo ...
excellent	excelente	ek·se·len·te
long	larga	lar·ga
OK	bien	byen

There are three ways of saying 'you' (singular) in Costa Rica. In formal situations or when you don't know someone well, it's best to use the polite (**pol**) form *usted* oos·*ted*. When the situation is informal or you're well acquainted with someone, the informal (**inf**) form *vos* vos is used. *Tú* too may also be used for informal situations, although it's less common than *vos*. In plural, however, there's only one 'you' form for both polite and informal situations – *ustedes* oos·*te*·des.

The words *usted*, *tú* and *vos* take different verb forms. Throughout this book the correct verb forms are given according to the real-life context of the phrases. Note that the pronouns are often left out in Spanish, as the verb endings tell you who's doing the action. For more information, see the **phrasebuilder**, page 23.

I (don't) like …	*(No) Me gusta/ gustan …* sg/pl	(no) me *goos*·ta/ *goos*·tan …
action movies	*las películas de acción* pl	las pe·*lee*·koo·las de ak·*syon*
animated films	*las películas animadas* pl	las pe·*lee*·koo·las a·nee·*ma*·das
(Costa Rican) cinema	*el cine (costarricense)* sg	el *see*·ne (kos·ta·ree·*sen*·se)
comedies	*las comedias* pl	las ko·*me*·dyas
documentaries	*los documentales* pl	los do·koo·men·*ta*·les
drama	*el drama* sg	el *dra*·ma
horror movies	*las películas de miedo* pl	las pe·*lee*·koo·las de *mye*·do
sci-fi	*la ciencia ficción* sg	la *syen*·sya feek·*syon*
short films	*los cortos* pl	los *kor*·tos
thrillers	*las películas de terror* pl	las pe·*lee*·koo·las de te·*ror*
war movies	*las películas de guerras* pl	las pe·*lee*·koo·las de *ge*·ras

interests

111

limón creole

If you're visiting popular destinations along the Caribbean coast, in the province of Limón, you'll notice striking differences in the language spoken by its Afro-Costa Rican community. This idiom, often referred to as *criollo limones* kree·o·yo lee·*mo*·nes (Limón Creole) is a mix of various languages and cultures in the region.

Limón Creole isn't a standardised language like English or Spanish – it changes from generation to generation and even from speaker to speaker. The idiom is a colourful hybrid of Jamaican Creole (a variation of English) and Spanish, which gradually developed among the descendents of the black 19th-century Jamaican immigrants.

An example that shows the great degree of Spanish influence in Limón Creole, particularly among younger people, is the y sound – just like the Costa Rican pronunciation of the Spanish letter *ll* – so that, for instance, the 'zh' sound in the word *gendarme* is actually pronounced as the 'y' in 'yes'.

Words in Limón Creole which are derived from English vocabulary don't necessarily have the same meaning. 'All right' often means 'hello' and 'OK' can mean 'thank you' or 'goodbye'. The Spanish phrase *es que* es ke (lit: it's that) is a common way to begin a sentence.

Looking at the same sentence in standard English, Spanish, Jamaican Creole and Limón Creole can give a good indication of the interaction between the languages and the way sentences are formed. Note that the sentences in both Jamaican and Limón Creole are spelled only phonetically to give a better idea of how they actually sound (and because the languages exist primarily in spoken form):

English	In three years, he will be ten.
Spanish	*Le faltan tres años para cumplir diez.*
	le *fal*·tan tres *a*·nyos *pa*·ra koom·*pleer* dyes
	(lit: him need three years to turn ten)
Jamaican Creole	heem *a*·ve tree *yee*·as lef fe toon ten
Limón Creole	*fal*·ta tree *yee*·as eem get ten

In this chapter, phrases are given in the informal *tú* and *vos* forms. For more details on polite and informal forms, see the **phrasebuilder**, page 23.

feelings

Feelings are described with either nouns or adjectives. The nouns use forms of the verb *tener* (have) in Spanish (eg 'I have hunger'), while the adjectives use forms of *estar* (be).

I'm (not) ...	(No) Tengo ...	(no) ten·go ...
Are you ...?	*¿Tenés ...?*	te·nes ...
cold	*frío*	free·o
hot	*calor*	ka·lor
hungry	*hambre*	am·bre
thirsty	*sed*	sed

I'm (not) ...	(No) Estoy ...	(no) es·toy ...
Are you ...?	*¿Estás ...?*	es·tas ...
happy	*contento/a* m/f	kon·ten·to/a
OK	*bien* m&f	byen
sad	*triste* m&f	trees·te
tired	*cansado/a* m/f	kan·sa·do/a

pregnant pause

If you want to say in Spanish that you're embarrassed, beware the following pitfall or you could end up with red faces all round. The word *embarazada* em·ba·ra·sa·da might look like the translation equivalent of 'embarrassed', but in actual fact means 'pregnant', as in the phrase *Estoy embarazada* es·toy em·ba·ra·sa·da (I'm pregnant). The correct word for embarrassed is *avergonzado/a* a·ver·gon·sa·do/a m/f.

mixed emotions		
not at all	*para nada*	pa·ra na·da
I don't care at all.	*No me importa*	no me eem·por·ta
	para nada.	pa·ra na·da
a little	*un poco*	oon po·ko
I'm a little sad.	*Estoy un poco*	es·toy oon po·ko
	triste.	trees·te
very	*muy*	mooy
I feel very tired.	*Estoy muy*	es·toy mooy
	cansado/a. m/f	kan·sa·do/a
extremely	*muchísimo*	moo·chee·see·mo
I'm extremely sorry.	*Lo siento*	lo syen·to
	muchísimo.	moo·chee·see·mo

If you're not feeling well, see **health**, page 183.

opinions

opiniones

Did you like it?
   ¿Te gustó?   te goos·to

What do you think of it?
   ¿Qué opinás?   ke o·pee·nas

I thought	*Pienso que*	pyen·so ke
it was ...	*estuvo ...*	es·too·vo ...
It's ...	*Es ...*	es ...
awful	*pésimo/a* m/f	pe·see·mo/a
bad	*malo/a* m/f	ma·lo/a
beautiful	*muy bonito/a* m/f	mooy bo·nee·to/a
boring	*aburrido/a* m/f	a·boo·ree·do/a
(too)	*(demasiado)*	(de·ma·sya·do)
expensive	*caro/a* m/f	ka·ro/a
great	*excelente* m&f	ek·se·len·te
interesting	*interesante* m&f	een·te·re·san·te
strange	*raro/a* m/f	ra·ro/a

politics & social issues

Costa Rica is a progressive country and has by far the most stable government and economy in Central America. The country hasn't had a military for over 50 years. Immigration, drugs, the ongoing battle against deforestation, political corruption and how to properly manage and develop the tourism boom are issues of social and political interest and debate. A growing problem in Costa Rica is also the high number of young thieves (*chapulines* cha·poo·*lee*·nes).

Who do you vote for?
   ¿Por quién votaste?   por kyen vo·*tas*·te

I support the ... party.	*Yo soy ...*	yo soy ...
I'm a member of the ... party.	*Yo soy ...*	yo soy ...
communist	*comunista* m&f	ko·moo·*nees*·ta
conservative	*conservador/*	kon·ser·va·*dor/*
	conservadora m/f	kon·ser·va·*do*·ra
democratic	*demócrata* m&f	de·*mo*·kra·ta
green	*verde* m&f	*ver*·de
liberal	*liberal* m&f	lee·be·*ral*
social	*social*	so·*syal*
democratic	*demócrata* m&f	de·*mo*·kra·ta
socialist	*socialista* m&f	so·sya·*lees*·ta

masculine or feminine?

In this phrasebook, masculine forms of nouns, pronouns and adjectives appear before the feminine forms. If you see a word ending in -*o/a*, it means the masculine form ends in -*o*, and the feminine form ends in -*a* (that is, you replace the -*o* ending with the -*a* ending to make it feminine). The same goes for the plural endings -*os/as*. In other cases we spell out the whole word.

feelings & opinions

115

party on

The two major political parties in Costa Rica are:

Partido Liberación Nacional (PLN)
par·*tee*·do lee·be·ra·*syon* na·syo·*nal*
National Liberation Party

Partido Unidad Social Cristiana (PUSC)
par·*tee*·do oo·nee·*dad* so·*syal* krees·*tya*·na
United Christian Social Party

Is there help for (the) ...?	¿Hay ayuda para los ...?	ai a·*yoo*·da *pa*·ra los ...
aged	ancianos	an·*sya*·nos
beggars	mendigos	men·*dee*·gos
disabled	discapacitados	dees·ka·pa·see·*ta*·dos
homeless	indigentes	een·dee·*khen*·tes
street kids	niños de la calle	*nee*·nyos de la *ka*·ye

Did you hear about ...?
¿Escuchaste que ...?
es·koo·*chas*·te ke ...

Do you agree with ...?
¿Estás de acuerdo con ...?
es·*tas* de a·*kwer*·do kon ...

I don't agree with ...
No estoy de acuerdo con ...
no es·*toy* de a·*kwer*·do kon ...

How do people feel about ...?
¿Qué piensa la gente sobre ...?
ke *pyen*·sa la *khen*·te *so*·bre ...

How can we protest against ...?
¿Cómo podemos protestar contra ...?
ko·mo po·*de*·mos pro·tes·*tar kon*·tra ...

How can we support ...?
¿Cómo podemos apoyar ...?
ko·mo po·*de*·mos a·po·*yar* ...

English	Spanish	Pronunciation
abortion	*aborto* m	a·*bor*·to
animal rights	*derechos de los animales* m pl	de·*re*·chos de los a·nee·*ma*·les
corruption	*corrupción* f	ko·roop·*syon*
crime	*crimen* m	*kree*·men
discrimination	*discriminación* f	dees·kree·mee·na·*syon*
drugs	*drogas* f pl	*dro*·gas
the economy	*economía* f	e·ko·no·*mee*·a
education	*educación* f	e·doo·ka·*syon*
the environment	*medio ambiente* m	*me*·dyo am·*byen*·te
equal opportunity	*igualdad de oportunidades* f	ee·gwal·*dad* de o·por·too·nee·*da*·des
euthanasia	*eutanasia* f	e·oo·ta·*na*·sya
globalisation	*globalización* f	glo·ba·lee·sa·*syon*
human rights	*derechos humanos* m pl	de·*re*·chos oo·*ma*·nos
immigration	*inmigración* f	een·me·gra·*syon*
indigenous issues	*Indígenas* m pl	een·*dee*·khe·nas
inequality	*desigualdad* f	des·ee·gwal·*dad*
party politics	*partidos políticos* m pl	par·*tee*·dos po·*lee*·tee·kos
poverty	*pobreza* f	po·*bre*·sa
privatisation	*privatización* f	pree·va·tee·sa·*syon*
racism	*racismo* m	ra·*sees*·mo
sexism	*sexismo* m	sek·*sees*·mo
social welfare	*bienestar social* m	byen·es·*tar* so·*syal*
terrorism	*terrorismo* m	te·ro·*rees*·mo
the war in (Iraq)	*la guerra en (Irak)* f	la *ge*·ra en (ee·*rak*)
unemployment	*desempleo* m	des·em·*ple*·o

---

tongue torture

Tongue twisters are known as *trabalenguas* tra·ba·*len*·gwas. Try rolling this tricky number off the tip of your tongue:

Tres tristes tigres trigo comieron.

tres *trees*·tes *tee*·gres *tree*·go ko·*mye*·ron	Three sad tigers ate wheat.

the environment

Is there a … problem here?
   ¿Hay un problema   ai oon pro·*ble*·ma
   de … aquí?   de … a·*kee*

What should be done about …?
   ¿Qué se debería   ke se de·be·*ree*·a
   hacer con respecto a …? a·*ser* kon re·*spek*·to a …

conservation	*protección*	pro·tek·*syon*
	del medio	del *me*·dyo
	ambiente f	am·*byen*·te
deforestation	*deforestación* f	de·fo·res·ta·*syon*
drought	*sequías* f pl	se·*kee*·as
ecosystem	*ecosistema* m	e·ko·sees·*te*·ma
endangered	*especies en*	es·*pe*·syas en
species	*peligro de*	pe·*lee*·gro de
	extinción f pl	eks·teen·*syon*
genetically	*alimentos*	a·lee·*men*·tos
modified food	*transgénicos* m pl	trans·*khe*·nee·kos
hunting	*caza* f	*ka*·sa
hydroelectricity	*proyectos*	pro·*yek*·tos
	hidroeléctricos m pl	ee·dro·e·*lek*·tree·kos
irrigation	*irrigación* f	ee·ree·ga·*syon*
nuclear energy	*energía*	e·ner·*khee*·a
	nuclear f	noo·kle·*ar*
nuclear testing	*pruebas*	*prwe*·bas
	nucleares f pl	noo·kle·*a*·res
ozone layer	*capa de ozono* f	*ka*·pa de o·*so*·no
pesticides	*pesticidas* m pl	pes·tee·*see*·das
pollution	*contaminación* f	kon·ta·mee·na·*syon*
recycling	*programas*	pro·*gra*·mas
programme	*de reciclaje* m pl	de re·see·*kla*·khe
toxic waste	*desechos*	de·*se*·chos
	tóxicos m pl	*tok*·see·kos
water supply	*suministro*	soo·mee·*nees*·tro
	de agua m	de *a*·gwa
wildlife poaching	*caza ilegal* f	*ka*·sa ee·le·*gal*

In this chapter, phrases are given in the informal *tú* and *vos* forms. For more details on polite and informal forms, see the **phrasebuilder**, page 23.

where to go

a dónde ir

What's there to do in the evenings?

¿Qué se puede hacer en la noche?		ke se *pwe*·de a·*ser* en la *no*·che

What's on …?	*¿Qué actividades hay …?*	ke ak·tee·vee·*da*·des ai …
locally	*por aquí*	por a·*kee*
this weekend	*este fin de semana*	*es*·te feen de se·*ma*·na
today	*hoy*	oy
tonight	*hoy en la noche*	oy en la *no*·che

out of the closet

Homosexuality is generally kept hidden in the closet in Costa Rica – as is the case throughout Central America. While most locals will be familiar with the terms *gay* gay and *lesbiana* les·*bya*·na, gay travellers should also be on the lookout for the term *playo* pla·yo. This is an offensive term for a gay man and might signal a potentially threatening situation.

On the bright side, Costa Rica does have some gay-friendly beaches and international resorts. Check ahead of your departure for information about these facilities.

Where are the ...?	¿Dónde hay ...?	don·de ai ...
bars	bares	ba·res
clubs	discotecas	dees·ko·te·kas
gay/lesbian venues	lugares gay/ lesbianas	loo·ga·res gay/ les·bya·nas
places to eat	lugares para comer	loo·ga·res pa·ra ko·mer
pubs	bares	ba·res

Is there a local ... guide?	¿Existe una guía local ...?	ek·sees·te oo·na gee·a lo·kal ...
entertainment	de entretenimiento	de en·tre·te·nee·myen·to
film	de películas	de pe·lee·koo·las
gay/lesbian	para personas gay/lesbianas	pa·ra per·so·nas gay/les·bya·nas
music	de música	de moo·see·ka

I feel like going to a ...	Tengo ganas de ir a ...	ten·go ga·nas de eer a ...
bar	un bar	oon bar
café	un café	oon ka·fe
concert	un concierto	oon kon·syer·to
film	ver una película	ver oo·na pe·lee·koo·la
(football) game	un partido de (fútbol)	oon par·tee·do de (foot·bol)
karaoke bar	un karaoke	oon ka·ra·o·ke
nightclub	un club	oon kloob
party	una fiesta	oo·na fyes·ta
performance	una presentación	oo·na pre·sen·ta·syon
play	una obra de teatro	oo·na o·bra de te·a·tro
pub	un bar	oon bar
restaurant	un restaurante	oon res·tow·ran·te

For more on bars, drinks and partying, see **romance**, page 125, and **eating out**, page 153.

invitations

What are you doing …?	¿Qué vas a hacer …?	ke vas a a·ser …
now	ahora	a·o·ra
this weekend	el fin de semana	el feen de se·ma·na
tonight	hoy en la noche	oy en la no·che

I feel like going (for a) …	Tengo ganas de ir a …	ten·go ga·nas de eer a …
Would you like to go (for a) …?	¿Querés ir a …?	ke·res eer a …
coffee	tomar un café	to·mar oon ka·fe
dancing	bailar	bai·lar
drink	tomar algo	to·mar al·go
meal	comer algo	ko·mer al·go
out somewhere	algún lado	al·goon la·do
walk	caminar	ka·mee·nar

My round.
Me toca.   me to·ka

Do you know a good restaurant?
¿Conocés un buen restaurante?   ko·no·ses oon bwen res·tow·ran·te

Do you want to come to the concert with me?
¿Querés acompañarme al concierto?   ke·res a·kom·pa·nyar·me al kon·syer·to

We're having a party.
Tenemos una fiesta.   te·ne·mos oo·na fyes·ta

You should come.
Vení.   ve·nee

responding to invitations

Sure!
¡Claro! — kla·ro

Yes, I'd love to.
Si, me encantaría. — see me en·kan·ta·ree·a

That's very kind of you.
Qué amable. — ke a·ma·ble

Where shall we go?
¿Adónde vamos? — a·don·de va·mos

No, I'm afraid I can't.
No, no puedo. — no no pwe·do

What about tomorrow?
¿Y mañana? — ee ma·nya·na

Sorry, I can't sing/dance.
Perdoná, no sé cantar/bailar. — per·do·na no se kan·tar/bai·lar

arranging to meet

What time will we meet?
¿A qué hora nos vemos? — a ke o·ra nos ve·mos

Where will we meet?
¿Adónde nos vemos? — a·don·de nos ve·mos

Let's meet at …	*Veámonos …*	ve·a·mo·nos …
(eight) o'clock	*a las (ocho)*	a las (o·cho)
the entrance	*en la entrada*	en la en·tra·da

I'll pick you up.
   Yo paso por vos.   yo *pa*·so por vos

Are you ready?
   ¿Estás listo/a? m/f   es·*tas lees*·to/a

I'm ready.
   Yo estoy listo/a. m/f   yo es·*toy lees*·to/a

I'll be coming later.
   Voy a llegar más tarde.   voy a ye·*gar* mas *tar*·de

Where will you be?
   ¿Dónde vas a estar?   *don*·de vas a es·*tar*

If I'm not there by (nine), don't wait for me.
   Si no he llegado a (las   see no e ye·*ga*·do a (las
   nueve) no me esperés.   *nwe*·ve) no me es·pe·*res*

I'll see you then.
   Nos vemos.   nos *ve*·mos

See you later.
   Nos vemos más tarde.   nos *ve*·mos mas *tar*·de

See you tomorrow.
   Nos vemos mañana.   nos *ve*·mos ma·*nya*·na

Sorry I'm late.
   Perdoná que llegara tarde. per·*do*·na ke ye·*ga*·ra *tar*·de

Never mind.
   No importa.   no eem·*por*·ta

don't worry, don't hurry

The ideas about punctuality are more relaxed in Costa Rica than in English-speaking countries. You can expect *Ticos* to be at least half an hour late for most social occasions. Costa Ricans do differentiate, however, between formal and social situations and are usually more punctual for the former.

Where punctuality is important, you could try adding the expression *en punto* en *poon*·to – meaning 'exactly' – after arranging to meet. If it's a rendez-vous for a football match you're trying to arrange, you can count on your Costa Rican friends being on time!

drugs

I don't take drugs.
Yo no uso drogas.   yo no *oo*·so *dro*·gas

I take/smoke … occasionally.
Yo uso/fumo …   yo *oo*·so/*foo*·mo …
de vez en cuando.   de ves en *kwan*·do

Do you want to have a smoke?
¿Querés fumarte un puro?   ke·*res* foo·*mar*·te oon *poo*·ro

Do you have a light?
¿Tenés fuego?   te·*nes* *fwe*·go

I'm high.
Estoy pijiado/a. m/f   es·*toy* pee·khee·*a*·do/a

If the police are talking to you about drugs, see **police**, page 180, for useful phrases.

---

fiesta fiends

Various local festivals, known as *fiestas* *fyes*·tas, add plenty of colour to life in Costa Rica. These are a few festivals of national significance:

día de los muertos   *dee*·a de los *mwer*·tos
All Souls' Day (November 2nd) – families visit graveyards to make flower offerings to their loved ones. Religious parades are also held in honour of the deceased.

semana santa   se·*ma*·na *san*·ta
Holy Week – the week leading up to Easter, celebrated with colourful religious processions and masses.

virgen de los ángeles   *veer*·khen de los *an*·khe·les
Costa Rica's patron saint is celebrated on 2 August with a particularly important procession from San José to Cartago.

In this chapter, phrases are given in the informal *tú* and *vos* forms. For more details on polite and informal forms, see the **phrasebuilder**, page 23.

asking someone out

invitando a alguien a salir

Where would you like to go (tonight)?
¿Adónde te gustaría   a·*don*·de te goos·ta·*ree*·a
ir (hoy en la noche)?   eer (oy en la *no*·che)

Would you like to do something (tomorrow)?
¿Querés hacer algo (mañana)?   ke·*res* a·*ser al*·go (ma·*nya*·na)

Yes, I'd love to.
Sí, me encantaría.   see me en·kan·ta·*ree*·a

Sorry, I can't.
Perdoná, no puedo.   per·do·*na* no *pwe*·do

local talk

How …!	*¡Qué …!*	ke …
cool	*buena nota*	*bwe*·na *no*·ta
sexy	*sexy*	*sek*·see
He/She …	*Él/Ella es …*	el/e·ya es …
is hot	*rico/a* m/f	*ree*·ko/a
gets around	*un perro/*	oon *pe*·ro/
	una perra m/f	*oo*·na *pe*·ra

He/She is a babe.
Él/Ella está guapo/a. m/f   el/e·ya es·ta *gwa*·po/a

He's a bastard.
Él es un hijueputa.   el es oon ee·khwe·*poo*·ta

She's a bitch.
Ella es una zorra.   *e*·ya es *oo*·na *so*·ra

pick-up lines

Would you like a drink?
¿Querés tomar algo?   ke·*res* to·*mar* al·go

You look like someone I know.
Me parecés conocido/a. m/f   me pa·re·*ses* ko·no·*see*·do/a

You're a fantastic dancer.
Sos un/una excelente   sos oon/*oo*·na ek·se·*len*·te
bailarín/bailarina. m/f   bai·la·*reen*/bai·la·*ree*·na

Can I …?	*¿Puedo …?*	*pwe*·do …
dance with you	*bailar contigo*	bai·*lar* kon·*tee*·go
sit here	*sentarme acá*	sen·*tar*·me a·*ka*
take you home	*llevarte a la casa*	ye·*var*·te a la *ka*·sa

macho a go go

When it comes to mating, *machismo* ma·*chees*·mo is Costa Rica's law of the jungle – men initiate most flirting. Typically a man will ask a woman to dance and will also buy drinks. Even merely striking up a conversation is usually left to the initiative of men. Feminists need not despair though, as in San José and other more cosmopolitan areas, women will sometimes make the first move and have even been known to whistle at passing men.

rejections

You're cool, but no thanks.
Me caes muy bien,   me *ka*·es mooy byen
pero no gracias.   *pe*·ro no *gra*·syas

I love you like a friend.
Te quiero como amigo/a. m/f   te *kye*·ro ko·mo a·*mee*·go/a

I'm here with my girlfriend/boyfriend.
   Estoy aquí con mi   es·*toy* a·*kee* kon mee
   novio/novia.   *no*·vyo/*no*·vya

I'd rather not.
   Mejor no.   me·*khor* no

No, thank you.
   No, gracias.   no *gra*·syas

Excuse me, I have to go now.
   Con permiso, ya   kon per·*mee*·so ya
   me tengo que ir.   me *ten*·go ke eer

giving someone the flick

Get out of here!   *¡Andáte ya!*   an·*da*·te ya
Leave me in peace!   *¡Dejáme en paz!*   de·*kha*·me en pas
Piss off!   *¡Largáte!*   lar·*ga*·te

getting closer

acercando

I really like you.
   Me gustás mucho.   me goos·*tas moo*·cho

You're great.
   Sos muy tuanis.   sos mooy too·*a*·nees

Can I kiss you?
   ¿Te puedo dar un beso?   te *pwe*·do dar oon *be*·so

Do you want to come inside for a while?
   ¿Querés entrar un rato?   ke·*res* en·*trar* oon *ra*·to

Do you want a massage?
   ¿Querés que te dé   ke·*res* ke te de
   un masaje?   oon ma·*sa*·khe

Would you like to stay over?
   ¿Te querés quedar?   te ke·*res* ke·*dar*

Can I stay over?
   ¿Me puedo quedar?   me *pwe*·do ke·*dar*

sex

sexo

Kiss me.
Dáme un beso.   *da*·me oon *be*·so

I want you.
Te deseo.   te de·*se*·o

Let's go to bed.
Vamos a la cama.   *va*·mos a la *ka*·ma

Touch me here.
Tocáme aquí.   to·*ka*·me a·*kee*

Do you like this?
¿Ésto te gusta?   *es*·to te *goos*·ta

I (don't) like that.
Éso (no) me gusta.   *e*·so (no) me *goos*·ta

I think we should stop now.
Mejor paremos ya.   me·*khor* pa·*re*·mos ya

Do you have a (condom)?
¿Tenés (preservativo)?   te·*nes* (pre·ser·va·*tee*·vo)

Let's use a (condom).
Usémos (preservativo).   oo·*se*·mos (pre·ser·va·*tee*·vo)

I won't do it without protection.
No lo voy a hacer   no lo voy a a·*ser*
sin protección.   seen pro·tek·*syon*

It's my first time.
Es mi primera vez.   es mee pree·*me*·ra ves

Don't worry, I'll do it myself.
No te preocupés,   no te pre·o·koo·*pes*
yo lo hago solo/a. m/f   yo lo *a*·go so·lo/a

SOCIAL

128

Oh my god!	¡Dios mío!	dee·os mee·o
That's great.	¡Qué bueno!	ke bwe·no
Easy tiger!	¡Suave tigre!	swa·ve tee·gre
faster	más rápido	mas ra·pee·do
harder	más duro	mas doo·ro
slower	más lento	mas len·to
softer	suave	swa·ve
That was ...	Eso estuvo ...	e·so es·too·vo ...
amazing	increíble	een·kre·ee·ble
romantic	romántico	ro·man·tee·ko
wild	salvaje	sal·va·khe

love

amor

I think we're good together.
Hacemos buena pareja. a·se·mos bwe·na pa·re·kha

I love you.
Te amo. te a·mo

Will you go out with me?
¿Saldrías conmigo? sal·dree·as kon·mee·go

Will you marry me?
¿Te casarías conmigo? te ka·sa·ree·as kon·mee·go

Will you meet my parents?
¿Conocerías a mis papás? ko·no·se·ree·as a mees pa·pas

pillow talk

It's a peculiarity of Costa Rican Spanish that seemingly unflattering turns of phrase are, in fact, terms of endearment:

My ...	Mi ...	mee ...
baby	bebé m&f	be·be
chicken	pollo/a m/f	po·yo/a
fatty	gordo/a m/f	gor·do/a
love	amor m&f	a·mor

problems

Are you seeing someone else?
¿Me estás dando vuelta?   me es·*tas dan*·do *vwel*·ta

He's just a friend.
Él es sólo un amigo.   el/e·ya es *so*·lo oon a·*mee*·go

She's just a friend.
Ella es sólo una amiga.   el/e·ya es *so*·lo *oo*·na a·*mee*·ga

You're just using me for sex.
Sólo estás   *so*·lo es·*tas*
jugando conmigo.   khoo·*gan*·do kon·*mee*·go

I never want to see you again.
No te quiero ver   no te *kye*·ro ver
nunca más.   *noon*·ka mas

I don't think it's working out.
Creo que no está   *kre*·o ke no es·*ta*
funcionando.   foon·see·o·*nan*·do

We'll work it out.
Vamos a resolverlo.   *va*·mos a re·sol·*ver*·lo

leaving

I have to leave (tomorrow).
(Mañana) Me tengo que ir.   (ma·*nya*·na) me *ten*·go ke eer

I'll call you.
Yo te llamo.   yo te *ya*·mo

I'll write to you.
Yo te escribo.   yo te es·*kree*·bo

I'll miss you.
Me vas a hacer falta.   me vas a a·*ser fal*·ta

For more phrases, see **farewells**, page 106.

religion

religión

What's your religion?
¿De qué religión es/sos? pol/inf   de ke re·lee·*khyon* es/sos

I'm not religious.
No soy religioso/a. m/f   no soy re·lee·*khyo*·so/a

I'm (a/an) ...	Soy ...	soy ...
agnostic	*agnóstico/a* m/f	ag·*nos*·tee·ko/a
Buddhist	*budista* m&f	boo·*dees*·ta
Catholic	*católico/a* m/f	ka·*to*·lee·ko/a
Christian	*cristiano/a* m/f	krees·*tya*·no/a
Hindu	*hindú* m&f	een·*doo*
Jewish	*judío/a* m/f	khoo·*dee*·o/a
Muslim	*musulmán/*	moo·sool·*man/*
	musulmána m/f	moo·sool·*ma*·na
Rastafarian	*rastafarián/*	ras·ta·fa·*ryan/*
	rastafariana m/f	ras·ta·fa·*rya*·na

I (don't)	Yo (no)	yo (no)
believe in ...	*creo en ...*	*kre*·o en ...
astrology	*la astrología*	la as·tro·lo·*khee*·a
fate	*el destino*	el des·*tee*·no
God	*Dios*	dee·*os*

Can I ... here?	¿Puedo ... aquí?	pwe·do ... a·kee
Where can I ...?	*¿Adónde puedo ...?*	a·*don*·de *pwe*·do ...
attend a	*participar en*	par·tee·see·*par* en
service	*un servicio*	oon ser·*vee*·syo
attend mass	*ir a misa*	eer a *mee*·sa
pray	*rezar*	re·*sar*

cultural differences

Is this a local or national custom?
¿Ésto es una costumbre   es·to es *oo*·na kos·*toom*·bre
local o del país?   lo·*kal* o del pa·*ees*

I don't want to offend you.
No quiero ofenderle/   no *kye*·ro o·fen·*der*·le/
ofenderte. pol/inf   o·fen·*der*·te

I'm not used to this.
No estoy acostumbrado/a   no es·*toy* a·kos·toom·*bra*·do/a
a ésto. m/f   a es·to

I'd rather not join in.
Prefiero no participar.   pre·*fye*·ro no par·tee·see·*par*

I'll try it.
Lo voy a probar.   lo voy a pro·*bar*

I didn't mean to do/say anything wrong.
No era mi intención   no *e*·ra mee een·ten·*syon*
hacer/decir algo malo.   a·*ser*/de·*seer* al·go *ma*·lo

I'm sorry, it's   *Lo siento, pero éso*   lo *syen*·to *pe*·ro *e*·so
against my ...   *va en contra de ...*   va en *kon*·tra de ...
  beliefs   *mis creencias*   mees kre·*en*·syas
  religion   *mi religión*   mee re·lee·*khyon*

This is ...   *Ésto es ...*   *es*·to es ...
  different   *diferente*   dee·fe·*ren*·te
  fun   *divertido*   dee·ver·*tee*·do
  interesting   *interesante*   een·te·re·*san*·te

---

mind your p's

As Roman Catholicism is the dominant religion in Costa Rica, be careful not to confuse *la papa* la *pa*·pa (with a lower case 'p'), which means 'potato', with *el Papa* el *pa*·pa (with an upper case 'P'), meaning 'Pope'. Best not to mix up your tubers and your pontiffs if you don't want to cause an unholy row.

SOCIAL

In this chapter, phrases are given in the informal *tú* and *vos* forms. For more details on polite and informal forms, see the **phrasebuilder**, page 23.

When's the gallery open?
 ¿Cuándo está abierta   kwan·do es·ta a·byer·ta
 la galería?   la ga·le·ree·a

When's the museum open?
 ¿Cuándo está abierto   kwan·do es·ta a·byer·to
 el museo?   el moo·se·o

What's in the collection?
 ¿Qué hay en la colección?   ke ai en la ko·lek·syon

It's an exhibition of …
 Es una exhibición de …   es oo·na ek·see·bee·syon de …

What do you think of …?
 ¿Qué opinas de …?   ke o·pee·nas de …

I like the works of …
 Me gusta la obra de …   me goos·ta la o·bra de …

It reminds me of …
 Me recuerda a …   me re·kwer·da a …

What kind of art are you interested in?
 ¿Qué tipo de arte te gusta?   ke tee·po de ar·te te goos·ta

I'm interested	Me interesa	me een·te·re·sa
in … art.	el arte …	el ar·te …
graphic	*gráfico*	gra·fee·ko
impressionist	*impresionista*	eem·pre·syo·nees·ta
indigenous	*autóctono*	ow·tok·to·no
modern	*moderno*	mo·der·no
performance	*de desempeño*	de de·sem·pe·nyo
Renaissance	*renacentista*	re·na·sen·tees·ta
traditional	*tradicional*	tra·dee·syo·nal
tropical art	*tropical*	tro·pee·kal

architecture	*arquitectura* f	ar·kee·tek·*too*·ra
art	*arte* m	*ar*·te
artwork	*obra de arte* f	o·bra de *ar*·te
curator	*curador* m	koo·ra·*dor*
exhibit n	*exhibición* f	ek·see·bee·*syon*
installation	*instalación* f	eens·ta·la·*syon*
painter	*pintor/pintora* m/f	peen·*tor*/peen·*to*·ra
painting (artwork)	*cuadro* m	*kwa*·dro
painting (technique)	*pintura* f	peen·*too*·ra
period	*periodo* m	pe·*ryo*·do
collection	*colección* f	ko·lek·*syon*
pottery	*alfarería* f	al·fa·re·*ree*·a
print n	*impresión* f	eem·pre·*syon*
sculptor	*escultor/escultora* m/f	es·kool·*tor*/es·kool·*to*·ra
sculpture	*escultura* f	es·kool·*too*·ra
statue	*estatua* f	es·*ta*·too·a
studio	*estudio* m	es·*too*·dyo
style n	*estilo* m	es·*tee*·lo

talking *tiquismos*

Ticos (Costa Ricans) colour their speech with a healthy smattering of distinctively Costa Rican expressions and slang words called *tiquismos* tee·*kees*·mos. These two phrases are ubiquitous:

¡Pura vida!   poo·ra *vee*·da
This expression embodies Costa Rican life. Meaning literally 'pure life', it's really a more profound concept encompassing wellbeing, positivity and harmony. It can variously be translated as 'great, cool, right on' etc.

¡Tuanis!   too·*a*·nees
A very popular phrase with younger folk, similar in meaning to *pura vida*. It's thought to have come from the English expression 'too nice'.

For more *tiquismos*, see the box **talking like a tico**, page 31.

In this chapter, phrases are given in the informal *tú* and *vos* forms. For more details on polite and informal forms, see the **phrasebuilder**, page 23.

sporting interests

What sport do you ...?	*¿Qué deporte ...?*	ke de·*por*·te ...
follow	*te gusta*	te *goos*·ta
play	*practicas*	prak·*tee*·kas
I follow ...	*Me gusta el ...*	me *goos*·ta el ...
I play/do ...	*Yo juego/ hago el ...*	yo *khwe*·go/ *a*·go el ...
athletics	*atletismo*	at·le·*tees*·mo
football/soccer	*fútbol*	*foot*·bol
scuba diving	*buceo*	boo·*se*·o
volleyball	*voleibol*	vo·lay·*bol*
I ...	*Yo ...*	yo ...
cycle (for fun)	*ando en bicicleta*	*an*·do en bee·see·*kle*·ta
cycle (in races)	*practico ciclismo*	prak·*tee*·ko see·*klees*·mo
run	*corro*	*ko*·ro

Do you like (surfing)?
¿Te gusta (surfear)? te *goos*·ta (soor·fe·*ar*)

Yes, very much.
Sí, mucho. see *moo*·cho

Not really.
No, en realidad no. no en re·a·lee·*dad* no

I like watching it.
    Me gusta verlo.   me *goos*·ta ver·lo

Who's your favourite athlete/player?
    ¿Quién es tu atleta/   kyen es too at·*le*·ta/
    jugador preferido?   khoo·ga·*dor* pre·fe·*ree*·do

What's your favourite team?
    ¿Cuál es tu equipo   kwal es too e·*kee*·po
    preferido?   pre·fe·*ree*·do

For more sports, see the **dictionary**.

going to a game

para ir a un partido

Would you like to go to a game?
    ¿Querés ir a un partido?   ke·*res* eer a oon par·*tee*·do

Who are you supporting?
    ¿Con quién vas?   kon kyen vas

Who's …?	*¿Quién …?*	kyen …
playing	*está jugando*	es·ta khoo·*gan*·do
winning	*va ganando*	va ga·*nan*·do

That was a	*¡Qué partido*	ke par·*tee*·do
… game!	*más …!*	mas …
bad	*malo*	*ma*·lo
boring	*aburrido*	a·boo·*ree*·do
great	*bueno*	*bwe*·no

scoring

What's the score?	*¿Cuánto van?*	*kwan*·to van
draw/even	*empate* m	em·*pa*·te
love/nil (zero)	*cero* m	*se*·ro
match-point	*punto de*	*poon*·to de
	juego m	*khwe*·go

sports talk

What a ...!	¡Qué ...!	ke ...
goal	golazo	go·la·so
hit	tiro	tee·ro
kick	patada	pa·ta·da
pass	pase	pa·se
performance	buena	bwe·na
	presentación	pre·sen·ta·syon

playing sport

practicando deporte

Do you want to play?
¿Querés jugar?
ke·res khoo·gar

Can I join in?
¿Puedo jugar?
pwe·do khoo·gar

Sure.
Claro.
kla·ro

Yes, I'd love to.
Sí, me encantaría.
see me en·kan·ta·ree·a

I can't.
No puedo.
no pwe·do

I have an injury.
Estoy lesionado/a. m/f
es·toy le·syo·na·do/a

Your/My point.
Punto mío/tuyo.
poon·to mee·o/too·yo

Kick/Pass it to me!
¡Pasámela!
pa·sa·me·la

You're a good player.
Jugás bien.
khoo·gas byen

Thanks for the game.
Gracias por el partido.
gra·syas por el par·tee·do

Where's a good place to …?	¿Dónde hay un buen lugar para …?	don·de ai oon bwen loo·gar pa·ra …
fish	pescar	pes·kar
go horse riding	montar a caballo	mon·tar a ka·ba·yo
run	correr	ko·rer
snorkel	esnorclear	e·snor·kle·ar
surf	surfear	soor·fe·ar

Where's the nearest …?	¿Dónde está … más cercano/a? m/f	don·de es·ta … mas ser·ka·no/a
golf course	el campo de golf m	el kam·po de golf
gym	el gimnasio m	el kheem·na·syo
swimming pool	la piscina f	la pee·see·na
tennis court	la cancha de tenis m	la kan·cha de te·nees

What's the charge per …?	¿Cuánto cobra por …?	kwan·to ko·bra por …
day	día	dee·a
game	juego	khwe·go
hour	hora	o·ra
visit	visita	vee·see·ta

Can I hire a …?	¿Puedo alquilar una …?	pwe·do al·kee·lar oo·na …
ball	bola	bo·la
bicycle	bicicleta	be·see·kle·ta
court	cancha	kan·cha
racquet	raqueta	ra·ke·ta

Do I have to be a member to attend?
  ¿Tengo que ser   *ten*·go ke ser
  miembro para ir?   *myem*·bro *pa*·ra eer

Is there a women-only session?
  ¿Hay alguna sesión   ai al·*goo*·na se·*syon*
  sólo para mujeres?   *so*·lo *pa*·ra moo·*khe*·res

Where are the changing rooms?
  ¿Dónde están   *don*·de es·*tan*
  los vestidores?   los ves·tee·*do*·res

diving

Where's a good diving site?
  ¿Dónde hay un buen   *don*·de ai oon bwen
  sitio para bucear?   *see*·tyo *pa*·ra boo·se·*ar*

Is the visibility good?
  ¿La visibilidad es buena? la vee·see·bee·lee·*dad* es *bwe*·na

How deep is the dive?
  ¿Qué tan hondo es el buzo? ke tan *on*·do es el *boo*·so

Is it a boat dive?
  ¿Es un buzo desde un bote? es oon *boo*·so *des*·de oon *bo*·te

Is it a shore dive?
  ¿Es un buzo desde la orilla? es oon *boo*·so *des*·de la o·*ree*·ya

I'd like to …	*Me gustaría …*	me goos·ta·*ree*·a …
explore caves/	*explorar*	eks·plo·*rar*
wrecks	*cuevas/ruinas*	*kwe*·vas/*rwee*·nas
go night diving	*bucear de*	boo·se·*ar* de
	noche	*no*·che
go scuba diving	*ir a bucear*	eer a boo·se·*ar*
go snorkelling	*ir a esnorclear*	eer a es·nor·kle·*ar*
join a diving	*ir a bucear con*	eer a boo·se·*ar* kon
tour	*un tour*	oon toor
learn to dive	*aprender a*	a·pren·*der* a
	bucear	boo·se·*ar*

Are there …?	¿Hay …?	ai …
currents	corrientes	ko·ryen·tes
sharks	tiburones	tee·boo·ro·nes
whales	ballenas	ba·ye·nas
I want to hire (a) …	Quiero alquilar …	kye·ro al·kee·lar …
buoyancy vest	un chaleco salvavidas	oon cha·le·ko sal·va·vee·das
diving equipment	equipo de buceo	e·kee·po de boo·se·o
fins	unas patas de rana	oo·nas pa·tas de ra·na
mask	una mascarilla	oo·na mas·ka·ree·ya
regulator	un regulador	oon re·goo·la·dor
snorkel	un esnórquel	oon e·snor·kel
tank	un tanque	oon tan·ke
weight belt	un cinturón de pesas	oon seen·too·ron de pe·sas
wetsuit	un traje de buzo	oon tra·khe de boo·so

buddy	compañero/a m/f	kom·pa·nye·ro/a
cave n	cueva f	kwe·va
dive n	buceo m	boo·se·o
dive v	bucear	boo·se·ar
diving boat	bote de buceo m	bo·te de boo·se·o
diving course	curso de buceo m	koor·so de boo·se·o
night dive	buceo nocturno m	boo·se·o nok·toor·no
wreck n	ruinas f pl	rwee·nas

extreme sports

I'd like to go ...	Quiero ...	kye·ro ...
bungee jumping	tirarme de bungee	tee·rar·me de boon·gee
caving	ir a explorar cavernas	eer a eks·plo·rar ka·ver·nas
canopying	ir al canopy	eer al ka·no·pee
game fishing	ir de pesca	eer de pes·ka
mountain biking	practicar ciclismo de montaña	prak·tee·kar see·klees·mo de mon·ta·nya
sea-kayaking	andar en kayak en el mar	an·dar en ka·yak en el mar
sky-diving	tirarme en paracaídas	tee·rar·me en pa·ra·ka·ee·das
white-water rafting	ir a los rápidos	eer a los ra·pee·dos

Is the equipment secure?
¿Está bien puesto el equipo?   es·ta byen pwes·to el e·kee·po

Is this safe?
¿Ésto es seguro?   es·to es se·goo·ro

This is insane.
Ésto es de locos.   es·to es de lo·kos

football/soccer

Who plays for (Saprissa)?
¿Quién juega con (Saprissa)?   kyen khwe·ga kon (sa·pree·sa)

He's a great (player).
Él es un (jugador) buenísimo.   el es oon (khoo·ga·dor) bwe·nee·see·mo

He played brilliantly in the match against (Brazil).

Jugó muy bien en	khoo·*go* mooy byen en
el partido contra (Brasil).	el par·*tee*·do *kon*·tra (bra·*seel*)

Which team is at the top of the league?

¿Cuál equipo está de	kwal e·*kee*·po es·*ta* de
primero en la tabla?	pree·*me*·ro en la *ta*·bla

What a great/terrible team!

¿Qué equipo más	ke e·*kee*·po mas
bueno/malo!	*bwe*·no/*ma*·lo

ball	*bola* f	*bo*·la
coach n	*entrenador* m	en·tre·na·*dor*
corner (kick) n	*tiro de esquina* m	*tee*·ro de es·*kee*·na
fan	*aficionado/a* m/f	a·fee·syo·*na*·do/a
foul n	*falta* f	*fal*·ta
free kick	*tiro libre* m	*tee*·ro *lee*·bre
goal	*gol* m	gol
goalkeeper	*portero/a* m/f	por·*te*·ro/a
manager	*director* m	dee·rek·*tor*
offside	*posición*	po·see·*syon*
	prohibida f	pro·ee·*bee*·da
penalty	*penal* m	pe·*nal*
red card	*tarjeta roja* f	tar·*khe*·ta *ro*·kha
referee	*árbitro* m	*ar*·bee·tro
throw in v	*meter*	me·*ter*

Off to see a match? Check out **going to a game**, page 136.

surfing

How do I get to the surf beaches?

¿Cómo llego a las	*ko*·mo *ye*·go a las
playas de surfear?	*pla*·yas de soor·fe·*ar*

Which beach has the best conditions today?

¿Cuál playa tiene las	kwal *pla*·ya *tye*·ne las
mejores condiciones hoy?	me·*kho*·res kon·dee·*syo*·nes oy

Where's the nearest beach/point break?
  ¿Dónde está el beach/   *don·*de es·*ta* el beech/
  point break más cerca?   poynt brek mas *ser*·ka

Where's the best beach/point break?
  ¿Dónde está el mejor   *don·*de es·*ta* el me·*khor*
  beach/point break?   beech/poynt brek

What are the best times to surf there?
  ¿Cuál es la mejor   kwal es la me·*khor*
  hora para surfear ahí?   *o*·ra *pa*·ra soor·fe·*ar* a·*ee*

Is the swell big?
  ¿Son grandes las olas?   son *gran*·des las *o*·las

Does it barrel?
  ¿Hay tubos?   ai *too*·bos

Does it work at high/low tide?
  ¿Sirve en marea   *seer*·ve en ma·*re*·a
  alta/baja?   *al*·ta/*ba*·kha

Do you know any secret spots?
  ¿Conocés algún   ko·no·*ses* al·*goon*
  lugar secreto?   loo·*gar* se·*kre*·to

Where can I find a surf shop?
  ¿Dónde hay una   *don*·de ai *oo*·na
  tienda de surf?   *tyen*·da de soorf

Where can I ...	*¿Dónde puedo ...*	*don*·de *pwe*·do ...
(equipment)?	*(equipo)?*	(e·*kee*·po)
buy	*comprar*	kom·*prar*
rent	*alquilar*	al·kee·*lar*
repair	*arreglar*	a·re·*glar*

board bag	bolsa para la tabla f	bol·sa pa·ra la ta·bla
body board	bodyboard m	bo·dee·bord
fin(s)	pata(s) de rana f	pa·ta(s) de ra·na
sailboarding	tabla de vela f	ta·bla de ve·la
sailing boat	bote de vela m	bo·te de ve·la
set n	set m	set
surfing n	surf m	soorf
surf v	surfear	soor·fe·ar
surfboard	tabla de surf f	ta·bla de soorf
wave n	ola f	o·la
wax n	cera f	se·ra

water sports

deportes acuáticos

Can I book a lesson?

| ¿Puedo apuntarme | pwe·do a·poon·tar·me |
| en una clase? | en oo·na kla·se |

Can I hire (a) ...?	¿Puedo alquilar ...?	pwe·do al·kee·lar ...
boat	un bote	oon bo·te
canoe	una canoa	oo·na ka·no·a
kayak	un kayak	oon ka·yak
life jacket	un chaleco	oon cha·le·ko
	salvavidas	sal·va·va·vee·das
snorkelling	equipo para	e·kee·po pa·ra
gear	esnorclear	e·snor·kle·ar
water-skis	esquís de agua	es·kees de a·gwa
wetsuit	un traje de	oon tra·khe de
	neoprene	ne·o·pre·ne

Are there	¿Hay algunos/	ai al·goo·nos/
any ...?	algunas ...? m/f	algunas ...
reefs	arrecifes m	a·re·see·fes
rips	corrientes f	ko·ryen·tes

guide n	guía m	gee·a
motorboat	bote de motor m	bo·te de mo·tor
oars	paletas f pl	pa·le·tas

hiking

caminatas

Where can I …?	¿Dónde puedo …?	don·de pwe·do …
buy supplies	comprar provisiones	kom·prar pro·vee·syo·nes
find someone who knows this area	encontrar a alguien que conozca la zona	en·kon·trar a al·gyen ke ko·nos·ka la so·na
get a map	conseguir un mapa	kon·se·geer oon ma·pa
hire hiking gear	alquilar equipo para la caminata	al·kee·lar e·kee·po pa·ra la ka·mee·na·ta

How …?	¿Qué tan …?	ke tan …
high is the climb	alta es la subida	al·ta es la soo·bee·da
long is the trail	largo es el sendero	lar·go es el sen·de·ro

Is the route scenic?
¿Es panorámica la ruta? — es pa·no·ra·mee·ka la roo·ta

Do we need a guide?
¿Ocupamos un guía? — o·koo·pa·mos oon gee·a

Are there guided treks?
¿Hay caminatas con guía? — ai ka·mee·na·tas kon gee·a

Is it safe?
¿Es seguro? — es se·goo·ro

Is there a hut?
¿Hay un rancho? — ai oon ran·cho

When does it get dark?
¿A qué hora oscurece? — a ke o·ra os·koo·re·se

Do we need to take …?	¿Tenemos que llevar …?	te·*ne*·mos ke ye·*var* …
bedding	*ropa de cama*	*ro*·pa de *ka*·ma
food	*comida*	ko·*mee*·da
water	*agua*	*a*·gwa
Is the track …?	¿El sendero está …?	el sen·*de*·ro es·*ta* …
(well) marked	*(bien) marcado*	(byen) mar·*ka*·do
open	*abierto*	a·*byer*·to
Which is the … route?	¿Cuál es el camino más …?	kwal es el ka·*mee*·no mas …
easiest	*fácil*	*fa*·seel
shortest	*corto*	*kor*·to
Where can I find the …?	¿Dónde queda/ quedan …? sg/pl	*don*·de *ke*·da/ *ke*·dan …
camping ground	*la zona para acampar* sg	la *so*·na *pa*·ra a·kam·*par*
showers	*las duchas* pl	las *doo*·chas
toilets	*los baños* pl	los *ba*·nyos

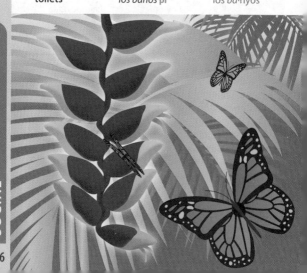

Where have you come from?
¿De dónde viene/vienen? sg/pl   de *don*·de *vye*·ne/*vye*·nen

How long did it take you?
¿Cuánto duró/duraron   *kwan*·to doo·*ro*/doo·*ra*·ron
en llegar? sg/pl   en ye·*gar*

Does this path go to (Arenal)?
¿Este camino   *es*·te ka·*mee*·no
llega a (Arenal)?   *ye*·ga a (a·re·*nal*)

Can I go through here?
¿Puedo pasar por aquí?   *pwe*·do pa·*sar* por a·*kee*

Is the water OK to drink?
¿Se puede beber el agua?   se *pwe*·de be·*ber* el *a*·gwa

I'm lost.
Estoy perdido/a. m/f   es·*toy* per·*dee*·do/a

beach

playa

Where's the ... beach?	¿Dónde está la ...?	*don*·de es·*ta* la ...
best	mejor playa	me·*khor* pla·ya
nearest	playa más cercana	*pla*·ya mas ser·*ka*·na
How much to rent a/an ...?	¿Cuánto cuesta alquilar ...?	*kwan*·to *kwes*·ta al·kee·*lar* ...
chair	una silla	*oo*·na *see*·ya
hut	un rancho	oon *ran*·cho
umbrella	una sombrilla	*oo*·na som·*bree*·ya

signs

Prohibido Hacer Clavados	pro·ee·*bee*·do a·*ser* kla·*va*·dos	**No Diving**
Prohibido Nadar	pro·ee·*bee*·do na·*dar*	**No Swimming**

outdoors

147

Is it dangerous to dive/swim here?
    ¿Será peligroso bucear/   se·ra pe·lee·gro·so boo·se·ar/
    nadar aquí?   na·dar a·kee

What time is high/low tide?
    ¿A qué hora es la   a ke o·ra es la
    marea alta/baja?   ma·re·a al·ta/ba·kha

weather

tiempo

What's the weather like?
    ¿Cómo está el tiempo?   ko·mo es·ta el tyem·po

It's ...	*Está ...*	es·ta ...
cloudy	*nublado*	noo·bla·do
cold	*frío*	free·o
hot	*haciendo*	a·syen·do
	mucho calor	moo·cho ka·lor
raining	*lloviendo*	yo·vyen·do
sunny	*haciendo sol*	a·syen·do sol
warm	*caliente*	ka·lyen·te
windy	*ventoso*	ven·to·so

Where can I	*¿Dónde puedo*	don·de pwe·do
buy a/an ...?	*comprar una ...?*	kom·prar oo·na ...
rain jacket	*capa*	ka·pa
umbrella	*sombrilla*	som·bree·ya

dry season	*estación seca* f	es·ta·syon se·ka
wet season	*estación lluviosa* f	es·ta·syon yoo·vyo·sa

ecotourism

ecoturismo

Costa Rica boasts some of the most diverse flora and fauna in the world, and opportunities for wildlife enthusiasts are endless. The country is known for its serious approach to conservation and protection of the environment, which includes one of the best park systems in the Western Hemisphere. Costa Rica also has numerous privately owned parks and ecotourism projects.

What ... is that?	¿Qué es ...?	ke es ...
animal	ese animal	e·se a·nee·mal
flower	esa flor	e·sa flor
plant	esa mata	e·sa ma·ta
tree	ese árbol	e·se ar·bol

What's it used for?
¿Para qué se usa?　　　pa·ra ke se oo·sa

Can you eat the fruit?
¿Esa fruta se come?　　e·sa froo·ta se ko·me

Is it ...?	¿Es ...?	es ...
dangerous	peligroso/a m/f	pe·lee·gro·so/a
poisonous	venenoso/a m/f	ve·ne·no·so/a

Is it ...?	¿Está ...?	es·ta ...
endangered	en peligro	en pe·lee·gro
	de extinción	de eks·teen·syon
protected	protegido/a m/f	pro·te·khee·do/a

Is this a	¿Este/Esta es ...	es·te/es·ta es ...
protected ...?	protegido/a? m/f	pro·te·khee·do/a
park	un parque m	oon par·ke
species	una especie f	oo·na es·pe·sye

ecotourism

149

What time is best for seeing …?
  ¿Cuál es la mejor   kwal es la me·*khor*
  hora para ver …?   o·ra *pa*·ra ver …

Can I see … here?
  ¿Puedo ver … aquí?   *pwe*·do ver … a·*kee*

Are there active volcanoes in this area?
  ¿Hay volcanes activos   ai vol·*ka*·nes ak·*tee*·vos
  en esta zona?   en *es*·ta *so*·na

Is that an active volcano?
  ¿Es un volcán activo?   es oon vol·*kan* ak·*tee*·vo

wildlife & habitat

flora, fauna y hábitat

geography

cave	*cueva* f	*kwe*·va
cliff	*acantilado* m	a·kan·tee·*la*·do
estuary	*estuario* m	es·too·*a*·ryo
forest	*bosque* m	*bos*·ke
hill	*colina* f	ko·*lee*·na
island	*isla* f	*ees*·la
lake	*lago* m	*la*·go
lava	*lava* f	*la*·va
mountain	*montaña* f	mon·*ta*·nya
mountain range	*sierra* f	*sye*·ra
ocean	*océano* m	o·*se*·a·no
river	*río* m	*ree*·o
sea	*mar* m	mar
swamp	*pantano* m	pan·*ta*·no
valley	*valle* m	*va*·ye
volcano	*volcán* m	vol·*kan*
waterfall	*salto* m	*sal*·to
wildlife	*flora y fauna*	*flo*·ra ee *fow*·na
	silvestre f	seel·*ves*·tre

flora

ceiba (silk cotton tree)	*ceiba* f	*say*·ba
cloud forest	*bosque nuboso* m	*bos*·ke noo·*bo*·so
guanacaste tree (national tree)	*árbol de guanacaste* m	*ar*·bol de gwa·na·*kas*·te
jungle	*selva* f	*sel*·va
mangrove	*manglar* m	man·*glar*
orchid	*orquídea* f	or·*kee*·de·a
palm tree	*palma* f	*pal*·ma
purple orchid (national flower)	*guaria morada* f	*gwa*·ree·a mo·*ra*·da
rain forest	*bosque lluvioso* m	*bos*·ke yoo·*vyo*·so
tropical dry forest	*bosque seco tropical* m	*bos*·ke *se*·ko tro·pee·*kal*
tropical plains	*llanura tropical* f	ya·*noo*·ra tro·pee·*kal*

mammals

agouti	*guatusa* f	gwa·*too*·sa
anteater	*oso hormiguero* m	*o*·so or·mee·*ge*·ro
armadillo	*armadillo* m	ar·ma·*dee*·yo
capuchin monkey	*mono capuchín* m	*mo*·no ka·poo·*cheen*
coati	*pizote* m	pee·*so*·te
howler monkey	*mono congo* m	*mo*·no *kon*·go
jaguar	*jaguar* m	kha·*gwar*
kinkajou	*martilla* f	mar·*tee*·ya
monkey	*mono* m	*mo*·no
opossum	*zorro* m	*so*·ro
paca	*tepezcuintle* m	te·pes·*kweent*·le
peccary	*chancho del monte* m	*chan*·cho del *mon*·te
sloth	*oso perezoso* m	*o*·so pe·re·*so*·so
spider monkey	*mono araña* m	*mo*·no a·*ra*·nya
squirrel	*ardilla* f	ar·*dee*·ya
squirrel monkey	*mono tití* m	*mo*·no tee·*tee*
tapir	*danta* f	*dan*·ta

ecotourism

151

insects & birds

ant	*hormiga* f	or·*mee*·ga
butterfly	*mariposa* f	ma·ree·*po*·sa
eagle	*águila* m	*a*·gee·la
heron	*garza* f	*gar*·sa
hummingbird	*colibrí* m	ko·lee·*bree*
jacana	*jacana* f	kha·*ka*·na
macaw	*lapa* f	*la*·pa
morpho butterfly	*morfo* m	*mor*·fo
mosquito	*zancudo* m	san·*koo*·do
parakeet	*perico* m	pe·*ree*·ko
pelican	*pelícano* m	pe·*lee*·ka·no
pigeon	*paloma* f	pa·*lo*·ma
quetzal	*quetzal* m	ket·*sal*
toucan	*tucán* m	too·*kan*
vulture	*buitre* m	*bwee*·tre
yigüirro (national bird)	*yigüirro* m	yee·*gwee*·ro

reptiles

bushmaster (snake)	*cascabel muda* f	kas·ka·*bel moo*·da
crocodile	*cocodrilo* m	ko·ko·*dree*·lo
fer-de-lance (snake)	*terciopelo* m	ter·syo·*pe*·lo
iguana	*iguana* f/*garrobo* m	ee·*gwa*·na/ga·*ro*·bo
lizard	*lagarto* m	la·*gar*·to
snake	*culebra* f	koo·*le*·bra

marine life

dolphin	*delfín* m	del·*feen*
fish	*pes* m	pes
frog	*rana* f	*ra*·na
manatee	*manatí* m	ma·na·*tee*
otter	*nutria* f	noo·*tree*·a
turtle	*tortuga* f	tor·*too*·ga
whale	*ballena* f	ba·*ye*·na

basics

breakfast	*desayuno* m	de·sa·*yoo*·no
lunch	*almuerzo* m	al·*mwer*·so
dinner	*cena* f	*se*·na
snack n	*merienda* f	me·*ryen*·da
eat v	*comer*	ko·*mer*
drink v	*beber*	be·*ber*
I'd like ...	*Me gustaría ...* pol	me goos·ta·*ree*·a ...
	Quiero ... inf	*kye*·ro ...
Please.	*Por favor.*	por fa·*vor*
Thank you.	*Gracias.*	*gra*·syas
Enjoy your meal.	*(Buen) Provecho.*	(bwen) pro·*ve*·cho
Cheers!	*¡Salud!*	sa·*lood*

a match made in heaven

The traditional lunch and dinner are variations on the famous *casado* ka·*sa*·do (lit: married couple). This match-made-in-heaven is a hearty combination plate of rice, beans, shredded cabbage salad, vegetable or fruit *picadillo* pee·ka·*dee*·yo (mince) and a meat of choice (beef, fish, pork or chicken). The whole is garnished with fried plantains, tortillas and a slice or two of tomato. It's cheap and more than enough to keep body and soul together! Specify what meat you want by asking for *bife* bee·fe (beef), *pescado* pes·*ka*·do (fish), *puerco* pwer·ko (pork) or *pollo* po·yo (chicken).

finding a place to eat

Can you recommend a ...?	¿Podría recomendar ...?	po·dree·a re·ko·men·dar ...
bar	un bar	oon bar
café	un café	oon ka·fe
lunch counter	una soda	oo·na so·da
(Chinese) restaurant	un restaurante (chino)	oon res·tow·ran·te (chee·no)

Where would you go for (a) ...?	¿Dónde podría ir para ...?	don·de po·dree·a eer pa·ra ...
celebration	una celebración	oo·na se·le·bra·syon
cheap meal	comer barato	ko·mer ba·ra·to
local specialities	comer comida local	ko·mer ko·mee·da lo·kal

I'd like to reserve a table for ...	Quiero reservar una mesa para ...	kye·ro re·ser·var oo·na me·sa pa·ra ...
(two) people	(dos) personas	(dos) per·so·nas
(eight) o'clock	las (ocho)	las (o·cho)

at the counter

If it's snacks you're after, you should be on the lookout for a *soda* so·da. You shouldn't have to look too far because they abound and come in various guises ranging from a lean-to or shack with a couple of makeshift tables to a small café-style restaurant.

Sodas dispense drinks and *casados* ka·sa·dos (combination plates of rice and meat or vegetables) in addition to snacks. They usually also sell *empanadas* em·pa·na·das (turnovers), *gallos* ga·yos (tortilla sandwiches) or *enchiladas* en·chee·la·das (pastries with spicy meat). Grilled beef or pork kebabs known as *pinchos* peen·chos are also a popular snack on the go. For more on these items and Costa Rican cuisine generally, see the **culinary reader**.

Are you still serving food?
¿Todavía están sirviendo comida?
to·da·*vee*·a es·*tan* seer·*vyen*·do ko·*mee*·da

How long is the wait?
¿Cuánto tengo que esperar? *kwan*·to *ten*·go ke es·pe·*rar*

listen for ...		
Está cerrado.	es·*ta* se·*ra*·do	**We're closed.**
Está lleno.	es·*ta* ye·no	**We're full.**
Un momento.	oon mo·*men*·to	**One moment.**

at the restaurant

en el restaurante

I'd like (a/the) ...	*Quisiera ..., por favor.*	kee·*sye*·ra ... por fa·*vor*
(non)smoking section	*el área de (no) fumado*	el *a*·re·a de (no) foo·*ma*·do
table for (five)	*una mesa para (cinco)*	*oo*·na *me*·sa *pa*·ra (*seen*·ko)
that dish	*ese plato*	*e*·se *pla*·to

What would you recommend?
¿Qué me recomienda? ke me re·ko·*myen*·da

What's in that dish?
¿Ese plato qué trae? *e*·se *pla*·to ke *tra*·e

What's that called?
¿Éso cómo se llama? *e*·so *ko*·mo se *ya*·ma

I'll have that.
Yo quiero éso. yo *kye*·ro *e*·so

Does it take long to prepare?
¿Se dura mucho preparándolo? se *doo*·ra *moo*·cho pre·pa·*ran*·do·lo

Is it self-serve?
¿Es de auto-servicio? es de ow·to·ser·*vee*·syo

eating out

155

Is there a cover/service charge?
¿Hay que pagar   ai ke pa·*gar*
entrada/servicio?   en·*tra*·da/ser·*vee*·syo

Is service included in the bill?
¿El servicio está incluído?   el ser·*vee*·syo es·*ta* een·kloo·*ee*·do

Are these complimentary?
¿Son gratis?   son *gra*·tees

Could I see the wine list?
¿Podría ver la lista   po·*dree*·a ver la *lees*·ta
de vinos, por favor?   de *vee*·nos por fa·*vor*

Bring me a/the ..., please.	*Tráigame ..., por favor.*	*trai*·ga·me ... por fa·*vor*
children's menu	*el menú para niños*	el me·*noo* pa·ra *nee*·nyos
drink list	*la lista de tragos*	la *lees*·ta de *tra*·gos
half portion	*media porción*	*me*·dya por·*syon*
local speciality	*una especialidad local*	*oo*·na es·pe·sya·lee·*dad* lo·*kal*
menu (in English)	*el menú (en inglés)*	el me·*noo* (en een·*gles*)

listen for ...

¿Cómo lo/la quiere? m/f
ko·mo lo/la *kye*·re   **How would you like that?**

¿Dónde se quiere sentar?
don·de se *kye*·re sen·*tar*   **Where would you like to sit?**

¿Qué le puedo traer?
ke le *pwe*·do tra·*er*   **What can I get for you?**

¡Aquí está!   a·*kee* es·*ta*   **Here you go!**
Buen provecho.   bwen pro·*ve*·cho   **Enjoy your meal.**
¿Le gusta ...?   le *goos*·ta ...   **Do you like ...?**
Le recomiendo ...   le re·ko·*myen*·do ...   **I suggest the ...**

FOOD

I'd like it with/	Lo quiero	lo kye·ro
without ...	con/sin ...	kon/seen ...
cheese	queso	ke·so
chilli sauce	salsa picante	sal·sa pee·kan·te
garlic	ajo	a·kho
ketchup	ketchup	ke·tchoop
nuts	nueces	nwe·ses
oil	aceite	a·say·te
pepper	pimienta	pee·myen·ta
Salsa Lizano	Salsa Lizano	sal·sa lee·sa·no
salt	sal	sal
vinegar	vinagre	vee·na·gre

For other specific meal requests, see **vegetarian & special meals**, page 169.

at the table

en la mesa

Please bring	Por favor	por fa·vor
(a/the) ...	tráigame ...	trai·ga·me ...
bill	la cuenta	la kwen·ta
cutlery	los cubiertos	los koo·byer·tos
glass	un vaso	oon va·so
serviette	una servilleta	oo·na ser·vee·ye·ta

There's a mistake in the bill.
    Hay un error en la cuenta.   ai oon e·ror en la kwen·ta

I didn't order this.
    No pedí esto.   no pe·dee es·to

talking food

I'm starving!
*¡Me estoy muriendo
de hambre!*
me es·*toy* moo·*ryen*·do
de *am*·bre

The food is very good.
La comida está muy rica.
la ko·*mee*·da es·*ta* mooy *ree*·ka

I love the local cuisine.
*Me encanta la
comida de aquí.*
me en·*kan*·ta la
ko·*mee*·da de a·*kee*

I love this dish.
Me encanta este plato.
me en·*kan*·ta es·te *pla*·to

That was delicious!
¡Estuvo delicioso!
es·*too*·vo de·lee·*syo*·so

I'm full.
Estoy lleno/a. m/f
es·*toy ye*·no/a

ashtray
cenicero m
se·nee·*se*·ro

spoon
cuchara f
koo·*cha*·ra

fork
tenedor m
te·ne·*dor*

plate
plato m
pla·to

knife
cuchillo m
koo·*chee*·yo

wineglass
copa f
ko·pa

glass
vaso m
va·so

table
mesa f
me·sa

This is ...	*Está ...*	es·ta ...
burnt	*quemado*	ke·ma·do
cold	*frío*	free·o
hot	*caliente*	ka·lyen·te
(too) spicy	*(demasiado)*	(de·ma·sya·do)
	condimentado	kon·dee·men·ta·do

look for ...

Aperitivos	a·pe·ree·tee·vos	Appetisers
Sopas	so·pas	Soups
Entradas	en·tra·das	Entrées
Ensaladas	en·sa·la·das	Salads
Platos Fuertes	pla·tos fwer·tes	Main Courses
Guarniciónes	gwar·nee·syo·nes	Side Dishes (at restaurants)
Acompañamientos	a·kom·pa·nya·myen·tos	Side Dishes (at bars & lunch counters)
Postres	pos·tres	Desserts
Bebidas	be·bee·das	Drinks
Refrescos	re·fres·kos	Soft Drinks
Cocteles	kok·te·les	Spirits
Cervezas	ser·ve·sas	Beers
Vinos ...	vee·nos ...	... Wines
Blancos	blan·kos	White
Digestivos	dee·khes·tee·vos	Dessert
Espumantes	es·poo·man·tes	Sparkling
Tintos	teen·tos	Red

For more words you might see on a menu, see the **culinary reader**, page 171.

eating out

159

methods of preparation

I'd like it …	*Lo quiero …*	lo *kye*·ro …
I don't want it …	*No lo quiero …*	no lo *kye*·ro …
boiled	*hervido*	er·*vee*·do
broiled	*asado*	a·*sa*·do
fried	*frito*	*free*·to
grilled	*a la parrilla*	a la pa·*ree*·ya
mashed	*en puré*	en poo·*re*
medium	*término medio*	*ter*·mee·no *me*·dyo
rare	*crudo*	*kroo*·do
reheated	*recalentado*	re·ka·len·*ta*·do
steamed	*al vapor*	al va·*por*
well-done	*bien cocinado*	byen ko·see·*na*·do
with the dressing	*con el aderezo*	kon el a·de·*re*·so
on the side	*al lado*	al *la*·do
without …	*sin …*	seen …

nonalcoholic drinks

boiled water	*agua*	*a*·gwa
	hervida f	er·*vee*·da
bottled water	*agua*	*a*·gwa
	embotellada f	em·bo·te·*ya*·da
freshly-squeezed fruit drink	*fresco* m	*fres*·ko
fruit shake	*batido* m	ba·*tee*·do
hot water	*agua caliente* f	*a*·gwa ka·*lyen*·te
iced tea	*té con hielo* m	te kon *ye*·lo
(orange) juice	*jugo*	*khoo*·go
	(de naranja) m	(de na·*ran*·kha)
mineral water	*agua mineral* f	*a*·gwa mee·ne·*ral*
soft drink	*gaseosa* f	ga·se·*o*·sa
sparkling mineral water	*soda* f	*so*·da
with/without ice	*con/sin hielo*	kon/seen *ye*·lo

(cup of) coffee …	(taza de) café …	(ta·sa de) ka·fe …
(cup of) tea …	(taza de) té …	(ta·sa de) te …
with (milk)	con (leche)	kon (le·che)
without (sugar)	sin (azúcar)	seen (a·soo·kar)
… coffee	café …	ka·fe …
black	negro	ne·gro
decaffeinated	descafeinado	des·ka·fay·na·do
strong	fuerte	fwer·te
weak	ralo	ra·lo
white	con leche	kon le·che

juicy treats

There are many delicious ways to quench your thirst in Costa Rica. Top of the list are the seemingly infinite varieties of *refrescos naturales* re·fres·kos na·too·ra·les, usually known simply as *frescos* fres·kos. These consist of almost any kind of fruit squeezed or blended with water and sugar or milk. You can specify whether you want water or milk by saying *con agua* kon a·gwa (with water) or *con leche* kon le·che (with milk). When ordering, simply refer to the flavour you want, eg *mora con leche* mo·ra kon le·che (blackberry with milk). Also popular are *batidos* ba·tee·dos (fruit shakes) which are essentially the same as *frescos* but thicker. Below are some of the most popular fruit flavours for both *frescos* and *batidos*:

barley	cebada f	se·ba·da
blackberry	mora f	mo·ra
cantaloupe	melón m	me·lon
carrot	zanahoria f	sa·na·o·rya
cas	cas m	kas
mango	mango m	man·go
naranjilla	naranjilla f	na·ran·khee·ya
papaya	papaya f	pa·pa·ya
pineapple	piña f	pee·nya
soursop	guanábana f	gwa·na·ba·na
star fruit	carambola f	ka·ram·bo·la
strawberry	fresa f	fre·sa
tamarind	tamarindo m	ta·ma·reen·do
watermelon	sandía f	san·dee·a

Coffee is the most popular beverage in the country and wherever you go, someone is likely to offer you a *cafecito* ka·fe·*see*·to (an affectionate term for a cup of coffee). Traditionally it's served strong and mixed with hot milk to taste. This is known as a *café con leche* ka·fe kon *le*·che. Some prefer a *café negro* ka·fe *ne*·gro (black coffee), but those who want a little milk can ask for *leche al lado* le·che al *la*·do (milk on the side). Many trendier places also serve capuccinos and espressos which you can ask for by these names.

alcoholic drinks

bebidas alcohólicas

a bottle/glass	*una botella/copa*	oo·na bo·*te*·ya/*ko*·pa
of … wine	*de vino …*	de *vee*·no …
dessert	*digestivo*	dee·khes·*tee*·vo
red	*tinto*	*teen*·to
rosé	*rosado*	ro·*sa*·do
sparkling	*espumante*	es·poo·*man*·te
white	*blanco*	*blan*·ko
a … of beer	*… de cerveza*	… de ser·*ve*·sa
glass	*un vaso*	oon *va*·so
jug	*una jarra*	*oo*·na *kha*·ra
large bottle	*una botella grande*	*oo*·na bo·*te*·ya *gran*·de
pitcher	*un pichel*	oon pee·*chel*
small bottle	*una botella pequeña*	*oo*·na bo·*te*·ya pe·*ke*·nya
champagne	*champán* m	cham·*pan*
cocktail	*coctél* m	kok·*tel*
gin	*ginebra* f	khee·*ne*·bra
rum	*ron* m	ron
tequila	*tequila* f	te·*kee*·la
vodka	*vodka* m	*vod*·ka
whisky	*whisky* m	*wee*·skee

in the bar

Most bars offer bar snacks called *bocas* bo·kas (lit: mouths). Typical offerings include black beans, *ceviche* se·vee·che (marinated shrimp or raw fish), chicken stew, potato chips, varieties of tacos or pieces of beef.

Excuse me!	*¡Con permiso!*	kon per·*mee*·so
I'm next.	*Sigo yo.*	*see*·go yo
I'll have (Cacique).	*Quiero (Cacique).*	*kye*·ro (ka·*see*·ke)
No ice, thanks.	*Sin hielo,*	seen *ye*·lo
	gracias.	*gra*·syas

Same again, please.
  Lo mismo, por favor.   lo *mees*·mo por fa·*vor*

I'll buy you a drink.
  Te invito a un trago.   te en·*vee*·to a oon *tra*·go

It's my round.
  Me toca.   me *to*·ka

What would you like?
  ¿Que querés?   ke ke·*res*

I don't drink alcohol.
  Yo no tomo.   yo no *to*·mo

Do you serve meals here?
  ¿Sirven comida aquí?   *seer*·ven ko·*mee*·da a·*kee*

down the hatch

The most popular alcoholic drinks are *cerveza* ser·ve·sa (beer) and the cane alcohol *guaro* gwa·ro which has the kick of a mule and a hangover to match. Beer is served *cruda* kroo·da (as a draft), in a *jarra* kha·ra (jug) or in a *pichel* pee·*chel* (pitcher). *Guaro* comes in a shot or is mixed with a soft drink or juice. The most popular brand of *guaro* is *Cacique* ka·*see*·ke (meaning 'chief').

eating out

163

listen for...

Creo que ya tomaste suficiente.
kre·o ke ya to·*mas*·te
soo·fee·*syen*·te
I think you've had enough.

¿Que vas a pedir?
ke vas a pe·*deer*
What are you having?

Última orden.
ool·tee·ma *or*·den
Last orders.

drinking up

tomando

Cheers!
¡Salud!
sa·*lood*

I feel fantastic!
¡Me siento fenomenal!
me *syen*·to fe·no·me·*nal*

I think I've had one too many.
Ya me llegaron.
ya me ye·*ga*·ron

I'm feeling drunk.
Estoy tapis.
es·*toy* ta·pees

I'm pissed.
Estoy hasta el culo.
es·*toy as*·ta el *koo*·lo

I feel ill.
Me siento mal.
me *syen*·to mal

Where's the toilet?
¿Dónde está el baño?
don·de es·*ta* el *ba*·nyo

I'm tired, I'd better go home.
Estoy cansado/a,
mejor me voy. m/f
es·*toy* kan·*sa*·do/a
me·*khor* me voy

I don't think you should drive.
No deberías manejar.
no de·be·*ree*·as ma·ne·*khar*

Can you call a taxi for me?
¿Me podrías llamar
un taxi?
me po·*dree*·as ya·*mar*
oon *tak*·see

FOOD

164

buying food

What's the local speciality?
*¿Cuál es la
especialidad local?*
kwal es la
es·pe·sya·lee·*dad* lo·*kal*

What's that?
¿Qué es éso?
ke es *e*·so

Can I taste it?
¿Puedo probarlo?
pwe·do pro·*bar*·lo

How much is (a kilo of cheese)?
*¿Cuánto cuesta
(un kilo de queso)?*
kwan·to *kwes*·ta
(oon *kee*·lo de *ke*·so)

Can I have a bag, please?
¿Me da una bolsa, por favor?
me da *oo*·na *bol*·sa por fa·*vor*

I don't need a bag, thanks.
No necesito bolsa, gracias.
no ne·se·*see*·to *bol*·sa *gra*·syas

I'd like …	*Quiero …*	*kye*·ro …
(200) grams	*(doscientos) gramos*	(do·*syen*·tos) *gra*·mos
a kilo	*un kilo*	oon *kee*·lo
half a kilo	*medio kilo*	*me*·dyo *kee*·lo
(two) kilos	*(dos) kilos*	(dos) *kee*·los
a dozen	*una docena*	*oo*·na do·*se*·na
half a dozen	*media docena*	*me*·dya do·*se*·na
a bottle	*una botella*	*oo*·na bo·*te*·ya
a jar	*una jarra*	*oo*·na *kha*·ra
a packet	*un paquete*	oon pa·*ke*·te
a piece	*un pedazo*	oon pe·*da*·so
(three) pieces	*(tres) pedazos*	(tres) pe·*da*·sos
a slice	*una tajada*	*oo*·na ta·*kha*·da
(six) slices	*(seis) tajadas*	(says) ta·*kha*·das

I'd like ...	Quiero ...	kye·ro ...
a little	un poquitito	oon po·kee·tee·to
some (of ...)	un poco (de ...)	oon po·ko (de ...)
more	más	mas
that one	ése/a m/f	e·se/a
this one	éste/a m/f	es·te/a

Less.	Menos.	me·nos
A bit more.	Un poquito más.	oon po·kee·to mas
Enough.	Suficiente.	soo·fee·syen·te

Do you have ...?	¿Tiene ...?	tye·ne ...
anything cheaper	algo más barato	al·go mas ba·ra·to
other kinds	otros tipos	o·tros tee·pos

Where can I find the ... section?	¿Dónde está/ están ... sg/pl	don·de es·ta/ es·tan ...
dairy	los lácteos pl	los lak·te·yos
fish	el pescado sg	el pes·ka·do
frozen goods	las comidas congeladas pl	las ko·mee·das kon·khe·la·das
fruit and vegetable	las frutas y verduras pl	las froo·tas ee ver·doo·ras
meat	las carnes pl	las kar·nes
poultry	las aves pl	las a·ves

For food items, see the **culinary reader**, page 171.

food stuff

cooked	cocinado/a m/f	ko·see·na·do/a
cured	adobado/a m/f	a·do·ba·do/a
dried	seco/a m/f	se·ko/a
fresh	fresco/a m/f	fres·ko/a
frozen	congelado/a m/f	kon·khe·la·do/a
raw	crudo/a m/f	kroo·do/a
smoked	ahumado/a m/f	a·oo·ma·do/a

¿Algo más? *al·*go mas	**Anything else?**
¿Le puedo ayudar en algo? le *pwe·*do a·yoo·*dar* en *al·*go	**Can I help you with something?**
No hay. no ai	**There isn't any.**
¿Qué quiere? ke *kye·*re	**What would you like?**

cooking utensils

utensilios de cocina

Can I borrow a ...?	*¿Podría* *prestarme ...?*	po·*dree·*a pres·*tar·*me ...
I need a ...	*Necesito ...*	ne·se·*see·*to ...
can opener	*un abrelatas*	oon a·bre·*la·*tas
chopping board	*una tabla para* *picar*	*oo·*na *ta·*bla *pa·*ra pee·*kar*
corkscrew	*un sacacorchos*	oon sa·ka·*kor·*chos
cup	*una taza*	*oo·*na *ta·*sa
frying pan	*un sartén*	oon sar·*ten*
knife	*un cuchillo*	oon koo·*chee·*yo
saucepan	*un sartén hondo*	oon sar·*ten on·*do
spoon	*una cuchara*	*oo·*na koo·*cha·*ra

For more cooking implements, see the **dictionary**.

One of the joys of a trip to Costa Rica is to sample some of the delicious varieties of healthy tropical fruits on offer. Some of these you'll discover in the guise of refreshing drinks called *frescos* fres·kos (see the box **juicy treats**, page 161). Note that not all local fruits have names in English.

caimito m   kai·*mee*·to
star apple – similar to a star fruit but has a purplish skin and soft sweet flesh

cas m   kas
small sour guava-like fruit which is whitish on the inside and frequently used in *frescos*

guanábana f   gwa·*na*·ba·na
soursop – large dark green fruit with spines on the outside and tart white flesh on the inside

jocote m   kho·*ko*·te
plum-sized fruit with a large pit, sometimes eaten green with salt (an acquired taste) or eaten when red and ripe – popular street snack

manzana de agua f   man·*sa*·na de *a*·gwa
'water apple' (relative of the rose apple) – has a crisp white juicy apple-like flesh

manzana rosa f   man·*sa*·na *ro*·sa
'rose apple' – round whitish-green to apricot-yellow fruit with a rose perfume and a sweet crispy and juicy flesh

naranjilla f   na·ran·*khee*·ya
orange tomato-like fruit with a juicy acidic pulp used in drinks and sherbets

zapote m   sa·*po*·te
sapote – fruit with a pinky-red flesh that has a sweet pumpkin-like flavour

zapote negro m   sa·*po*·te *ne*·gro
'black sapote' – fruit with a delicious jelly-like flesh, similar in flavour to a chocolate pudding (unrelated to sapote)

vegetarian & special meals
comidas vegetarianas y especiales

ordering food

ordenando comida

If you don't mind rice and beans, Costa Rica is a relatively comfortable place for vegetarians to travel. Most restaurants will do *casados vegetarianos* ka·*sa*·dos ve·khe·ta·*rya*·nos (ie vegetarian *casados*) on request – see the box **a match made in heaven**, page 153, for more information on this dish.

Is there a ...	*¿Hay un*	ai oon
restaurant	*restaurante ...*	res·tow·*ran*·te ...
near here?	*cerca de aquí?*	*ser*·ka de a·*kee*
Do you have	*¿Tienen*	*tye*·nen
... food?	*comida ...?*	ko·*mee*·da ...
halal	*halal*	a·*lal*
kosher	*kosher*	*ko*·sher
vegetarian	*vegetariana*	ve·khe·ta·*rya*·na

I don't eat ...	*No como ...*	no *ko*·mo ...
Is it cooked	*¿Está cocinado*	es·*ta* ko·see·*na*·do
with ...?	*con ...?*	kon ...
butter	*mantequilla*	man·te·*kee*·ya
eggs	*huevos*	*we*·vos
fish (stock)	*(caldo de)*	(*kal*·do de)
	pescado	pes·*ka*·do
meat (stock)	*(caldo de) carne*	(*kal*·do de) *kar*·ne
oil	*aceite*	a·*say*·te
pork	*cerdo*	*ser*·do
poultry	*ave*	*a*·ve
red meat	*carne roja*	*kar*·ne *ro*·kha

Could you prepare a meal without …?
¿Podría preparar   po·*dree*·a pre·pa·*rar*
un plato sin …?   oon *pla*·to seen …

Does it contain animal produce?
¿Tiene productos   *tye*·ne pro·*dook*·tos
animales?   a·nee·*ma*·les

Is this …?	*¿Es …?*	es …
decaffeinated	*descafeinado*	des·ka·fay·*na*·do
genetically	*genéticamente*	khe·*ne*·tee·ka·men·te
modified	*modificado*	mo·dee·fee·*ka*·do
gluten-free	*sin gluten*	seen *gloo*·ten
low-fat	*de poca grasa*	de *po*·ka *gra*·sa
low in sugar	*de poca azúcar*	de *po*·ka a·*soo*·kar
organic	*orgánico*	or·*ga*·nee·ko
salt-free	*sin sal*	seen sal

special diets & allergies

dietas especiales y alergias

I'm on a special diet.
Estoy en una dieta especial.   es·*toy* en *oo*·na *dye*·ta es·pe·*syal*

I'm a vegan.
Soy vegano/a. m/f   soy ve·*ga*·no/a

I'm allergic to …	*Soy alérgico/a …* m/f	soy a·*ler*·khee·ko/a …
dairy produce	*a los lácteos*	a los *lak*·te·os
eggs	*a los huevos*	a los *we*·vos
gelatine	*a la gelatina*	a la khe·la·*tee*·na
gluten	*al gluten*	al *gloo*·ten
honey	*a la miel*	a la myel
MSG	*al GMS*	al khe e·me e·se
nuts	*a las nueces*	a las *nwe*·ses
peanuts	*al maní*	al ma·*nee*
seafood	*a los mariscos*	a los ma·*rees*·kos
shellfish	*a las conchas*	a las *kon*·chas

To explain your dietary restrictions with reference to religious beliefs, see **beliefs & cultural differences**, page 131.

This miniguide to Costa Rican cuisine lists ingredients in Spanish alphabetical order (see the box **spanish alphabet**, page 13). It's designed to help you navigate menus and get the most out of your gastronomic experience in Costa Rica. ¡Buen provecho!

A

aceitunas ① pl a·say·too·nas *olives*
 — **negras** ne·gras *black olives*
 — **rellenas** re·ye·nas *stuffed olives*
 — **verdes** ver·des *green olives*
adobo ⓜ a·do·bo *garlic, oregano, paprika, peppercorn, salt, olive, lime juice & vinegar paste for seasoning meat*
agua ⓜ a·gwa *water*
 — **del tubo** del too·bo *tap water*
 — **de manantial** de ma·nan·tyal *spring water*
 — **mineral** mee·ne·ral *mineral water*
 — **sin gas** seen gas *still water*
aguacate ⓜ a·gwa·ka·te *avocado*
ahumado/a ⓜ/① a·oo·ma·do/a *smoked*
ají ⓜ a·khee *red chilli pepper*
ajillo, al a·khee·yo, al *cooked in garlic*
ajo ⓜ a·kho *garlic*
albahaca ① al·ba·a·ka *basil*
albaricoque ⓜ al·ba·ree·ko·ke *apricot*
albóndigas ① pl al·bon·dee·gas *meatballs*
alcachofa ① al·ka·cho·fa *artichoke*
alcaparra ① al·ka·pa·ra *caper*
alita ① a·lee·ta *wing (poultry)*
almejas ① pl al·me·khas *clams*
almendra ① al·men·dra *almond*
alubias ① a·loo·byas *red kidney beans*
anchoas ① pl an·cho·as *anchovies*
anguila ① an·gee·la *eel*
anís ⓜ a·nees *anise · aniseed*
apio ⓜ a·pyo *celery*
arreglado ⓜ a·re·gla·do *sandwich or tiny puff pastry stuffed with beef cheese or chicken*
arrollado/a ⓜ/① a·ro·ya·do/a *rolled*
arroz ⓜ a·ros *rice*
 — **con atún** kon a·toon *rice & tuna*
 — **con camarones** kon ka·ma·ro·nes *rice with shrimps*
 — **con leche** kon le·che *milky sweet rice pudding with a hint of cinnamon*
 — **con pollo** kon po·yo *rice & chicken*
 — **guacho** gwa·cho *rice with onion, garlic, pork & cilantro (coriander)*
 — **y frijoles** ee free·kho·les *rice with black beans*
arvejas ① pl ar·ve·khas *peas (also known as* **petipoas***)*
 — **secas** se·kas *split peas*
asado ⓜ a·sa·do *mixed grill*
atún ⓜ a·toon *tuna*
ave ① a·ve *poultry*
avellana ① a·ve·ya·na *hazelnut*
avena ① a·ve·na *oats*
ayote ⓜ a·yo·te *gourd · squash*
azafrán ⓜ a·sa·fran *saffron*
azúcar ⓜ a·soo·kar *sugar*

B

bacalao ⓜ ba·ka·low *cod*
 — **seco** se·ko *dried salted cod*
bagre ⓜ ba·gre *catfish*
banano ⓜ ba·na·no *banana*
batido ⓜ ba·tee·do *fresh fruit shake made with water (***con agua***) or milk (***con leche***) – see the box* **juicy treats***, page 161, for popular flavours*
berberechos ⓜ pl be·be·re·chos *cockles*
berenjena ① be·ren·khe·na *aubergine · eggplant*
berro ⓜ be·ro *watercress*
bien asado/a ⓜ/① byen a·sa·do/a *well done*
bien cocido/a ⓜ/① byen ko·see·do/a *well done*

bien hecho/a ⓜ/ⓕ byen e-cho/a *well done*

bistec ⓜ bees-*tek* steak

— con papas kon *pa*-pas *steak & chips*

bocadillo ⓜ bo-ka-*dee*-yo *snack*

bocas ⓕ pl *bo*-kas

bar snacks such as black beans, **ceviche**, chicken stew, potato chips, varieties of tacos, or pieces of beef – served with drinks

bollos ⓜ pl *bo*-yos *bread rolls*

brócoli ⓜ *bro*-ko-lee *broccoli*

budín ⓜ boo-*deen* *pudding*

buey ⓜ bwey *ox*

C

cabra ⓕ *ka*-bra *goat*

cacho ⓜ *ka*-cho *sweet horn-shaped pastry filled with* **dulce de leche**

caimito ⓜ kai-*mee*-to

star apple – similar to a star fruit but has a purplish skin & a soft sweet flesh

cajeta ⓕ ka-*khe*-ta *thick caramel fudge*

calabaza ⓕ ka-la-*ba*-sa *pumpkin*

calamares ⓜ pl ka-la-*ma*-res *squid*

— a la romana a la ro-*ma*-na

squid rings fried in butter

caldo ⓜ *kal*-do *broth • consommé • stock*

camarón ⓜ ka-ma-*ron* *shrimp*

— grande *gran*-de *large prawn*

camote ⓜ ka-*mo*-te *sweet potato*

canela ⓕ ka-*ne*-la *cinnamon*

canelones ⓜ pl ka-ne-*lo*-nes *cannelloni*

cangrejo ⓜ kan-*gre*-kho *crab*

caracol ⓜ ka-ra-*kol* *snail*

carambola ⓕ ka-ram-*bo*-la

star fruit – mild sweet tropical fruit eaten fresh or juiced in **frescos**

carbón, al kar-*bon*, al *chargrilled*

carne ⓕ *kar*-ne

meat – usually synonymous with beef

— de caballo de ka-*ba*-yo *horsemeat*

— de res de res *beef*

— de vaca de *va*-ka *beef*

— dorada al horno do-*ra*-da al or-no *roast meat*

— fría *free*-ya *cold meat*

— molida mo-*lee*-da *ground meat*

— picada pee-*ka*-da *minced meat*

— rotisada ro-tee-*sa*-da *roast meat*

carpa ⓕ *kar*-pa *carp*

cas ⓜ kas *tropical fruit – relative of the guava but very sour & whitish on the inside*

casado ⓜ ka-*sa*-do set platter with rice, black beans, fried plantains, chopped cabbage, tomato & usually a choice of beef, chicken or fish (often an egg, a lime or an avocado are included)

— vegetariano ve-khe-ta-*rya*-no

casado without the meat

castaña ⓕ kas-*ta*-nya *chestnut*

caza ⓕ *ka*-sa *game (meat)*

— de temporada de tem-po-*ra*-da *game in season*

cazuela ⓕ ka-*swe*-la *casserole*

cebada ⓕ se-*ba*-da *barley*

cebolla ⓕ se-*bo*-ya *onion*

cebollín ⓜ se-bo-*yeen* *shallot • spring onion*

cele ⓜ *se*-le

green mango – usually eaten with salt

cerdo ⓜ *ser*-do *pork*

cereza ⓕ se-*re*-sa *cherry*

cerveza ⓕ ser-*ve*-sa *beer*

— en botella en bo-*te*-ya *bottled beer*

ceviche ⓜ se-*vee*-che raw fish, shrimp or conch marinated in lemon juice, chilli, cilantro (coriander) & onions

chancho ⓜ *chan*-cho *pork*

chayote ⓜ cha-*yo*-te *pear-shaped vegetable similar in flavour to a squash*

chicharrón ⓜ chee-cha-*ron*

fried pork crackling – popular as ingredient

chifrijo ⓜ chee-*free*-kho

beans & **chicharrón** with minced tomato, onion, cilantro (coriander) & lime juice

chile ⓜ *chee*-le *chilli pepper*

chirimoya ⓕ chee-ree-*mo*-ya *custard apple*

chivo ⓜ *chee*-vo *kid*

choclo ⓜ *cho*-klo *corn • maize (off the cob)*

chorizo ⓜ cho-*ree*-so

spicy red or white pork sausage

— al horno al *or*-no

spicy sausage baked in the oven

chorreadas ⓕ pl cho-re-*a*-das

fried pancakes of fresh corn mash served with sour cream

chuleta ⓕ choo-*le*-ta *chop • cutlet*

— de cerdo de *ser*-do *pork cutlet*

churrasco ⓜ choo-*ras*-ko *rib steak*

chuzo ⓜ *choo*-so

kebab – also know as **pincho**

ciruela ① see-*rwe*-la *plum*
cocinado/a ⓜ/① ko-see-*na*-do/a *cooked*
coco ⓜ *ko*-ko *coconut*
coctel ⓜ kok-*tel* *appetiser in sauce • cocktail*
codorniz ① ko-dor-*nees* *quail*
coles de bruselas ⓜ pl *ko*-les de broo-*se*-las *Brussels sprouts*
coliflor ① ko-lee-*flor* *cauliflower*
con agua kon *a*-gwa
'with water' – refers to the preparation of a **batido** *or* **refresco natural** *with water*
conejo ⓜ ko-*ne*-kho *rabbit*
con leche kon *le*-che
'with milk' – refers to the preparation of a **batido** *or* **refresco natural** *with milk*
corazón ⓜ ko-ra-*son* *heart*
cordero ⓜ kor-*de*-ro *lamb*
corvina ① kor-*vee*-na *bass*
costilla ① kos-*tee*-ya *loin • spare rib*
costillas de cordero ①
kos-*tee*-yas de kor-*de*-ro *rack of lamb*
crema ① *kre*-ma *cream*
— **chantillí** chan-tee-*lee* *whipped cream*
crudo/a ⓜ/① *kroo*-do/a *raw*
crustáceos ⓜ pl kroos-*ta*-se-os *shellfish*
cuajada ① kwa-*kha*-da
milk junket with honey
culantro ⓜ koo-*lan*-tro *cilantro • coriander*

D

dátil ⓜ *da*-teel *date*
dorado ① do-*ra*-do *sea bass*
dorado/a ⓜ/① do-*ra*-do/a *seared*
dulce ⓜ&① *dool*-se *sweet* a
dulce de leche ⓜ *dool*-se de *le*-che
caramelised condensed milk used as a filling for pastries or eaten on bread

E

ejote ⓜ e-*kho*-te *string bean*
elote ⓜ e-*lo*-te *corn • maize (on the cob)*
— **asado** a-*sa*-do *corn roasted on the cob*
— **hervido** er-*vee*-do *boiled corn*
empanada ① em-pa-*na*-da *baked or fried turnover usually containing fried meat & vegetables though it can have fruit fillings*
enchilada ① en-chee-*la*-da *pastry stuffed with potatoes & cheese & sometimes meat*

eneldo ⓜ e-*nel*-do *dill*
ensalada ① en-sa-*la*-da *salad*
— **de remolacha** de re-mo-*la*-cha *beetroot salad*
— **mixta** *mees*-ta *mixed salad*
— **rusa** *roo*-sa *'Russian salad' – vegetable salad with mayonnaise*
— **verde** *ver*-de *green salad*
espagueti ⓜ es-pa-*ge*-tee *spaghetti*
espárragos ⓜ pl es-*pa*-ra-gos *asparagus*
espinaca ① es-pee-*na*-ka *spinach*
estofado ⓜ es-to-*fa*-do *stew*
estofado/a ⓜ/① es-to-*fa*-do/a *braised*

F

faisán ⓜ fai-*san* *pheasant*
fideos ⓜ pl fee-*de*-os *noodles*
filete ⓜ fee-*le*-te *fillet*
— **de carne** de *kar*-ne *beef fillet*
— **de pescado** de pes-*ka*-do *fish fillet*
flan ⓜ flan *crème caramel • egg custard*
frambuesa ① fram-*bwe*-sa *raspberry*
fresa ① *fre*-sa *strawberry*
fresco ⓜ *fres*-ko
fresh fruit drink – short for **refresco natural**
frijol ⓜ free-*khol* *bean*
— **blanco** *blan*-ko *large butter bean*
frijoles ⓜ pl free-*kho*-les *beans*
— **con arroz** kon a-*ros* *beans & rice*
frito ⓜ *free*-to *scraps of fried or roast pork*
frito/a ⓜ/① *free*-to/a *fried*
— **al sartén** al sar-*ten* *pan-fried*
fruta ① *froo*-ta *fruit*
frutilla ① froo-*tee*-ya *berry*

G

galleta ① ga-*ye*-ta *biscuit • cookie*
— **salada** sa-*la*-da *cracker*
gallo ⓜ *ga*-yo *tortilla sandwich containing a meat, bean, cheese or* **picadillo** *filling*
— **de queso con cebolla** de *ke*-so kon se-*bo*-ya
soft cheese & onions folded in a **tortilla**
— **pinto** *peen*-to
'spotted rooster' – lightly spiced mixture of rice & black beans traditionally served for breakfast, sometimes with sour cream or fried eggs (Costa Rica's signature dish)

ganso ⓜ gan·so goose
garbanzo ⓜ gar·ban·so
chickpea · garbanzo bean
gazpacho ⓜ gas·pa·cho
cold tomato & vegetable soup
granadilla ⓕ gra·na·dee·ya pomegranate
grasa ⓕ gra·sa
fat · grease (also called **manteca**)
gratinado ⓜ gra·tee·na·do
dish cooked au gratin
guacamole ⓜ gwa·ka·mo·le
mashed avocado combined with onion,
chilli, lemon & tomato
guanábana ⓕ gwa·na·ba·na prickly custard
apple · soursop (fruit with a tart pulp)
guaro ⓜ gwa·ro
local firewater made from sugar cane
guayaba ⓕ gwa·ya·ba guava
guineo ⓜ gee·ne·o
small banana similar to a plantain
guisantes pl gee·san·tes peas
guiso ⓜ gee·so stew

H

haba ⓕ a·ba broad bean
hamburguesa ⓕ am·boor·ge·sa
hamburger
harina ⓕ a·ree·na flour
helado ⓜ e·la·do ice cream
helado/a ⓜ/ⓕ e·la·do/a chilled · iced
hervido/a ⓜ/ⓕ er·vee·do/a boiled
— **a fuego lento** a fwe·go len·to
simmered
hielo ⓜ ye·lo ice
hierba ⓕ yer·ba herb
hígado ⓜ ee·ga·do liver
higo ⓜ ee·go fig
hocico ⓜ o·see·ko snout
hongo ⓜ on·go button mushroom
hongos al ajillo ⓜ pl on·gos al a·khee·yo
garlic mushrooms
horchata ⓕ or·cha·ta
rice-based drink flavoured with cinnamon
horneado/a ⓜ/ⓕ or·ne·a·do/a baked
horno, al or·no, al baked
hueso ⓜ we·so bone
huevos ⓜ pl we·vos eggs
— **de tortuga** de tor·too·ga
turtle eggs – environmentally suspect dish
due to a dwindling turtle population

— **duros** doo·ros hard-boiled eggs
— **fritos** free·tos fried eggs
— **hervidos** er·vee·dos boiled eggs
— **pateados** pa·te·a·dos scrambled eggs
— **revueltos** re·vwel·tos scrambled eggs

J

jabalí ⓜ kha·ba·lee wild boar
jalea ⓕ kha·le·a jam
jamón ⓜ kha·mon ham
— **dulce** dool·se boiled ham
— **serrano** se·ra·no cured ham
jarrete ⓜ kha·re·te
bone marrow · knuckle · shank
jengibre ⓜ khen·khee·bre ginger
jocote ⓜ kho·ko·te
plum-sized fruit with a large pit,
sometimes eaten green with salt (an
acquired taste) or eaten when red & ripe
jugo ⓜ khoo·go juice
— **de naranja** de na·ran·kha orange juice
— **natural** na·too·ral
freshly-squeezed juice
— **puro** poo·ro pure juice

L

langosta ⓕ lan·gos·ta spiny lobster
langostino ⓜ lan·gos·tee·no
crawfish · crayfish
leche ⓕ le·che milk
— **descremada** des·kre·ma·da
skimmed milk
— **de soya** de so·ya soya milk
lechón ⓜ le·chon suckling pig
lechuga ⓕ le·choo·ga lettuce
legumbre ⓕ le·goom·bre pulse
lengua ⓕ len·gwa tongue
lenguado ⓜ len·gwa·do dab · lemon sole
lentejas ⓕ len·te·khas lentils
limón ⓜ lee·mon lemon · lime
lomo ⓜ lo·mo sirloin

M

macarela ⓕ ma·ka·re·la mackerel
macarrones ⓜ pl ma·ka·ro·nes macaroni
maduro/a ⓜ/ⓕ ma·doo·ro/a ripe
maíz ⓜ ma·ees corn · maize

mandarina ① man·da·*ree*·na
  mandarin • tangerine
mango ⓜ *man*·go *mango*
maní ⓜ ma·*nee* *peanut*
manteca ① man·*te*·ka
  grease • fat (also known as **grasa***)*
mantequilla ① man·te·*kee*·ya *butter*
manzana ① man·*sa*·na *apple*
  — **de agua** de *a*·gwa
  *'water apple' (relative of the rose apple) –
  has a crisp, white, juicy, apple-like flesh*
  — **rosa** *ro*·sa *'rose apple' – fruit with an
  apple-like taste but with a rose perfume*
maracuyá ① ma·ra·koo·*ya passionfruit*
margarina ① mar·ga·*ree*·na *margarine*
marinado/a ⓜ/① ma·ree·*na*·do/a
  marinated
mariscos ⓜ pl ma·*rees*·kos
  seafood • shellfish
mayonesa ① ma·yo·*ne*·sa *mayonnaise*
mazapán ⓜ ma·sa·*pan*
  almond paste • marzipan
medio crudo/a ⓜ/① *me*·dyo *kroo*·do/a
  rare
mejilla ① me·*khee*·ya *cheek*
mejillones ⓜ pl me·khee·*yo*·nes *mussels*
  — **al vapor** al va·*por steamed mussels*
melocotón ⓜ me·lo·ko·*ton peach*
melón ⓜ me·*lon melon*
menta ① *men*·ta *mint*
menudo de pollo ⓜ me·*noo*·do de *po*·yo
  gizzard • poultry entrails
menudos ⓜ pl me·*noo*·dos *giblets*
merluza ① mer·*loo*·sa *hake*
  — **a la plancha** a la *plan*·cha *fried hake*
mermelada ① mer·me·*la*·da *marmalade*
miel ⓜ myel *honey*
milanesa ① mee·la·*ne*·sa
  schnitzel – pounded, breaded & fried meat
mil hojas ⓜ pl meel o·khas
  *'thousand leaves' – layers of thin pastry
  filled with an almond & honey paste*
mojarra ① mo·*kha*·ra *perch*
mondongo ⓜ mon·*don*·go *tripe*
mora ① *mo*·ra *blackberry*
morcilla ① mor·*see*·ya *black pudding •
  blood sausage – common* **asado** *dish*
mostaza ① mos·*ta*·sa *mustard*
muslo ⓜ *moos*·lo *thigh*
muy cocinado/a ⓜ/①
  mooy ko·see·*na*·do/a *well done*

N

nabo ⓜ *na*·bo *turnip*
naranja ① na·*ran*·kha *orange*
naranjilla ① na·ran·*khee*·ya
  *orange-coloured, tomato-like fruit with a
  juicy acidic pulp used in drinks & sherbets*
nata ① *na*·ta *cream*
natilla ① na·*tee*·ya *sour cream*
natural ⓜ na·too·*ral*
  fresh fruit drink – short for **refresco natural**
nuez ⓜ nwes *nut • walnut*

O

olla de carne ① *o*·ya de *kar*·ne
  *hearty soup containing beef, potatoes,
  corn,* **chayote***, plantains & cassava*
omelet ⓜ o·me·*let*
  omelette (also known as **torta de huevo***)*
oreja ① o·*re*·kha
  'ear' – sweet biscuit of flaky pastry
ostión ⓜ os·tee·*on scallop*
ostra ① *os*·tra *oyster*
oveja ① o·*ve*·kha *ewe*

P

paleta ① pa·*le*·ta *shoulder*
palmitos ⓜ pl pal·*mee*·tos *palm hearts –
  usually served in a vinegar dressing*
paloma ① pa·*lo*·ma *pigeon*
pan ⓜ pan *bread*
  — **dulce** *dool*·se *sweet bread*
panqueque ⓜ pan·*ke*·ke *pancake*
papas ① pl *pa*·pas *potatoes*
  — **fritas** *free*·tas *chips • French fries*
papaya ① pa·*pa*·ya *papaya*
papitas ① pl pa·*pee*·tas *crisps • potato chips*
pargo ⓜ *par*·go *red snapper*
parrilla ① pa·*ree*·ya *grill*
parrilla, a la pa·*ree*·ya, a la
  grilled over charcoal
parrillada ① pa·ree·*ya*·da
  *mixed grill – huge slabs of grilled meat
  prepared over hot coals & served with spicy
  sauces & vegetables*
pasa ① *pa*·sa *raisin*
pasado/a al agua ⓜ/① pa·*sa*·do/a al *a*·gwa
  boiled

pasta ① *pas*·ta *pasta*
pastel ⓜ *pas*·tel *cake • pastry*
pata ① *pa*·ta *leg*
patacones ⓜ pl pa·ta·*ko*·nes
  fried green plantains cut into thin pieces,
  salted & then pressed & fried – popular on
  the Caribbean coast
patita de cerdo/chancho ①
  pa·*tee*·ta de ser·*do*/*chan*·cho *pig's trotter*
pato ⓜ *pa*·to *duck*
pavo ⓜ *pa*·vo *turkey*
pechuga ① pe·*choo*·ga *breast meat*
pejibaye ⓜ pe·khee·*ba*·ye
  starchy palm fruit boiled & frequently
  eaten with mayonnaise
pepinillo ⓜ pe·pee·*nee*·yo *pickle*
pepino ⓜ pe·*pee*·no *cucumber*
pera ① *pe*·ra *pear*
perejil ⓜ pe·re·*kheel* *parsley*
pescado ⓜ pes·*ka*·do *fish*
  — **ahumado** a·oo·*ma*·do *smoked fish*
  — **al ajillo** al a·*khee*·yo *fish in garlic sauce*
  — **de agua dulce** de a·gwa *dool*·se
  freshwater fish
  — **de mar** de mar *saltwater fish*
pescaíto ⓜ pes·ka·*ee*·to *tiny fried fish*
petipoas ⓜ pl pe·tee·*po*·as
  peas – another word for **arvejas**
pez espada ⓜ pes es·*pa*·da *swordfish*
pez hoja ⓜ pes o·kha *bottom fish • flounder*
picadillo ⓜ pee·ka·*dee*·yo
  'minced' – side dish of minced vegetables
  and/or fruit & ground meat (usually beef)
picante ⓜ&① pee·*kan*·te *spicy*
pimentón ⓜ pee·men·*ton*
  bell pepper • capsicum
pimienta ① pee·*myen*·ta *pepper*
pincho ⓜ *peen*·cho
  kebab – also know as **chuzo**
piña ① *pee*·nya *pineapple*
pipa ① *pee*·pa
  green coconut – picked for its milk which is
  often drunk straight from the shell
pistacho ⓜ pees·*ta*·cho *pistachio nut*
plancha ① *plan*·cha *grill • hot plate*
plancha, a la *plan*·cha, a la *grilled*
plátano ⓜ *pla*·ta·no
  plantain – savoury banana-like fruit that's
  cooked & often served with main dishes
poco cocido/a ⓜ/① po·ko ko·*see*·do/a *rare*
poco hecho/a ⓜ/① po·ko e·*cho*/a *rare*

pollo ⓜ *po*·yo *chicken*
polvo ⓜ *pol*·vo *powder*
postre ⓜ *pos*·tre *dessert*
prestiño ⓜ pres·*tee*·nyo
  very thin fried pastry eaten with syrup
puerco ⓜ *pwer*·ko *pork*
pulpo ⓜ *pool*·po *octopus*
  — **a la gallega** a la ga·*ye*·ga
  octopus in a garlicky wine & tomato sauce
  with bell pepper & potatoes thrown in
punto, a *poon*·to, a *medium (steak)*

Q

queque ⓜ *ke*·ke *cake • pastry*
  — **seco** *se*·ko *pound cake*
queso ⓜ *ke*·so *cheese*

R

rábano ⓜ *ra*·ba·no *radish*
rabo ⓜ *ra*·bo *tail*
rape ⓜ *ra*·pe *monkfish*
refresco ⓜ re·*fres*·ko *soft drink*
  — **natural** na·too·*ral*
  frequently referred to simply as **frescos** *or*
  naturales*, these are fruit juices made to*
  order **con agua** *(with water) or* **con leche**
  (with milk) – see the box **juicy treats***, page*
  161, for common flavours
relleno/a ⓜ/① re·*ye*·no/a *stuffed*
remolacha ① re·mo·*la*·cha *beetroot*
repollo ⓜ re·*po*·yo *cabbage*
res, carne de ① res, *kar*·ne de *beef*
riñón ⓜ ree·*nyon* *kidney*
romero ⓜ ro·*me*·ro *rosemary*
rosado ⓜ ro·*sa*·do *rosé*
rostisado/a ⓜ/① ros·tee·*sa*·do/a *roasted*
  — **al espiedo** al es·*pye*·do *spit-roasted*
  — **a la parilla** a la pa·*ree*·ya *grilled*
  — **al horno** al or·no *oven roasted*

S

sal ① sal *salt*
salado/a ⓜ/① sa·*la*·do/a *salted • salty*
salchichas ① pl sal·*chee*·chas
  sausages similar to hot dogs
salmón ⓜ sal·*mon* *salmon*

salsa ① *sal*·sa *sauce*
  — **de carne** de *kar*·ne *gravy*
  — **picante** pee·*kan*·te *chilli sauce*
Salsa Lizano ① *sal*·sa lee·*sa*·no
  the secret sauce of Costa Rica (added to everything, especially **gallo pinto**) – *a tangy, yet somewhat sweet concoction, with tamarind as the main ingredient*
salteado/a ⓜ/① sal·te·*a*·do/a *sautéed*
salvaje ⓜ&① sal·*va*·khe *wild*
sandía ① san·*dee*·a *watermelon*
sandwich ⓜ *sand*·weech *sandwich*
sandwiche ⓜ *sand*·wee·che
  alternate spelling of **sandwich**
sangre ① *san*·gre *blood*
sangría ① san·*gree*·a
  sangria (red-wine punch)
sardina ① sar·*dee*·na *sardine*
secado/a ⓜ/① se·*ka*·do/a *dried*
seco/a ⓜ/① se·*ko*/a *dry • dried*
semilla de marañón ①
  se·*mee*·ya de ma·ra·*nyon* *cashew*
semolina ① se·mo·*lee*·na *semolina*
sepia ① *se*·pya *cuttlefish*
sésamo ⓜ *se*·sa·mo *sesame*
sesos ⓜ pl *se*·sos *brains*
sidra ① *see*·dra *cider*
sin grasa seen *gra*·sa *lean*
sopa ① *so*·pa *soup*
  — **de albóndigas** de al·*bon*·dee·gas
    meatball soup
  — **de espinacas** de es·pee·*na*·kas
    spinach soup
  — **de frijoles negros**
    de free·*kho*·les ne·gros *black bean soup*
  — **de mariscos** de ma·*rees*·kos
    shellfish soup
  — **de mondongo** de mon·*don*·go
    tripe soup
  — **de pescado** de pes·*ka*·do *fish soup*
  — **de pollo** de *po*·yo *chicken soup*
  — **negra** *ne*·gra *creamy black bean soup, often with a hard-boiled egg & vegetables soaking in the bean broth*
soya ① *so*·ya *soy*
suflé ⓜ soo·*fle* *soufflé*

T

tacos ⓜ pl *ta*·kos *Costa Rican-style tacos (*tortillas *filled with meat, beans & other ingredients) – deep-fried & served with shredded cabbage, mayonnaise & ketchup*

tajadas ① pl ta·*kha*·das *slices*
tallarines ⓜ pl ta·ya·*ree*·nes *noodles mixed with pork, chicken, beef or vegetables*
tamales ⓜ pl ta·*ma*·les
  cornmeal dough filled with spiced beef or pork, vegetables & potatoes, then wrapped in a maize husk or banana leaf & fried, grilled or baked
  — **asado** a·*sa*·do *sweet cornmeal cake*
tamarindo ⓜ ta·ma·*reen*·do *tamarind*
té ⓜ te *tea*
término medio *ter*·mee·no *me*·dyo *medium*
ternera ① ter·*ne*·ra *veal*
tiburón ⓜ tee·boo·*ron* *shark*
tinto ⓜ *teen*·to *red (wine)*
tocineta ① to·see·*ne*·ta *bacon*
  — **ahumada** a·oo·*ma*·da *smoked bacon*
tocino ⓜ to·*see*·no *cold bacon*
  — **con queso** kon *ke*·so
    cold bacon & cheese
tomate ⓜ to·*ma*·te *tomato*
toronja ① to·*ron*·kha *grapefruit*
  — **rellena** ① re·*ye*·na *caramelised grapefruit peel filled with milk* **cajeta**
torta ① *tor*·ta *cake • tart*
  — **de huevo** de *we*·vo
    plain omelette also known as **omelet**
  — **española** es·pa·*nyo*·la
    egg & potato omelette
tortilla ① tor·*tee*·ya *thin round of pressed corn (or sometimes wheat) dough cooked on a griddle • another name for an* **omelet**
  — **con queso** kon *ke*·so
    tortilla with cheese
tortuga ① tor·*too*·ga
  turtle – not for the environmentally aware as turtle numbers are dwindling
tostada ① tos·*ta*·da *toast*
tres leches ⓜ tres *le*·ches
  moist cake prepared with cream, condensed & evaporated milk
tripas ① pl *tree*·pas *offal*
trucha ① *troo*·cha *trout*
trufa ① *troo*·fa *truffle*
turrón ⓜ too·*ron* *almond nougat*

U

ubre ① *oo*·bre *udder*
uva ① *oo*·va *grape*

V

vaca, carne de ① *va*-ka, *kar*-ne de *beef*
vainilla ① vai-*nee*-ya *vanilla*
vapor ⓜ va-*por* *steam*
vapor, al va-*por*, al *steamed*
vegetal ⓜ ve-khe-*tal* *vegetable* n
vegetales ⓜ pl ve-khe-*ta*-les *vegetables*
venado ⓜ ve-*na*-do *venison*
verdes ⓜ pl *ver*-des *greens*
verduras ① pl ver-*doo*-ras *green vegetables*
vieira ① *vyay*-ra *scallop*
vigorón ⓜ vee-go-*ron* *boiled cassava top served with cabbage salad,* **chicharrón,** *tomatoes, onions & lime juice*
vinagre ⓜ vee-*na*-gre *vinegar*
vino ⓜ *vee*-no *wine*
  — blanco *blan*-ko *white wine*
  — espumoso es-poo-*mo*-so *sparkling wine*
  — rosado ro-*sa*-do *rosé*
  — tinto *teen*-to *red wine*
vualve a la vida caribeño ⓜ *vwal*-ve a la *vee*-da ka-ree-*be*-nyo *thick seafood-based soup blended with coconut milk*

Y

yogur ⓜ yo-*gur* *yogurt*
yuca ① *yoo*-ka *cassava – common staple in Latin American cuisine*

Z

zanahoria ① sa-na-o-*rya* *carrot*
zapote ⓜ sa-*po*-te *sapote – fruit with a pinky red flesh & a pumpkin-like flavour*

SAFE TRAVEL > essentials
esenciales

emergencies

emergencias

Help!	¡Socorro!	so·ko·ro
Stop!	¡Pare!	pa·re
Go away!	¡Váyase!	va·ya·se
Thief!	¡Ladrón!	la·dron
Fire!	¡Incendio!	een·sen·dyo
Watch out!	¡Cuidado!	kwee·da·do

Call ...	Llame a ...	ya·me a ...
an ambulance	una ambulancia	oo·na am·boo·lan·sya
a doctor	un doctor	oon dok·tor
the police	la policía	la po·lee·see·a

It's an emergency.
Es una emergencia.   es oo·na e·mer·khen·sya

There's been an accident.
Hubo un accidente.   oo·bo oon ak·see·den·te

Could you please help me/us?
¿Me/Nos podría ayudar,   me/nos po·dree·a a·yoo·dar
por favor?   por fa·vor

signs

Emergencias	e·mer·khen·syas	Emergency Department
Estación Policial	es·ta·syon po·lee·syal	Police Station (city)
Guardia Rural	gwar·dya roo·ral	Police Station (rural)
Hospital	os·pee·tal	Hospital
Policía	po·lee·see·a	Police

essentials

179

Can I use your phone?
¿Usted me prestaría el teléfono? — oos·*ted* me pres·ta·*ree*·a el te·*le*·fo·no

I'm lost.
Estoy perdido/a. m/f — es·*toy* per·*dee*·do/a

Where are the toilets?
¿Dónde está el baño? — *don*·de es·*ta* el *ba*·nyo

Is it dangerous …?	¿Es peligroso …?	es pe·lee·*gro*·so …
at night	en la noche	en la *no*·che
for gay people	para homosexuales	pa·ra o·mo·sek·*swa*·les
for travellers	para turistas	pa·ra too·*rees*·tas
for women	para mujeres	pa·ra moo·*khe*·res
on your own	si uno va solo/a m/f	see *oo*·no va *so*·lo/a

police

policía

Where's the police station?
¿Adónde está la estación de policía? — a·*don*·de es·*ta* la es·ta·*syon* de po·lee·*see*·a

Please telephone the police.
Por favor, llame a la policía. — por fa·*vor ya*·me a la po·lee·*see*·a

I want to report an offence.
Quiero reportar un delito. — *kye*·ro re·por·*tar* oon de·*lee*·to

It was him/her.
Fue él/ella. — fwe el/*e*·ya

I've been …	Me …	me …
He/She has been …	Lo/La …	lo/la …
assaulted	asaltaron	a·sal·*ta*·ron
raped	violaron	vyo·*la*·ron
robbed	robaron	ro·*ba*·ron

English	Spanish	Pronunciation
My ... was/were stolen.	*Me robaron ...*	me ro·*ba*·ron ...
I've lost my ...	*Perdí ...*	per·*dee* ...
backpack	*mi mochila*	mee mo·*chee*·la
credit card	*mi tarjeta de crédito*	mee tar·*khe*·ta de *kre*·dee·to
handbag	*mi bolso*	mee *bol*·so
jewellery	*mis joyas*	mees *kho*·yas
money	*mi plata*	mee *pla*·ta
papers	*mis documentos*	mees do·koo·*men*·tos
passport	*mi pasaporte*	mee pa·sa·*por*·te
travellers cheques	*mis cheques de viajero*	mee *che*·kes de vya·*khe*·ro
wallet	*mi billetera*	mee bee·ye·*te*·ra

the police may say ...

Es una multa por ...	es *oo*·na *mool*·ta por ...	It's a ... fine.
exceso de velocidad	ek·*se*·so de ve·lo·see·*dad*	speeding
parquear donde no se permite	par·ke·*ar don*·de no se per·*mee*·te	parking
A usted se le acusa de ...	a oos·*ted* se le a·*koo*·sa de ...	You're charged with ...
asaltar a alguien	a·sal·*tar* a *al*·gyen	assault
no tener visa	no te·*ner* *vee*·sa	not having a visa
permanecer ilegalmente en el país con documentos vencidos	per·ma·ne·*ser* ee·le·gal·*men*·te en el pa·*ees* kon do·koo·*men*·tos ven·*see*·dos	overstaying a visa
robo	*ro*·bo	theft
tenencia (de sustancias ilegales)	te·*nen*·sya (de soos·*tan*·syas ee·lee·*ga*·les)	possession (of illegal substances)

What am I accused of?
¿De que me están acusando? de ke me es·*tan* a·koo·*san*·do

I apologise.
Lo siento. lo *syen*·to

I didn't realise I was doing anything wrong.
No sabía que estaba no sa·*bee*·a ke es·*ta*·ba
haciendo algo malo. a·*syen*·do *al*·go *ma*·lo

I didn't do it.
Yo no fui. yo no fwee

Can I pay an on-the-spot fine?
¿Puedo pagar la *pwe*·do pa·*gar* la
multa aquí mismo? *mool*·ta a·*kee* mees·mo

I have insurance.
Tengo seguro. *ten*·go se·*goo*·ro

Do you have this form in (English)?
¿Tiene este formulario *tye*·ne *es*·te for·moo·*la*·ryo
en (inglés)? en (een·*gles*)

I want to contact my embassy/consulate.
Quiero contactar a mi *kye*·ro kon·tak·*tar* a mee
embajada/consulado. em·ba·*kha*·da/kon·soo·*la*·do

Can I make a phone call?
¿Puedo hacer una *pwe*·do a·*ser* oo·na
llamada telefónica? ya·*ma*·da te·le·*fo*·nee·ka

Can I have a lawyer (who speaks English)?
¿Me pueden traer un me *pwe*·den tra·*er* oon
abogado (que hable inglés)? a·bo·*ga*·do (ke *a*·ble een·*gles*)

I want to speak to a female police officer.
Quiero hablar con *kye*·ro ab·*lar* kon
una mujer policía. *oo*·na moo·*kher* po·lee·*see*·a

I have a prescription for this drug.
Tengo receta para *ten*·go re·*se*·ta *pa*·ra
este medicamento. *es*·te me·dee·ka·*men*·to

This drug is for personal use.
Esta droga es de *es*·ta *dro*·ga es de
uso personal. *oo*·so per·so·*nal*

doctor

doctor

Where's the nearest …?	¿Adónde está … más cercano/a? m/f	a·don·de es·ta … mas ser·ka·no/a
dentist	el dentista m	el den·tees·ta
doctor	el doctor m	el dok·tor
emergency department	la sección de emergencias f	la sek·syon de e·mer·khen·syas
hospital	el hospital m	el os·pee·tal
medical centre	la clínica f	la klee·nee·ka
optometrist	el optometrista m	el op·to·me·trees·ta
(24-hour) pharmacist	la farmacia (abierta 24 horas) f	la far·ma·sya (a·byer·ta vayn·tee·kwa·tro o·ras)

I need a doctor (who speaks English).
Necesito un doctor (que hable inglés).
ne·se·see·to oon dok·tor (ke a·ble een·gles)

Could I see a female doctor?
¿Podría atenderme una doctora?
po·dree·a a·ten·der·me oo·na dok·to·ra

Could the doctor come here?
¿El doctor podría venir acá? el dok·tor po·dree·a ve·neer a·ka

Is there an after-hours emergency number?
¿Hay un número de emergencias fuera de horas hábiles?
ai oon noo·me·ro de e·mer·khen·syas fwe·ra de o·ras a·bee·les

I've run out of my medication.
Se me acabó mi medicamento.
se me a·ka·bo mee me·dee·ka·men·to

This is my usual medicine.
Esta es mi medicina normal.
es·ta es mee me·dee·see·na nor·mal

My son/daughter weighs (20 kilos).
Mi hijo/hija pesa (20 kilos).
me ee·kho/ee·kha pe·sa (vayn·te kee·los)

What's the correct dosage?
¿Cuál es la dosis correcta?
kwal es la do·sees ko·rek·ta

I don't want a blood transfusion.
No quiero que me hagan una transfusión.
no kye·ro ke me a·gan oo·na trans·foo·syon

Please use a new syringe.
Por favor, use una jeringa nueva.
por fa·vor oo·se oo·na khe·reen·ga nwe·va

I have my own syringe.
Yo tengo mi propia jeringa.
yo ten·go mee pro·pya khe·reen·ga

the doctor may say ...

¿Cuál es el problema? kwal es el pro·ble·ma	**What's the problem?**
¿Adónde le duele? a·don·de le dwe·le	**Where does it hurt?**
¿Qué tiene? ke tye·ne	**What do you have?**
¿Tiene fiebre? tye·ne fye·bre	**Do you have a temperature?**
¿Cuánto tiene de estar así? kwan·to tye·ne de es·tar a·see	**How long have you been like this?**
¿Ha tenido esto mismo antes? ha te·nee·do es·to mees·mo an·tes	**Have you had this before?**
¿Es usted alérgico/a a algo? m/f es oos·ted a·ler·khee·ko/a a al·go	**Are you allergic to anything?**

the doctor may say ...

¿Está usted tomando algún medicamento?
es·*ta* oos·*ted* to·*man*·do
al·*goon* me·dee·ka·*men*·to
Are you on medication?

¿Usted es sexualmente activo/a? m/f
oos·*ted* es sek·swal·*men*·te
ak·*tee*·vo/a
Are you sexually active?

¿Ha tenido relaciones sexuales sin protección?
ha te·*nee*·do re·la·*syo*·nes
sek·*swa*·les seen pro·tek·*syon*
Have you had unprotected sex?

¿Usted fuma?
oos·*ted* foo·ma
Do you smoke?

¿Usted toma licor?
oos·*ted* to·ma lee·*kor*
Do you drink?

¿Usted usa drogas?
oos·*ted* oo·sa *dro*·gas
Do you take drugs?

¿Por cuánto tiempo es su viaje?
por *kwan*·to *tyem*·po
es soo *vya*·khe
How long are you travelling for?

Debería ir a revisarse eso cuando llegue a su casa.
de·be·*ree*·a eer a
re·vee·*sar*·se e·so *kwan*·do
ye·ge a soo *ka*·sa
You should have it checked when you go home.

Debería devolverse a su casa para que le den tratamiento.
de·be·*ree*·a de·vol·*ver*·se a
soo *ka*·sa pa·ra ke le
den tra·ta·*myen*·to
You should return home for treatment.

Vamos a tener que internarlo en el hospital.
va·mos a te·*ner* ke
een·ter·*nar*·lo en el
os·pee·*tal*
You need to be admitted to hospital.

Usted es hipocondríaco.
oos·*ted* es
ee·po·kon·*dree*·a·ko
You're a hypochondriac.

I've been	Yo estoy	yo es·toy
vaccinated	vacunado/a	va·koo·na·do/a
against ...	contra ... m/f	kon·tra ...
He/She has been	El/Ella está	el/e·ya es·ta
vaccinated	vacunado/a	va·koo·na·do/a
against ...	contra ...	kon·tra ...
hepatitis	hepatitis	e·pa·tee·tees
A/B/C	A/B/C	a/be/se
tetanus	tétano	te·ta·no
typhoid	fiebre tifoidea	fye·bre tee·foy·de·a

I need new ...	Necesito ...	ne·se·see·to ...
	nuevos/as. m/f	nwe·vos/as
contact	lentes de	len·tes de
lenses	contacto f	kon·tak·to
glasses	anteojos m	an·te·o·khos

My prescription is ...
Mi receta está ...   mee re·se·ta es·ta ...

How much will it cost?
¿Cuánto me va a costar?   kwan·to me va a kos·tar

Can I have a receipt for my insurance?
¿Me podría dar una   me po·dree·a dar oo·na
factura para mi   fak·too·ra pa·ra mee
seguro médico?   se·goo·ro me·dee·ko

symptoms & conditions

condiciones y síntomas

I'm sick.
Estoy enfermo/a. m/f   es·toy en·fer·mo/a

My friend is (very) sick.
Mi amigo/a está   mee a·mee·go/a es·ta
(muy) enfermo/a. m/f   (mooy) en·fer·mo/a

My son/daughter is (very) sick.
Mi hijo/hija está   mee ee·kho/ee·kha es·ta
(muy) enfermo/a.   (mooy) en·fer·mo/a

I've been injured.
Estoy herido/a. m/f   es·*toy* e·*ree*·do/a

He/She has been injured.
El/Ella está herido/a.   el/e·ya es·*ta* e·*ree*·do/a

I've been vomiting.
He estado vomitando.   e es·*ta*·do vo·mee·*tan*·do

He/She has been vomiting.
El/Ella ha estado   el/e·ya a es·*ta*·do
vomitando.   vo·mee·*tan*·do

She's having a baby.
Está teniendo el bebé.   es·*ta* te·*nyen*·do el be·*be*

He/She is having a/an …	*Le está dando …*	le es·*ta dan*·do …
allergic reaction	*una reacción alérgica*	*oo*·na re·ak·*syon* a·*ler*·khee·ka
asthma attack	*un ataque de asma*	oon a·*ta*·ke de *as*·ma
epileptic fit	*un ataque epiléptico*	oon a·*ta*·ke e·pee·*lep*·tee·ko
heart attack	*un ataque cardíaco*	oon a·*ta*·ke kar·*dee*·a·ko

I feel …	*Me siento …*	me *syen*·to …
anxious	*ansioso/a* m/f	an·*syo*·so/a
better	*mejor* m&f	me·*khor*
depressed	*deprimido/a* m/f	de·pree·*mee*·do/a
dizzy	*mareado/a* m/f	ma·re·a·do/a
hot and cold	*con calor y con frío*	kon ka·*lor* ee kon *free*·o
strange	*raro/a* m/f	*ra*·ro/a
weak	*débil* m&f	*de*·beel
worse	*peor* m&f	pe·*or*

I feel nauseous.
Tengo náuseas. ten·go now·se·as

I feel shivery.
Tengo escalofríos. ten·go es·ka·lo·free·os

It hurts here.
Me duele aquí. me dwe·le a·kee

I'm dehydrated.
Estoy deshidratado/a. m/f es·toy de·see·dra·ta·do/a

I can't sleep.
No puedo dormir. no pwe·do dor·meer

I think it's the medication I'm on.
Creo que son las medicinas kre·o ke son las me·dee·see·nas
que estoy tomando. ke es·toy to·man·do

I'm on medication for ...
Estoy tomando es·toy to·man·do
medicinas para ... me·dee·see·nas pa·ra ...

He/She is on medication for ...
Él/Ella está tomando el/e·ya es·ta to·man·do
medicinas para ... me·dee·see·nas pa·ra ...

I have (a/an) ...
Tengo (un/una) ... m/f ten·go (oon/oo·na) ...

He/She has (a/an) ...
Él/Ella tiene (un/una) ... m/f el/e·ya tye·ne (oon/oo·na) ...

asthma	*asma* f	as·ma
cold n	*resfrío* m	res·free·o
constipation	*estreñimiento* m	es·tre·nyee·myen·to
cough n	*tos* m	tos
diabetes	*diabetes* m	dee·a·be·tees
diarrhoea	*diarrea* f	dee·a·re·a
fever	*fiebre* f	fye·bre
flu	*gripe* f	gree·pe
headache	*dolor de cabeza* m	do·lor de ka·be·sa
migraine	*migraña* f	mee·gra·nya
nausea	*náuseas* f pl	now·se·as
pain n	*dolor* m	do·lor
sore throat	*dolor de*	do·lor de
	garganta m	gar·gan·ta

women's health

(I think) I'm pregnant.
(Creo que) Estoy embarazada. (kre·o ke) es·toy em·ba·ra·sa·da

I'm on the pill.
Estoy tomando pastillas es·toy to·man·do pas·tee·yas
anticonceptivas. an·tee·kon·sep·tee·vas

I haven't had my period for (six) weeks.
No me ha bajado la no me a ba·kha·do la
regla en (seis) semanas. re·gla en (says) se·ma·nas

I've noticed a lump here.
Noté una pelota aquí. no·te oo·na pe·lo·ta a·kee

Do you have something for (period pain)?
¿Tiene algo para tye·ne al·go pa·ra
(dolores menstruales)? (do·lo·res mens·trwa·les)

I have a ...	*Tengo una ...*	ten·go oo·na ...
urinary tract infection	*infección urinaria*	een·fek·syon oo·ree·na·rya
yeast infection	*infección vaginal*	een·fek·syon va·khee·nal

I need (a/the) ...	*Necesito ...*	ne·se·see·to ...
contraception	*un anti-conceptivo*	oon an·tee·kon·sep·tee·vo
morning-after pill	*una pastilla del día siguiente*	oo·na pas·tee·ya del dee·a see·gyen·te
pregnancy test	*una prueba de embarazo*	oo·na prwe·ba de em·ba·ra·so

¿Cuándo fue la última vez que tuvo la regla?	
kwan·do fwe la ool·tee·ma ves ke too·vo la re·gla	**When did you last have your period?**
¿ Está con la regla?	
es·ta kon la reg·la	**Are you menstruating?**
¿Está embarazada?	
es·ta em·ba·ra·sa·da	**Are you pregnant?**
Está embarazada.	
es·ta em·ba·ra·sa·da	**You're pregnant.**
¿Está usando algún anticonceptivo?	
es·ta oo·san·do al·goon an·tee·kon·sep·tee·vo	**Are you using contraception?**

allergies

alergias

I'm allergic to ...	*Soy alérgico/ alérgica ...* m/f	soy a·ler·khee·ko/ a·ler·khee·ka ...
He/She is allergic to ...	*Él/Ella es alérgico/a ...*	el/e·ya es a·ler·khee·ko/a ...
antibiotics	*a los antibióticos*	a los an·tee·byo·tee·kos
anti-inflammatories	*a los anti-inflamatorios*	a los an·tee·een·fla·ma·to·ryos
aspirin	*a la aspirina*	a la as·pee·ree·na
bees	*a las abejas*	a las a·be·khas
codeine	*a la codeína*	a la ko·de·ee·na
penicillin	*a la penicilina*	a la pe·nee·see·lee·na
pollen	*al polen*	al po·len
sulphur-based drugs	*a los medicamentos a base de azufre*	a los me·dee·ka·men·tos a ba·se de a·soo·fre

I have a skin allergy.

   Tengo una alergia   *ten·*go *oo·*na a·*ler·*khee·a
   en la piel.   en la pyel

antihistamines	*antihista-*	an·tee·ees·ta·
	mínicos m pl	*mee·*nee·kos
inhaler	*inhalador* m	een·a·la·*dor*
injection	*inyección* f	een·yek·*syon*

For phrases on food-related allergies, see **special diets & allergies**, page 170.

alternative treatments

tratamientos alternativos

I don't use (Western medicine).

   Yo no uso (la medicina   yo no *oo·*so (la me·dee·*see·*na
   occidental).   ok·see·den·*tal*)

I prefer …	*Prefiero …*	pre·*fye·*ro …
Can I see someone	*¿Podría ver a*	po·*dree·*a ver a
who practises …?	*alguien que*	*al·*gyen ke
	practique la …?	prak·*tee·*ke la …
acupuncture	*acupuntura*	a·koo·poon·*too·*ra
aromatherapy	*aromaterapia*	a·ro·ma·te·*ra·*pee·a
homeopathy	*homeopatía*	o·me·o·pa·*tee·*a
meditation	*meditación*	me·dee·ta·*syon*
naturopathy	*neuropatía*	ne·oo·ro·pa·*tee·*a
reflexology	*reflexología*	re·flek·so·lo·*khee·*a

health

191

parts of the body

My ... hurts.
Me duele el/la ... m/f   me *dwe*·le el/la ...

I can't move my ...
No puedo mover el/la ... m/f   no *pwe*·do mo·*ver* el/la ...
No puedo mover   no *pwe*·do mo·*ver*
los/las ... m/f pl   los/las ...

My ... is swollen.
Tengo el/la ...   *ten*·go el/la ...
hinchado/a. m/f   een·*cha*·do/a

For other parts of the body, see the **dictionary**.

eye
ojo m
o·kho

ear
oreja f
o·*re*·kha

nose
nariz f
na·*rees*

mouth
boca f
bo·ka

head
cabeza f
ka·*be*·sa

hand
mano f
ma·no

arm
brazo m
bra·so

chest
pecho m
pe·cho

stomach
estómago m
es·*to*·ma·go

bum
nalgas f pl
nal·gas

leg
pierna f
pyer·na

foot
pie m
pye

pharmacist

I need something for (a headache).
Necesito algo para   ne·se·*see*·to *al*·go *pa*·ra
(el dolor de cabeza).   (el do·*lor* de ka·*be*·sa)

Do I need a prescription for (antihistamines)?
¿Necesito una receta   ne·se·*see*·to *oo*·na re·*se*·ta
para (antihistamínicos)?   *pa*·ra (an·tee·ees·ta·*mee*·nee·kos)

I have a prescription.
Tengo una receta.   *ten*·go *oo*·na re·*se*·ta

How many times a day?
¿Cuántas veces al día?   *kwan*·tas *ve*·ses al *dee*·a

Will it make me drowsy?
¿Me va a dar sueño?   me va a dar *swe*·nyo

antiseptic n	*antiséptico* m	an·tee·*sep*·tee·ko
contraceptives	*anticonceptivo* m	an·tee·kon·sep·*tee*·vo
insect repellent	*repelente* m	re·pe·*len*·te
painkillers	*medicinas para*	me·dee·*see*·nas *pa*·ra
	el dolor f pl	el do·*lor*
rehydration	*sales*	*sa*·les
salts	*hidratantes* f pl	ee·dra·*tan*·tes
sunblock	*bloqueador* m	blo·ke·a·*dor*
thermometer	*termómetro* m	ter·*mo*·me·tro

---

the pharmacist may say ...

Antes de comer.   *an*·tes de ko·*mer*   **Before food.**
Con la comida.   kon la ko·*mee*·da   **With food.**
Después de comer.   des·*pwes* de ko·*mer*   **After food.**

Dos/Tres veces al día.
   dos/tres *ve*·ses al *dee*·a   **Twice/Three times a day.**

¿Ha tomado esto antes?
   ha to·*ma*·do *es*·to *an*·tes   **Have you taken this before?**

Tiene que terminar el tratamiento completo.
   tye·ne ke ter·mee·*nar* el   **You must complete the**
   tra·ta·*myen*·to kom·*ple*·to   **course.**

dentist

dentista

I have a ...	Tengo ...	ten·go ...
broken tooth	un diente quebrado	oon dyen·te ke·bra·do
cavity	una caries	oo·na ka·ryes
toothache	un dolor de muela	oon do·lor de mwe·la

I need a/an ...	Necesito ...	ne·se·see·to ...
anaesthetic	un anestésico	oon a·nes·te·see·ko
filling	una calza	oo·na kal·sa

I've lost a filling.
Se me cayó una calza.　　se me ka·yo oo·na kal·sa

My dentures are broken.
Mi dentadura　　mee den·ta·doo·ra
está quebrada.　　es·ta ke·bra·da

My gums hurt.
Me duelen las encías.　　me dwe·len las en·see·as

I don't want it extracted.
No quiero que me la saque.　　no kye·ro ke me la sa·ke

Ouch!
Ay!　　ai

the dentist may say ...

Abra grande.	a·bra gran·de	**Open wide.**
Enjuague.	en·khwa·ge	**Rinse.**
Esto no le va a doler.	es·to no le va a do·ler	**This won't hurt a bit.**
Muerda esto.	mwer·da es·to	**Bite down on this.**
No se mueva.	no se mwe·va	**Don't move.**
Vuelva, no he terminado.	vwel·va no e ter·mee·na·do	**Come back, I haven't finished.**

Spanish nouns in this dictionary have their gender indicated with ⓜ (masculine) and ⓕ (feminine). If adjectives and nouns have just one form for both genders, it's marked as ⓜ&ⓕ. Where adjectives and nouns have separate masculine and feminine forms, the endings are divided by a slash (eg *bello/a* ⓜ/ⓕ). In other cases we spell out the masculine and feminine forms in full for clarity of pronunciation (eg *embajador/ embajadora* ⓜ/ⓕ). See the **phrasebuilder** for more on gender. Words are also marked as n (noun), a (adjective), adv (adverb), v (verb), pl (plural), sg (singular), inf (informal) and pol (polite) where necessary. Verbs are given in the infinitive – for details on how to change verbs for use in a sentence, see the **phrasebuilder**, page 28.

A

aboard *a bordo* a·bor·do
abortion *aborto* ⓜ a·bor·to
about *sobre* so·bre
above *sobre* so·bre
abroad *en el extranjero*
  en el eks·tran·khe·ro
accident *accidente* ⓜ ak·see·den·te
accommodation *alojamiento* ⓜ
  a·lo·kha·myen·to
account (bill) *cuenta* ⓕ kwen·ta
acid *ácido* ⓜ a·see·do
across *a través* a tra·ves
activist *activista* ⓜ&ⓕ ak·tee·vees·ta
actor *actor/actriz* ⓜ/ⓕ ak·tor/ak·trees
acupuncture *acupuntura* ⓕ
  a·koo·poon·too·ra
adaptor *adaptador* ⓜ a·dap·ta·dor
addiction *adicción* ⓕ a·deek·syon
address *dirección* ⓕ dee·rek·syon
administration *administración* ⓕ
  ad·mee·nees·tra·syon
admission (price) *admisión* ⓕ ad·mee·syon
admit *admitir* ad·mee·teer
adult nⓐ *adulto/a* ⓜ/ⓕ a·dool·to/a
advertisement *anuncio* ⓜ a·noon·syo
advice *consejo* ⓜ kon·se·kho
aerobics *aeróbicos* ⓜ a·e·ro·bee·kos
aeroplane *avión* ⓜ a·vyon
Africa *África* ⓕ a·free·ka
after *después* des·pwes

afternoon *tarde* ⓕ tar·de
aftershave *loción para despues del afeitado*
  ⓕ lo·syon pa·ra des·pwes del a·fay·ta·do
again *otra vez* o·tra ves
age *edad* ⓕ e·dad
(three days) ago *hace (tres días)*
  a·se (tres dee·as)
agree *estar de acuerdo* es·tar de a·kwer·do
agriculture *agricultura* ⓕ a·gree·kool·too·ra
ahead *adelante* a·de·lan·te
AIDS *SIDA* ⓜ see·da
air *aire* ⓜ ai·re
air-conditioned *con aire acondicionado*
  kon ai·re a·kon·dee·syo·na·do
air conditioning *aire acondicionado* ⓜ
  ai·re a·kon·dee·syo·na·do
airline *aerolínea* ⓕ a·e·ro·lee·ne·a
airmail *correo aéreo* ⓜ ko·re·o a·e·re·o
airplane *avión* ⓜ a·vyon
airport *aeropuerto* ⓜ a·e·ro·pwer·to
airport tax *impuesto de salida* ⓜ
  eem·pwes·to de sa·lee·da
aisle (on plane) *pasillo* ⓜ pa·see·yo
alarm clock *reloj despertador* ⓜ
  re·lokh des·per·ta·dor
alcohol *alcohol* ⓜ al·kol
all *todo/a* ⓜ/ⓕ to·do/a
allergy *alergia* ⓕ a·ler·khee·a
all-terrain vehicle *camión de todo-terreno*
  ⓜ ka·myon de to·do te·re·no
almond *almendra* ⓕ al·men·dra
almost *casi* ka·see
alone *solo/a* ⓜ/ⓕ so·lo/a

already *ya* ya
also *también* tam·*byen*
altar *altar* ⓜ al·*tar*
altitude *altura* ⓕ al·*too*·ra
always *siempre* *syem*·pre
ambassador *embajador/embajadora* ⓜ/ⓕ em·ba·kha·*dor*/em·ba·kha·*do*·ra
ambulance *ambulancia* ⓕ am·boo·*lan*·sya
anaemia *anemia* ⓕ a·ne·*mya
anarchist n&a *anarquista* ⓜ&ⓕ a·nar·*kees*·ta
ancient *antiguo/a* ⓜ/ⓕ an·*tee*·gwo/a
and *y* ee
angry *enfadado/a* ⓜ/ⓕ en·fa·*da*·do/a
animal *animal* ⓜ a·nee·*mal
ankle *tobillo* ⓜ to·*bee*·yo
another *otro/a* ⓜ/ⓕ o·tro/a
answer *respuesta* ⓕ res·*pwes*·ta
answer v *responder* res·pon·*der
ant *hormiga* ⓕ or·*mee*·ga
antibiotics *antibióticos* ⓜ pl an·tee·*byo*·tee·kos
antinuclear *antinuclear* an·tee·noo·kle·*ar
antique *antigüedad* ⓕ an·tee·gwe·*dad
antiseptic *antiséptico* ⓜ an·tee·*sep*·tee·ko
any *cualquier/cualquiera* ⓜ/ⓕ kwal·*kyer*/kwal·*kye*·ra
apartment *apartamento* ⓜ a·par·ta·*men*·to
appendix (body) *apéndice* ⓜ a·*pen*·dee·se
apple *manzana* ⓕ man·*sa*·na
appointment *cita* ⓕ *see*·ta
apricot *albaricoque* ⓜ al·ba·ree·*ko*·ke
April *abril* ⓜ a·*breel
archaeological *arqueológico/a* ⓜ/ⓕ ar·ke·o·lo·*khee*·ko/a
architect *arquitecto/a* ⓜ/ⓕ ar·kee·*tek*·to/a
architecture *arquitectura* ⓕ ar·kee·tek·*too*·ra
argue *argumentar* ar·goo·men·*tar
arm (body) *brazo* ⓜ *bra*·so
aromatherapy *aromaterapia* ⓕ a·ro·ma·te·*ra*·pya
arrest *arrestar* a·res·*tar
arrivals *llegadas* ⓕ pl ye·*ga*·das
arrive *llegar* ye·*gar
art *arte* ⓜ *ar*·te
art gallery *galería de arte* ⓕ ga·le·*ree*·a de ar·te
artist *artista* ⓜ&ⓕ ar·*tees*·ta
ashtray *cenicero* ⓜ se·nee·*se*·ro
Asia *Asia* ⓕ *a*·sya

ask (a question) *preguntar* pre·goon·*tar
ask (for something) *pedir* pe·*deer
asparagus *espárragos* ⓜ es·pa·ra·gos
aspirin *aspirina* ⓕ as·pee·*ree*·na
asthma *asma* ⓕ *as*·ma
at *en* en
athletics *atletismo* ⓜ at·le·*tees*·mo
Atlantic Ocean *Océano Atlántico* ⓜ o·se·a·no at·*lan*·tee·ko
ATM *cajero automático* ⓜ ka·*khe*·ro ow·to·*ma*·tee·ko
atmosphere *atmósfera* ⓕ at·*mos*·fe·ra
aubergine *berenjena* ⓕ be·ren·*khe*·na
August *agosto* ⓜ a·*gos*·to
aunt *tía* ⓕ *tee*·a
Australia *Australia* ⓕ ows·*tra*·lya
autumn *otoño* ⓜ o·*to*·nyo
avenue *avenida* ⓕ a·ve·*nee*·da
avocado *aguacate* ⓜ a·gwa·*ka*·te
awful *horrible* ⓜ&ⓕ o·*ree*·ble

B

B&W (film) a *blanco y negro* *blan*·ko ee ne·gro
baby *bebé* ⓜ&ⓕ be·*be
baby food *comida de bebé* ⓕ ko·*mee*·da de be·be
baby powder *talcos* ⓜ pl *tal*·kos
babysitter *niñera* ⓕ nee·*nye*·ra
back (body) *espalda* ⓕ es·*pal*·da
back (position) *atrás* a·*tras
backpack *mochila* ⓕ mo·*chee*·la
bacon *tocineta* ⓕ to·see·*ne*·ta
bad *malo/a* ⓜ/ⓕ *ma*·lo/a
bag *bolsa* ⓕ *bol*·sa
baggage *equipaje* ⓜ e·kee·*pa*·khe
baggage allowance *límite de equipaje* ⓕ *lee*·mee·te de e·kee·*pa*·khe
baggage claim *reclamo de equipaje* ⓜ re·*kla*·mo de e·kee·*pa*·khe
bakery *panadería* ⓕ pa·na·de·*ree*·a
balance (account) *saldo* ⓜ *sal*·do
balcony *balcón* ⓜ bal·*kon
ball (sport) *bola* ⓕ *bo*·la
ballet *ballet* ⓜ ba·*let
banana *banano* ⓜ ba·*na*·no
band (music) *grupo musical* ⓜ *groo*·po moo·see·*kal

bandage *vendaje* ⓜ ven-*da*-khe
Band-Aid *curita* ① koo-*ree*-ta
bank *banco* ⓜ *ban*-ko
bank account *cuenta bancaria* ①
  kwen-ta ban-*ka*-rya
banknote *billete de banco* ⓜ
  bee-*ye*-te de *ban*-ko
baptism *bautismo* ⓜ bow-*tees*-mo
bar *bar* ⓜ bar
barber *barbero* ⓜ bar-*be*-ro
bar work *trabajo en el bar* ⓜ
  tra-*ba*-kho en el bar
baseball *béisbol* ⓜ *bays*-bol
basket *canasta* ① ka-*nas*-ta
basketball *básquetbol* ⓜ *bas*-ket-bol
bath *baño* ⓜ *ba*-nyo
bathing suit *vestido de baño* ⓜ
  ves-*tee*-do de *ba*-nyo
bathroom *baño* ⓜ *ba*-nyo
battery *batería* ① ba-te-*ree*-a
be (permanent) *ser* ser
be (temporary) *estar* es-*tar*
beach *playa* ① *pla*-ya
beach volleyball *volibol de playa* ⓜ
  vo-lee-*bol* de *pla*-ya
bean *frijol* ⓜ free-*khol*
beansprout *frijol nacido* ⓜ
  free-*khol* na-*see*-do
beautician *estilista* ⓜ&① es-tee-*lees*-ta
beautiful *bello/a* ⓜ/① *be*-yo/a
beauty salon *salón de belleza* ⓜ
  sa-*lon* de be-*ye*-sa
because *porque* *por*-ke
bed *cama* ① *ka*-ma
bedding *ropa de cama* ① *ro*-pa de *ka*-ma
bed linen *sábana* ① *sa*-ba-na
bedroom *cuarto* ⓜ *kwar*-to
bee *abeja* ① a-*be*-kha
beef *carne de res/vaca* ① *kar*-ne de res/*va*-ka
beer *cerveza* ① ser-*ve*-sa
before *antes* *an*-tes
beggar *mendigo/a* ⓜ/① men-*dee*-go/a
behind *detrás* de-*tras*
Belgium *Bélgica* ① *bel*-khee-ka
below *debajo* de-*ba*-kho
berth *litera* ① lee-*te*-ra
beside *junto a* *khoon*-to a
(the) best *el/la mejor* ⓜ/① el/la me-*khor*
bet *apuesta* ① a-*pwes*-ta
bet v *apostar* a-*pos*-tar

better *mejor* me-*khor*
between *entre* *en*-tre
Bible *Biblia* ① *bee*-blya
bicycle *bicicleta* ① bee-see-*kle*-ta
big *grande* ⓜ&① *gran*-de
bigger *más grande* ⓜ&① mas *gran*-de
(the) biggest *el/la más grande* ⓜ/①
  el/la mas *gran*-de
bike *bicicleta* ① bee-see-*kle*-ta
bike chain *cadena de bicicleta* ①
  ka-*de*-na de bee-see-*kle*-ta
bike lock *candado de bicicleta* ⓜ
  kan-*da*-do de bee-see-*kle*-ta
bike trail *sendero de bicicleta* ⓜ
  sen-*de*-ro de bee-see-*kle*-ta
bike shop *ciclo* ⓜ *see*-klo
bill (account/restaurant) *cuenta* ① *kwen*-ta
binoculars *binoculares* ⓜ pl
  bee-no-koo-*la*-res
bird *pájaro* ⓜ *pa*-kha-ro
birth certificate *certificado de nacimiento* ⓜ
  ser-tee-fee-*ka*-do de na-see-*myen*-to
birthday *cumpleaños* ⓜ koom-ple-*a*-nyos
biscuit (savoury) *pancito* ⓜ pan-*see*-to
biscuit (sweet) *galleta* ① ga-*ye*-ta
bite (dog) *mordida* ① mor-*dee*-da
bite (insect) *picada* ① pee-*ka*-da
bitter *amargo/a* ⓜ/① a-*mar*-go/a
black *negro/a* ⓜ/① *ne*-gro/a
black market *mercado negro* ⓜ
  mer-*ka*-do *ne*-gro
bladder *vejiga* ① ve-*khee*-ga
blanket *cobija* ① ko-*bee*-kha
blind *ciego/a* ⓜ/① *sye*-go/a
blister *ampolla* ① am-*po*-ya
blocked *bloqueado/a* ⓜ/① blo-ke-*a*-do/a
blood *sangre* ① *san*-gre
blood group *grupo sanguíneo* ⓜ
  groo-po san-*gee*-ne-o
blood pressure *presión sanguínea* ①
  pre-*syon* san-*gee*-ne-a
blood test *prueba de sangre* ①
  prwe-ba de *san*-gre
blue *azul* ⓜ&① a-*sool*
board (plane/ship) *abordar* a-bor-*dar*
boarding house *pensión* ① pen-*syon*
boarding pass *tiquete de abordaje* ⓜ
  tee-*ke*-te de a-bor-*da*-khe
boat *barco* ⓜ *bar*-ko
body *cuerpo* ⓜ *kwer*-po

B

english–costa rican spanish

197

boiled *hervido/a* ⓜ/ⓕ er-*vee*-do/a
bone *hueso* ⓜ *we*-so
book *libro* ⓜ *lee*-bro
book (make a booking) *reservar* re-ser-*var*
booked out *sin espacio* seen es-*pa*-syo
book shop *librería* ⓕ lee-bre-*ree*-a
boots *botas* ⓕ pl *bo*-tas
border (geographic) *frontera* ⓕ fron-*te*-ra
bored *aburrido/a* ⓜ/ⓕ a-boo-*ree*-do/a
boring *aburrido/a* ⓜ/ⓕ a-boo-*ree*-do/a
borrow *pedir prestado* pe-*deer* pres-*ta*-do
botanic garden *jardín botánico* ⓜ
khar-*deen* bo-*ta*-nee-ko
both *ambos/as* ⓜ/ⓕ pl am-bos/as
bottle *botella* ⓕ bo-*te*-ya
bottle opener *abridor* ⓜ a-bree-*dor*
bottle shop *licorera* ⓕ lee-ko-*re*-ra
bottom (body) *trasero* ⓜ tra-*se*-ro
bottom (position) *fondo* ⓜ *fon*-do
bowl *plato hondo* ⓜ *pla*-to on-do
box *caja* ⓕ *ka*-kha
boxer shorts *bóxer* ⓜ *bok*-ser
boxing *boxeo* ⓜ *bok*-se-o
boy *chico* ⓜ *chee*-ko
boyfriend *novio* ⓜ *no*-vyo
bra *bracier* ⓜ bra-*syer*
brakes *frenos* ⓜ pl *fre*-nos
brave *valiente* ⓜ&ⓕ va-*lyen*-te
bread *pan* ⓜ pan
bread rolls *bollos de pan* ⓜ pl *bo*-yos de pan
break (in general) *quebrar* ke-*brar*
break (smash) *romper* rom-*per*
break down (car) *quedarse varado*
ke-*dar*-se va-*ra*-do
breakfast *desayuno* ⓜ de-sa-*yoo*-no
breast (body) *pecho* ⓜ *pe*-cho
breast (poultry) *pechuga* ⓕ pe-*choo*-ga
breasts (body) *senos* ⓜ pl *se*-nos
bribe *soborno* ⓜ so-*bor*-no
bribe v *sobornar* so-bor-*nar*
bridge (structure) *puente* ⓜ *pwen*-te
briefcase *valija* ⓕ va-*lee*-kha
bring *traer* tra-*er*
brochure *panfleto* ⓜ pan-*fle*-to
broken *quebrado/a* ⓜ/ⓕ ke-*bra*-do/a
broken down (car) *descompuesto/a* ⓜ/ⓕ
des-kom-*pwes*-to/a
bronchitis *bronquitis* ⓕ bron-*kee*-tees
brother *hermano* ⓜ er-*ma*-no
brown *café* ⓜ&ⓕ ka-*fe*

bruise *moretón* ⓜ mo-re-*ton*
brush *cepillo* ⓜ se-*pee*-yo
bucket *balde* ⓜ *bal*-de
Buddhist n&a *budista* ⓜ&ⓕ boo-*dees*-ta
budget *presupuesto* ⓜ pre-soo-*pwes*-to
buffet *buffet* ⓜ boo-*fe*
bug *bicho* ⓜ *bee*-cho
build *construir* kons-troo-*eer*
builder *constructor/constructora* ⓜ/ⓕ
kons-trook-*tor*/kons-trook-*to*-ra
building *edificio* ⓜ e-dee-*fee*-syo
burn *quemadura* ⓕ ke-ma-*doo*-ra
burnt *quemado/a* ⓜ/ⓕ ke-*ma*-do/a
bus *bus* ⓜ boos
bus station *estación de bus* ⓕ
es-ta-*syon* de boos
bus stop *parada de bus* ⓕ pa-*ra*-da de boos
business *negocio* ⓜ ne-*go*-syo
business class *clase ejecutiva* ⓕ
kla-se e-khe-koo-*tee*-va
businessman *hombre de negocios* ⓜ
om-bre de ne-*go*-syos
businesswoman *mujer de negocios* ⓕ
moo-*kher* de ne-*go*-syos
busker *artista callejero* ⓜ&ⓕ
ar-*tees*-ta ka-ye-*khe*-ro
busy *ocupado/a* ⓜ/ⓕ o-koo-*pa*-do/a
but *pero* *pe*-ro
butcher *carnicero* ⓜ kar-nee-*se*-ro
butcher's shop *carnicería* ⓕ kar-nee-se-*ree*-a
butter *mantequilla* ⓕ man-te-*kee*-ya
butterfly *mariposa* ⓕ ma-ree-*po*-sa
button *botón* ⓜ bo-*ton*
buy *comprar* kom-*prar*

C

cabbage *repollo* ⓜ re-*po*-yo
cable car *teleférico* ⓜ te-le-*fe*-ree-ko
café *café* ⓜ ka-*fe*
cake *queque* ⓜ *ke*-ke
cake shop *pastelería* ⓕ pas-te-le-*ree*-a
calculator *calculadora* ⓕ kal-koo-la-*do*-ra
calendar *calendario* ⓜ ka-len-*da*-ryo
call (phone) *llamar* ya-*mar*
camera *cámara* ⓕ *ka*-ma-ra
camera shop *tienda de cámaras* ⓕ
tyen-da de *ka*-ma-ras
camp *acampar* a-kam-*par*

camping ground *área de acampar* ①
a·re·a de a·kam·par

camping store
tienda de artículos para acampar ①
tyen·da de ar·tee·koo·los pa·ra a·kam·par

camp site *sitio para acampar* ⑩
see·tyo pa·ra a·kam·par

can (be able/have permission) *poder* po·der

can (tin) *lata* ① la·ta

Canada *Canadá* ① ka·na·*da*

cancel *cancelar* kan·se·lar

cancer *cáncer* ⑩ kan·ser

candle *vela* ① ve·la

candy *confite* ⑩ kon·fee·te

canoe *canoa* ① ka·no·a

can opener *abrelatas* ⑩ a·bre·la·tas

cantaloupe *melón* ⑩ me·lon

capsicum *pimentón* ⑩ pee·men·ton

car *carro* ⑩ ka·ro

caravan *caravana* ① ka·ra·va·na

cardiac arrest *ataque cardíaco* ⑩
a·ta·ke kar·dee·a·ko

cards (playing) *naipes* ⑩ pl nai·pes

care (for someone) *cuidar de* kwee·dar de

car hire *alquiler de carros* ⑩
al·kee·ler de ka·ros

Caribbean Sea *Mar Caribe* ⑩ mar ka·ree·be

car owner's title *título de propiedad* ⑩
tee·too·lo de pro·pee·e·dad

car park *parqueo* ⑩ par·ke·o

carpenter *carpintero* ⑩ kar·peen·te·ro

car registration *registro del carro* ⑩
re·khees·tro del ka·ro

carrot *zanahoria* ① sa·na·o·rya

carry *llevar* ye·var

carton *cartón* ⑩ kar·ton

cash *efectivo* ⑩ e·fek·tee·vo

cash (a cheque) *cambiar (un cheque)*
kam·byar (oon che·ke)

cashew *semilla de marañón* ①
se·mee·ya de ma·ra·nyon

cashier *cajero/a* ⑩/① ka·khe·ro/a

cash register *caja* ① ka·kha

casino *casino* ⑩ ka·see·no

cassette *cassette* ① ka·se·te

castle *castillo* ⑩ kas·tee·yo

casual work *trabajo temporal* ⑩
tra·ba·kho tem·po·ral

cat *gato/a* ⑩/① ga·to/a

cathedral *catedral* ① ka·te·dral

Catholic n&a *católico/a* ⑩/① ka·to·lee·ko/a

cave *cueva* ① kwe·va

CD *CD* ⑩ se de

celebration *celebración* ① se·le·bra·syon

cell phone *teléfono celular* ⑩
te·le·fo·no se·loo·lar

cemetery *cementerio* ⑩ se·men·te·ryo

cent *centavo* ⑩ sen·ta·vo

centimetre *centímetro* ⑩ sen·tee·me·tro

centre *centro* ⑩ sen·tro

ceramics *cerámica* ① se·ra·mee·ka

cereal (breakfast) *cereal* ⑩ se·re·al

certificate *certificado* ⑩ ser·tee·fee·ka·do

chain *cadena* ① ka·de·na

chair *silla* ① see·ya

champagne *champaña* ① cham·pa·nya

championships *campeonatos* ⑩ pl
kam·pe·o·na·tos

chance *oportunidad* ① o·por·too·nee·dad

change *cambio* ⑩ kam·byo

change (coins) *vuelto* ⑩ vwel·to

change (money) v *cambiar* kam·byar

changing room *vestidores* ⑩ pl
ves·tee·do·res

charming *encantador/encantadora* ⑩/①
en·kan·ta·dor/en·kan·ta·do·ra

chat up (flirt) *ligar* lee·gar

cheap *barato/a* ⑩/① ba·ra·to/a

cheat *tramposo/a* ⑩/① tram·po·so/a

check v *revisar* re·vee·sar

check (banking) *cheque* ⑩ che·ke

check (bill) *cuenta* ① kwen·ta

check-in (desk) *chequeo* ⑩ che·ke·o

checkpoint (border) *punto de control* ⑩
poon·to de kon·trol

cheese *queso* ⑩ ke·so

chef *chef* ⑩ shef

chemist (pharmacist) *farmacéutico/a* ⑩/①
far·ma·se·oo·tee·ko/a

chemist (pharmacy) *farmacia* ① far·ma·sya

cheque (banking) *cheque* ⑩ che·ke

cherry *cereza* ① se·re·sa

chess *ajedrez* ⑩ a·khe·dres

chest (body) *pecho* ⑩ pe·cho

chewing gum *chicle* ⑩ chee·kle

chicken *pollo* ⑩ po·yo

chicken pox *varicela* ① va·ree·se·la

chickpea *garbanzo* ⑩ gar·ban·so

child *chiquito/a* ⑩/① chee·kee·to/a

child-minding service *guardería* ① gwar-de-*ree*-a

child seat *silla para niños* ① *see*-ya pa-ra *nee*-nyos

children *niños/as* ⓜ/① pl *nee*-nyos/as

chilli *chile* ⓜ *chee*-le

chilli sauce *salsa picante* ① *sal*-sa pee-*kan*-te

China *China* ① *chee*-na

chiropractor *qiropráctico* ⓜ kee-ro-*prak*-tee-ko

chocolate *chocolate* ⓜ cho-ko-*la*-te

choose *escoger* es-ko-*kher*

chopping board *tabla para picar* ① *ta*-bla pa-ra pee-*kar*

chopsticks *palillos chinos* ⓜ pl pa-*lee*-yos *chee*-nos

Christian n&a *cristiano/a* ⓜ/① krees-*tya*-no/a

Christian name *nombre cristiano* ⓜ *nom*-bre krees-*tya*-no

Christmas *Navidad* ① na-vee-*dad*

Christmas Day *día de Navidad* ⓜ *dee*-a de na-vee-*dad*

Christmas Eve *víspera de Navidad* ① *vees*-pe-ra de na-vee-*dad*

church *iglesia* ① ee-*gle*-sya

cider *cidra* ① *see*-dra

cigar *cigarro* ⓜ see-*ga*-ro

cigarette *cigarrillo* ⓜ see-ga-*ree*-yo

cigarette lighter *encendedor* ⓜ en-sen-de-*dor*

cinema *cine* ⓜ *see*-ne

circus *circo* ⓜ *seer*-ko

citizenship *ciudadanía* ① syoo-da-da-*nee*-a

city *ciudad* ① syoo-*dad*

city centre *centro de la ciudad* ⓜ *sen*-tro de la syoo-*dad*

civil rights *derechos civiles* ⓜ pl de-*re*-chos se-*vee*-les

clarinet *clarinete* ⓜ kla-ree-*ne*-te

class (category) *clase* ① *kla*-se

class system *escalas sociales* ① pl es-*ka*-la so-*sya*-les

classical *clásico/a* ⓜ/① *kla*-see-ko/a

clean *limpio/a* ⓜ/① *leem*-pyo/a

clean v *limpiar* leem-*pyar*

cleaning *limpieza* ① leem-*pye*-sa

client *cliente* ⓜ klee-*en*-te

cliff *precipicio* ⓜ pre-see-*pee*-syo

climb v *escalar* es-ka-*lar*

cloakroom *guardaropa* ⓜ gwar-da-*ro*-pa

clock *reloj* ⓜ re-*lokh*

close (by) *cerca* *ser*-ka

close v *cerrar* se-*rar*

closed *cerrado/a* ⓜ/① se-*ra*-do/a

clothesline *tendedero* ⓜ ten-de-*de*-ro

clothing *ropa* ① *ro*-pa

clothing store *tienda de ropa* ① *tyen*-da de *ro*-pa

cloud *nube* ① *noo*-be

cloud forest *bosque nuboso* ⓜ *bos*-ke noo-*bo*-so

cloudy *nublado/a* ⓜ/① noo-*bla*-do/a

clutch (car) *closh* ⓜ klosh

coach (bus) *bus* ⓜ boos

coach (trainer) *entrenador/entrenadora* ⓜ/① en-tre-na-*dor*/en-tre-na-*do*-ra

coach *entrenar* en-tre-*nar*

coast *costa* ① *kos*-ta

coat *abrigo* ⓜ a-*bree*-go

cocaine *cocaína* ① ko-ka-*ee*-na

cockroach *cucaracha* ① koo-ka-*ra*-cha

cocktail *coctel* ⓜ kok-*tel*

cocoa *cacao* ⓜ ka-*kow*

coconut *coco* ⓜ *ko*-ko

coffee *café* ⓜ ka-*fe*

coins *monedas* ① pl mo-*ne*-das

cold *frío/a* ⓜ/① *free*-o/a

cold (illness) *resfriado* ⓜ res-free-*a*-do

colleague *colega* ⓜ&① ko-*le*-ga

collect call *llamada a cobrar* ① ya-*ma*-da a ko-*brar*

college (university) *universidad* ① oo-nee-ver-see-*dad*

colour *color* ⓜ ko-*lor*

comb *peine* ⓜ *pay*-ne

come *venir* ve-*neer*

comedy *comedia* ① ko-*me*-dya

comfortable *cómodo/a* ⓜ/① *ko*-mo-do/a

commission *conmoción* ① kon-mo-*syon*

communications (profession) *comunicación* ① ko-moo-nee-ka-*syon*

communion *comunión* ① ko-moo-*nyon*

communist n&a *comunista* ⓜ&① ko-moo-*nees*-ta

companion *compañero/a* ⓜ/① kom-pa-*nye*-ro/a

company (firm) *compañía* ① kom-pa-*nyee*-a

compass *brújula* ① *broo*-khoo-la

complain *quejarse* ke-*khar*-se

complaint *queja* ① *ke*·kha
complimentary (free) *gratis* ⓜ&① *gra*·tees
computer *computadora* ①
  kom·poo·ta·*do*·ra
computer game *juego de computadora* ⓜ
  khwe·go de kom·poo·ta·*do*·ra
concert *concierto* ⓜ kon·*syer*·to
concussion *contusión* ① kon·too·*syon*
conditioner (hair) *acondicionador* ⓜ
  a·kon·dee·syo·na·*dor*
condom *preservativo* ⓜ pre·ser·va·tee·vo
conference (big) *congreso* ⓜ kon·*gre*·so
conference (small) *conferencia* ①
  kon·fe·*ren*·sya
confession (religious) *confesión* ①
  kon·fe·*syon*
confirm (a booking) *confirmar* kon·feer·*mar*
congratulations *felicidades* fe·lee·see·*da*·des
conjunctivitis *conjuntivitis* ①
  kon·khoon·tee·vee·tees
connection *conexión* ① ko·nek·*syon*
conservative n&a
  conservador/conservadora ⓜ/①
  kon·ser·va·*dor*/kon·ser·va·*do*·ra
constipation *estreñimiento* ⓜ
  es·tre·nyee·*myen*·to
consulate *consulado* ⓜ kon·soo·*la*·do
contact lenses *lentes de contacto* ⓜ pl
  len·tes de kon·*tak*·to
contact lens solution
  líquido para lentes de contacto ⓜ
  lee·kee·do *pa*·ra *len*·tes de kon·*tak*·to
contraceptives *anticonceptivos* ⓜ pl
  an·tee·kon·sep·*tee*·vos
contract *contrato* ⓜ kon·*tra*·to
convenience store *súper* ⓜ *soo*·per
convent *convento* ⓜ kon·*ven*·to
cook *cocinero/a* ⓜ/① ko·see·*ne*·ro/a
cook v *cocinar* ko·see·*nar*
cookie *galleta* ① ga·*ye*·ta
cooking *cocina* ① ko·*see*·na
cool (temperature) *fresco/a* ⓜ/① *fres*·ko/a
corkscrew *sacacorchos* ⓜ sa·ka·*kor*·chos
corn *maíz* ⓜ ma·*ees*
corner *esquina* ① es·*kee*·na
cornflakes *cornflakes* ⓜ pl *korn*·fleks
corrupt *corrupto/a* ⓜ/① ko·*roop*·to/a
corruption *corrupción* ① ko·roop·*syon*
cost (price) *precio* ⓜ *pre*·syo
cost v *costar* kos·*tar*
cotton *algodón* ⓜ al·go·*don*

cotton balls *bolitas de algodón* ① pl
  bo·*lee*·tas de al·go·*don*
cotton buds (swabs) *aplicadores* ⓜ pl
  a·plee·ka·*do*·res
cough *tos* ① tos
cough v *toser* to·*ser*
cough medicine *jarabe para la tos* ⓜ
  kha·*ra*·be *pa*·ra la tos
count *contar* kon·*tar*
counter (at bar) *barra* ① *ba*·ra
country *país* ⓜ pa·*ees*
countryside *campo* ⓜ *kam*·po
coupon *cupón* ① koo·*pon*
court (legal) *corte* ① *kor*·te
court (tennis) *cancha de tenis* ①
  kan·cha de te·nees
cover charge *entrada* ① en·*tra*·da
cow *vaca* ① *va*·ka
cracker *galleta salada* ① ga·*ye*·ta sa·*la*·da
crafts *artesanías* ① pl ar·te·sa·*nee*·as
crash *choque* ⓜ *cho*·ke
crazy *loco/a* ⓜ/① *lo*·ko/a
cream (food/lotion) *crema* ① *kre*·ma
crèche *cuna* ① *koo*·na
credit *crédito* ⓜ *kre*·dee·to
credit card *tarjeta de crédito* ①
  tar·*khe*·ta de *kre*·dee·to
cricket (sport) *cricket* ⓜ *kree*·ket
cross (religious) *cruz* ① kroos
crowded *lleno/a de gente* ⓜ/①
  ye·no/a de *khen*·te
cucumber *pepino* ⓜ pe·*pee*·no
cup *taza* ① *ta*·sa
cupboard *armario* ⓜ ar·*ma*·ryo
currency exchange *cambio de moneda* ⓜ
  kam·byo de mo·*ne*·da
current (electricity) *corriente* ① ko·*ryen*·te
current affairs *actualidad* ① ak·twa·lee·*dad*
custom *costumbre* ① kos·*toom*·bre
customs (immigration) *aduana* ①
  a·*dwa*·na
cut *cortada* ① kor·*ta*·da
cut v *cortar* kor·*tar*
cutlery *cubiertos* ⓜ pl koo·*byer*·tos
CV *currículum* ⓜ koo·*ree*·koo·loom
cycle (ride) *andar en bicicleta*
  an·*dar* en bee·see·*kle*·ta
cycling *ciclismo* ⓜ see·*klees*·mo
cyclist *ciclista* ⓜ&① see·*klees*·ta
cystitis *cistitis* ① sees·*tee*·tees

D

dad *papá* ⓜ pa·*pa*
daily adv *todos los días*
  to·dos los *dee*·as
dance *baile* ⓜ *bai*·le
dance v *bailar* bai·*lar*
dangerous *peligroso/a* ⓜ/ⓕ pe·lee·*gro*·so/a
dark (colour/night) *oscuro/a* ⓜ/ⓕ
  os·*koo*·ro/a
date (appointment) *cita* ⓕ *see*·ta
date (day) *fecha* ⓕ *fe*·cha
date (go out with) *salir con* sa·*leer* kon
date of birth *fecha de nacimiento* ⓕ
  fe·cha de na·see·*myen*·to
daughter *hija* ⓕ ee·*kha*
dawn *amanecer* ⓜ a·ma·ne·*ser*
day *día* ⓜ *dee*·a
day after tomorrow *pasado mañana* ⓜ
  pa·*sa*·do ma·*nya*·na
day before yesterday *anteayer* ⓜ
  an·te·a·*yer*
dead *muerto/a* ⓜ/ⓕ *mwer*·to/a
deaf *sordo/a* ⓜ/ⓕ *sor*·do/a
deal (cards) *repartir* re·par·*teer*
December *diciembre* ⓜ dee·*syem*·bre
decide *decidir* de·see·*deer*
deep *hondo/a* ⓜ/ⓕ *on*·do/a
deforestation *deforestación* ⓕ
  de·fo·res·ta·*syon*
degrees (temperature) *grados* ⓜ pl *gra*·dos
delay *atraso* ⓜ a·*tra*·so
delicatessen *delicatessen* ⓕ de·le·ka·*te*·sen
deliver *enviar* en·*vyar*
democracy *democracia* ⓕ de·mo·*kra*·sya
demonstration (display) *demostración* ⓕ
  de·mos·tra·*syon*
demonstration (rally) *manifestación* ⓕ
  ma·nee·fes·ta·*syon*
Denmark *Dinamarca* ⓕ dee·na·*mar*·ka
dental floss *hilo dental* ⓜ *ee*·lo den·*tal*
dentist *dentista* ⓜ&ⓕ den·*tees*·ta
deodorant *desodorante* ⓜ de·so·do·*ran*·te
depart *partir* par·*teer*
department store *tienda por departamentos*
  ⓕ *tyen*·da por de·par·ta·*men*·tos
departure *salida* ⓕ sa·*lee*·da
departure gate *puerta de salida* ⓕ
  pwer·ta de sa·*lee*·da
deposit (bank) *depósito* ⓜ de·po·*see*·to
descendent *descendiente* ⓜ de·sen·*dyen*·te

desert *desierto* ⓜ de·*syer*·to
design *diseño* ⓜ dee·*se*·nyo
dessert *postre* ⓜ *pos*·tre
destination *destino* ⓜ des·*tee*·no
details *detalles* ⓜ pl de·*ta*·yes
diabetes *diabetes* ⓕ dee·a·*be*·tes
dial tone *tono* ⓜ *to*·no
diaper *pañal* ⓜ pa·*nyal*
diaphragm (contraceptive) *diafragma* ⓜ
  dya·*frag*·ma
diarrhoea *diarrea* ⓕ dee·a·*re*·a
diary *agenda* ⓕ a·*khen*·da
dice *dados* ⓜ pl *da*·dos
dictionary *diccionario* ⓜ deek·syo·*na*·ryo
die *morir* mo·*reer*
diet *dieta* ⓕ *dye*·ta
different *diferente* ⓜ&ⓕ dee·fe·*ren*·te
difficult *difícil* ⓜ&ⓕ dee·*fee*·seel
digital *digital* ⓜ&ⓕ dee·khee·*tal*
dinner *cena* ⓕ *se*·na
direct *directo/a* ⓜ/ⓕ dee·*rek*·to/a
direct-dial *marcación directa* ⓕ
  mar·ka·*syon* dee·*rek*·ta
direction *dirección* ⓕ dee·rek·*syon*
director *director/directora* ⓜ/ⓕ
  dee·rek·*tor*/dee·rek·*to*·ra
dirty *sucio/a* ⓜ/ⓕ *soo*·syo/a
disabled *discapacitado/a* ⓜ/ⓕ
  dees·ka·pa·see·*ta*·do/a
disco *discoteca* ⓕ dees·ko·*te*·ka
discount *descuento* ⓜ des·*kwen*·to
discrimination *discriminación* ⓕ
  dees·kree·mee·na·*syon*
disease *enfermedad* ⓕ en·fer·me·*dad*
dish *plato* ⓜ *pla*·to
disk (CD-ROM) *CD-ROM* ⓜ se de rom
disk (floppy) *disquete* ⓜ dees·*ke*·te
diving *buceo* ⓜ boo·*se*·o
diving equipment *equipo de buceo* ⓜ
  e·*kee*·po de boo·*se*·o
divorced *divorciado/a* ⓜ/ⓕ
  dee·vor·*sya*·do/a
dizzy *mareado/a* ⓜ/ⓕ ma·re·*a*·do/a
do *hacer* a·*ser*
doctor *doctor/doctora* ⓜ/ⓕ
  dok·*tor*/dok·*to*·ra
documentary *documental* ⓜ
  do·koo·men·*tal*
dog *perro/a* ⓜ/ⓕ *pe*·ro/a
doll *muñeca* ⓕ moo·*nye*·ka
dollar *dólar* ⓜ *do*·lar

door *puerta* ① *pwer*·ta
dope (drugs) *hierba* ① • *mota* ①
 yer·ba • *mo*·ta
double *doble* ⓜ&① *do*·ble
double bed *cama matrimonial* ①
 ka·ma ma·tree·mo·*nyal*
double room *cuarto doble* ⓜ *kwar*·to *do*·ble
down *abajo* a·*ba*·kho
downhill *cuesta abajo* *kwes*·ta a·*ba*·kho
dozen *docena* ① do·*se*·na
drama *drama* ⓜ *dra*·ma
dream *sueño* ⓜ *swe*·nyo
dress *vestido* ⓜ ves·*tee*·do
dried *seco/a* ⓜ/① *se*·ko/a
dried fruit *frutas secas* ① pl *froo*·tas *se*·kas
drink *bebida* ① be·*bee*·da
drink v *beber* • *tomar* be·*ber* • to·*mar*
drink (alcoholic) *trago* ⓜ *tra*·go
drive *conducir* kon·doo·*seer*
driving licence *licencia de conductor* ①
 lee·*sen*·sya de kon·*dook*·tor
drug (illicit) *droga* ① *dro*·ga
drug (medicine) *medicamento* ⓜ
 me·dee·ka·*men*·to
drug addiction *drogadicción* ①
 dro·ga·deek·*syon*
drug dealer *narcotraficante* ⓜ&①
 nar·ko·tra·fee·*kan*·te
drug trafficking *narcotráfico* ⓜ
 nar·ko·*tra*·fee·ko
drug user *drogadicto/a* ⓜ/①
 dro·ga·*deek*·to/a
drum (instrument) *tambor* ⓜ tam·*bor*
drums (kit) *batería* ① ba·te·*ree*·a
drunk *borracho/a* ⓜ/① bo·*ra*·cho/a
dry *seco/a* ⓜ/① *se*·ko/a
dry (clothes, etc) *secar* se·*kar*
dry (oneself) *secarse* se·*kar*·se
duck *pato* ⓜ *pa*·to
dummy (pacifier) *chupeta* ① choo·*pe*·ta
DVD *DVD* ⓜ de ve de

E

each *cada* *ka*·da
ear *oreja* ① o·*re*·kha
early adv *temprano* tem·*pra*·no
earn *ganar* ga·*nar*
earplugs *tapones para los oídos* ⓜ pl
 ta·*po*·nes *pa*·ra los o·*ee*·dos

earrings *aretes* ⓜ pl a·*re*·tes
Earth *tierra* ① *tye*·ra
earthquake *terremoto* ⓜ te·re·*mo*·to
east *este* ⓜ *es*·te
Easter *Pascua* ① *pas*·kwa
easy *fácil* ⓜ&① *fa*·seel
eat *comer* ko·*mer*
economy class *clase económica* ①
 kla·se e·ko·no·mee·ka
ecstacy (drug) *éxtasis* ⓜ *eks*·ta·sees
eczema *eczema* ① ek·*se*·ma
education *educación* ① e·doo·ka·*syon*
egg *huevo* ⓜ *we*·vo
eggplant *berenjena* ① be·ren·*khe*·na
election *elección* ① e·lek·*syon*
electrical store *tienda de electrónicos* ①
 tyen·da de e·lek·*tro*·nee·kos
electrician *electricista* ⓜ&①
 e·lek·tree·*sees*·ta
electricity *electricidad* ① e·lek·tree·see·*dad*
elevator *ascensor* ⓜ a·sen·*sor*
email *correo electrónico* ⓜ
 ko·*re*·o e·lek·*tro*·nee·ko
embarrassed *avergonzado/a* ⓜ/①
 a·ver·gon·*sa*·do/a
embassy *embajada* ① em·ba·*kha*·da
emergency *emergencia* ① e·mer·*khen*·sya
emotional *emocional* ⓜ&① e·mo·syo·*nal*
employee *empleado/a* ⓜ/① em·ple·a·do/a
employer *empleador/empleadora* ⓜ/①
 em·ple·a·*dor*/em·ple·a·*do*·ra
empty *vacío/a* ⓜ/① va·*see*·o/a
end *fin* ⓜ feen
endangered species
 especie en peligro de extinción ①
 es·*pe*·sye en pe·*lee*·gro de eks·teen·*syon*
engaged (phone) *ocupado* o·koo·*pa*·do
engaged (to marry) *comprometido/a* ⓜ/①
 kom·pro·me·*tee*·do/a
engagement (to marry) *compromiso* ⓜ
 kom·pro·*mee*·so
engine *motor* ⓜ mo·*tor*
engineer *ingeniero/a* ⓜ/① een·khe·*nye*·ro/a
engineering *ingeniería* ① een·khe·nye·*ree*·a
England *Inglaterra* ① een·gla·*te*·ra
English (language) *inglés* ⓜ een·*gles*
English a *inglés/inglesa* ⓜ/①
 een·*gles*/een·*gle*·sa
enjoy (oneself) *disfrutar* dees·froo·*tar*
enough *suficiente* soo·fee·*syen*·te

enter *entrar* en·*trar*
entertainment guide
guía de entretenimiento ⊕
gee·a de en·tre·te·nee·*myen*·to
entry *entrada* ⊕ en·*tra*·da
envelope *sobre* ⊕ *so*·bre
environment *medio ambiente* ⊕
me·dyo am·*byen*·te
epilepsy *epilepsia* ⊕ e·pee·*lep*·sya
equality *igualdad* ⊕ ee·gwal·*dad*
equal opportunity
igualdad de oportunidades ⊕
ee·gwal·*dad* de o·por·too·nee·*da*·des
equipment *equipo* ⊕ e·*kee*·po
escalator *gradas* ⊕ pl *gra*·das
estate agent *agente de bienes raíces* ⊕
a·*khen*·te de bye·nes ra·ee·ses
estuary *estuario* ⊕ es·*twa*·ryo
euro *euro* ⊕ e·oo·ro
Europe *Europa* ⊕ e·oo·ro·pa
euthanasia *eutanasia* ⊕ e·oo·ta·*na*·sya
evening *noche* ⊕ *no*·che
every *todo/a* ⊕/⊕ *to*·do/a
everyone *todos/as* ⊕/⊕ pl *to*·dos/as
everything *todo* *to*·do
exactly *exactamente* ek·sak·ta·*men*·te
example *ejemplo* ⊕ e·*khem*·plo
excellent *excelente* ⊕&⊕ ek·se·*len*·te
excess baggage *exceso de equipaje* ⊕
ek·*se*·so de e·kee·*pa*·khe
exchange *cambio* ⊕ *kam*·byo
exchange (money) *cambiar* kam·*byar*
exchange rate *tipo de cambio* ⊕
tee·po de *kam*·byo
excluded *excluido/a* ⊕/⊕ eks·kloo·*ee*·do/a
exhaust (car) *escape* ⊕ es·*ka*·pe
exhibition *exhibición* ⊕ ek·see·bee·*syon*
exit *salida* ⊕ sa·*lee*·da
expensive *caro/a* ⊕/⊕ *ka*·ro/a
experience *experiencia* ⊕ eks·pe·*ryen*·sya
exploitation *explotación* ⊕ eks·plo·ta·*syon*
express *directo/a* ⊕/⊕ dee·*rek*·to/a
express mail *correo express* ⊕
ko·re·o eks·*pres*
extension (visa) *extensión* ⊕ eks·ten·*syon*
eyes *ojos* ⊕ pl o·khos
eye drops *gotas para los ojos* ⊕ pl
go·tas *pa*·ra los o·khos

F

fabric *tela* ⊕ *te*·la
face *cara* ⊕ *ka*·ra
face cloth *paño para la cara* ⊕
pa·nyo *pa*·ra la *ka*·ra
factory *fábrica* ⊕ *fa*·bree·ka
fall (autumn) *otoño* ⊕ o·*to*·nyo
fall (down) v *caer* ka·*er*
family *familia* ⊕ fa·*mee*·lya
family name *apellido* ⊕ a·pe·*yee*·do
famous *famoso/a* ⊕/⊕ fa·*mo*·so/a
fan (hand-held) *abanico* ⊕ a·ba·*nee*·ko
fan (machine) *ventilador* ⊕ ven·tee·la·*dor*
fan (sport, etc) *aficionado/a* ⊕/⊕
a·fee·syo·*na*·do/a
fanbelt *faja del abanico* ⊕
fa·kha del a·ba·*nee*·ko
far (away) *lejos* le·khos
fare *tarifa* ⊕ ta·*ree*·fa
farm *finca* ⊕ *feen*·ka
farmer *finquero/a* ⊕/⊕ feen·*ke*·ro/a
fashion *moda* ⊕ *mo*·da
fast *rápido/a* ⊕/⊕ *ra*·pee·do/a
fat *gordo/a* ⊕/⊕ *gor*·do/a
father *padre* ⊕ *pa*·dre
father-in-law *suegro* ⊕ *swe*·gro
faucet *tubo* ⊕ *too*·bo
fault (someone's) *culpa* ⊕ *kool*·pa
faulty *defectuoso/a* ⊕/⊕ de·fek·*two*·so/a
fax machine *fax* ⊕ faks
February *febrero* ⊕ fe·*bre*·ro
feed *dar de comer* dar de ko·*mer*
feel (emotions) *sentir* sen·*teer*
feelings *sentimientos* ⊕ pl
seen·tee·*myen*·tos
female *hembra* ⊕ *em*·bra
fence *cerca* ⊕ *ser*·ka
fencing (sport) *esgrima* ⊕ es·*gree*·ma
ferry *ferry* ⊕ fe·ree
festival *fiesta* ⊕ *fyes*·ta
fever *fiebre* ⊕ *fye*·bre
few *poco/a* ⊕/⊕ *po*·ko/a
fiancé *prometido* ⊕ pro·me·*tee*·do
fiancée *prometida* ⊕ pro·me·*tee*·da
fiction *ficción* ⊕ feek·*syon*
fig *higo* ⊕ ee·go
fight *pelea* ⊕ pe·*le*·a
fill *llenar* ye·nar
fillet *filete* ⊕ fee·*le*·te

film (cinema) *película* ① pe·lee·koo·la
film (for camera) *rollo* ⑩ ro·yo
film speed *asa* ⑩ a·sa
filtered *filtrado/a* ⑩/① feel·tra·do/a
find *encontrar* en·kon·trar
fine adv *bien* byen
fine (payment) *multa* ① mool·ta
finger *dedo* ⑩ de·do
finish *meta* ① me·ta
finish v *terminar* ter·mee·nar
Finland *Finlandia* ① feen·lan·dya
fire *fuego* ⑩ fwe·go
firewood *leña* ① le·nya
first *primero/a* ⑩/① pree·me·ro/a
first class *primera clase* ① pree·me·ra kla·se
first-aid kit *maletín de primeros auxilios* ⑩
 ma·le·teen de pree·me·ros owk·see·lyos
first name *nombre cristiano* ⑩
 nom·bre krees·tya·no
fish (animal) *pez* ⑩ pes
fish (meat) *pescado* ⑩ pes·ka·do
fishing *pesca* ① pes·ka
fishmonger *vendedor de pescado* ⑩
 ven·de·dor de pes·ka·do
fish shop *tienda de pesca* ①
 tyen·da de pes·ka
flag *bandera* ① ban·de·ra
flannel (face cloth) *franela* ① fra·ne·la
flash (camera) *flash* ⑩ flash
flashlight (torch) *foco* ⑩ fo·ko
flat *plano/a* ⑩/① pla·no/a
flat (apartment) *apartamento* ⑩
 a·par·ta·men·to
flea *pulga* ① pool·ga
fleamarket *mercado de pulgas* ⑩
 mer·ka·do de pool·gas
flight *vuelo* ⑩ vwe·lo
flood *inundación* ① ee·noon·da·syon
floor (ground) *suelo* ⑩ swe·lo
floor (storey) *piso* ⑩ pee·so
florist (shop) *floristería* ① flo·rees·te·ree·a
flour *harina* ① a·ree·na
flower *flor* ① flor
flu *gripe* ① gree·pe
flute *flauta* ① flow·ta
fly *mosca* ① mos·ka
fly v *volar* vo·lar
foggy *con neblina* kon ne·blee·na
follow *seguir* se·geer
food *comida* ① ko·mee·da

food supplies *provisiones* ① pl
 pro·vee·syo·nes
foot *pie* ⑩ pye
football (soccer) *fútbol* ⑩ foot·bol
footpath *sendero* ⑩ sen·de·ro
foreign *extranjero/a* ⑩/① eks·tran·khe·ro/a
forest *bosque* ⑩ bos·ke
forever *para siempre* pa·ra syem·pre
forget *olvidar* ol·vee·dar
forgive *perdonar* per·do·nar
fork *tenedor* ⑩ te·ne·dor
fortnight *quincena* ① keen·se·na
fortune teller *adivino/a* ⑩/①
 a·dee·vee·no/a
foul (soccer) *faul* ⑩ fa·ool
foyer *vestíbulo* ⑩ ves·tee·boo·lo
fragile *frágil* ⑩&① fra·kheel
France *Francia* ① fran·sya
free (available) *disponible* ⑩&①
 dees·po·nee·ble
free (gratis) *gratis* ⑩&① gra·tees
free (not bound) *libre* ⑩&① lee·bre
freeze *congelar* kon·khe·lar
French (language) *francés* fran·ses
fresh *fresco/a* ⑩/① fres·ko/a
Friday *viernes* ⑩ vyer·nes
fridge *refri* ⑩ re·free
fried *frito/a* ⑩/① free·to/a
friend *amigo/a* ⑩/① a·mee·go/a
from *de · desde* de · des·de
frost *escarcha* ① es·kar·cha
frozen *congelado/a* ⑩/① kon·khe·la·do/a
fruit *fruta* ① froo·ta
fry *freír* fre·eer
frying pan *sartén* ① sar·ten
full *lleno/a* ⑩/① ye·no/a
full time n *tiempo completo* ⑩
 tyem·po kom·ple·to
fun *divertido/a* ⑩/① dee·ver·tee·do/a
funeral *funeral* ⑩ foo·ne·ral
funny *vacilón/vacilona* ⑩/①
 va·see·lon/va·see·lo·na
furniture *muebles* ⑩ pl mwe·bles
future *futuro* ⑩ foo·too·ro

G

game (sport) *partido* ⑩ par·tee·do
garage *garaje* ⑩ ga·ra·khe
garbage *basura* ① ba·soo·ra

garbage can *basurero* ⓜ ba·soo·re·ro
garden *jardín* ⓕ khar·*deen*
gardener *jardinero/a* ⓜ/ⓕ khar·dee·*ne*·ro/a
gardening *jardinería* ⓕ khar·dee·ne·*ree*·a
garlic *ajo* ⓜ *a*·kho
gas (cooking) *gas* ⓜ gas
gas (petrol) *gasolina* ⓕ ga·so·*lee*·na
gas cartridge *cilindro de gas* ⓜ
   see·*leen*·dro de gas
gas station *bomba* ⓕ *bom*·ba
gastroenteritis *gastritis* ⓕ gas·*tree*·tees
gate (airport, etc) *puerta* ⓕ *pwer*·ta
gauze *gasa* ⓕ *ga*·sa
gay n&a *gay* gay
gearbox *caja de cambios* ⓕ
   ka·kha de *kam*·byos
German (language) *alemán* a·le·*man*
Germany *Alemania* ⓕ a·le·*ma*·nya
get *obtener* ob·te·*ner*
get off (bus, train) *bajar* ba·*khar*
gift *regalo* ⓜ re·*ga*·lo
gig *chivo* ⓜ *chee*·vo
gin *ginebra* ⓕ khee·*ne*·bra
girl *chiquita* ⓕ chee·*kee*·ta
girlfriend *novia* ⓕ *no*·vya
give *dar* dar
given name *nombre cristiano* ⓜ
   nom·bre krees·*tya*·no
glandular fever *mononucleosis* ⓕ
   mo·no·noo·kle·o·sees
glass (drinking) *vaso* ⓜ *va*·so
glasses (spectacles) *anteojos* ⓜ pl
   an·te·o·khos
gloves *guantes* ⓜ pl *gwan*·tes
glue *pegamento* ⓜ pe·ga·*men*·to
go *ir* eer
go out (with) *salir (con)* sa·*leer* (kon)
go shopping *ir de compras* eer de *kom*·pras
goal (sport) *gol* ⓜ gol
goalkeeper *portero* ⓜ por·*te*·ro
goat *cabra* ⓕ *ka*·bra
god *dios* ⓜ dee·os
goggles (diving) *mascara* ⓕ mas·*ka*·ra
goggles (swimming) *mascarilla* ⓕ
   mas·ka·*ree*·ya
gold *oro* ⓜ *o*·ro
golf ball *bola de golf* ⓕ *bo*·la de golf
golf course *campo de golf* ⓜ *kam*·po de golf
good *bueno/a* ⓜ/ⓕ *bwe*·no/a
goodbye *adiós* a·*dyos*

government *gobierno* ⓜ go·*byer*·no
gram *gramo* ⓜ *gra*·mo
grandchild *nieto/a* ⓜ/ⓕ *nye*·to/a
grandfather *abuelo* ⓜ a·*bwe*·lo
grandmother *abuela* ⓕ a·*bwe*·la
grapes *uvas* ⓕ pl *oo*·vas
grass (lawn) *zacate* ⓜ sa·*ka*·te
grateful *agradecido/a* ⓜ/ⓕ
   a·gra·de·*see*·do/a
grave *tumba* ⓕ *toom*·ba
great (fantastic) *fantástico/a* ⓜ/ⓕ
   fan·*tas*·tee·ko
green *verde* ⓜ&ⓕ *ver*·de
greengrocer *verdurería* ⓕ ve·doo·re·*ree*·a
grey *gris* ⓜ&ⓕ grees
grocery store *súper* ⓜ *soo*·per
grow *crecer* kre·*ser*
guaranteed *garantizado/a* ⓜ/ⓕ
   ga·ran·tee·*sa*·do/a
guess *adivinar* a·dee·vee·*nar*
guesthouse *pensión* ⓕ pen·*syon*
guide (audio) *guía* ⓕ *gee*·a
guide (person) *guía* ⓜ&ⓕ *gee*·a
guidebook *guía turística* ⓕ
   gee·a too·*rees*·tee·ka
guide dog *perro guía* ⓜ *pe*·ro *gee*·a
guided tour *tour con guía* ⓜ toor kon *gee*·a
guilty *culpable* ⓜ&ⓕ kool·*pa*·ble
guitar *guitarra* ⓕ gee·*ta*·ra
gum (chewing) *chicle* ⓜ *chee*·kle
gums (mouth) *encías* ⓕ pl en·*see*·as
gun *pistola* ⓕ pees·*to*·la
gym (place) *gimnasio* ⓜ kheem·*na*·syo
gymnastics *gimnasia* ⓕ kheem·*na*·sya
gynaecologist *ginecólogo/a* ⓜ/ⓕ
   khee·ne·ko·lo·go/a

H

hair *pelo* ⓜ *pe*·lo
hairbrush *cepillo* ⓜ se·*pee*·yo
haircut *corte de pelo* ⓜ *kor*·te de *pe*·lo
hairdresser *peluquero/a* ⓜ/ⓕ pe·loo·*ke*·ro/a
halal *halal* ⓜ&ⓕ a·*lal*
half *mitad* ⓕ mee·*tad*
hallucination *alucinación* ⓕ
   a·loo·see·na·*syon*
ham *jamón* ⓜ kha·*mon*
hammer *martillo* ⓜ mar·*tee*·yo

hammock *hamaca* ① a·ma·ka
hand *mano* ① ma·no
handbag *bolso* ⓜ bol·so
handball *balomano* ⓜ ba·lo·ma·no
handicraft *artesanías* ① pl ar·te·sa·nee·as
handkerchief *pañuelo* ⓜ pa·nywe·lo
handlebars *manillar* ① ma·nee·yar
handmade *hecho/a a mano* ⓜ/①
e·cho/a a ma·no
handsome *guapo/a* ⓜ/① gwa·po/a
happy *feliz* ⓜ&① fe·lees
harassment *acoso* ⓜ a·ko·so
harbour *puerto* ⓜ pwer·to
hard (not soft) *duro/a* ⓜ/① doo·ro/a
hard-boiled (eggs) *duro/a* ⓜ/① doo·ro/a
hardware store *ferretería* ① fe·re·te·ree·a
hashish *hachís* ⓜ a·chees
hat *sombrero* ⓜ som·bre·ro
have *tener* te·ner
have fun *divertirse* dee·ver·teer·se
hay fever *fiebre del heno* ① fye·bre del e·no
hazelnut *avellana* ① a·ve·ya·na
he *él* el
head *cabeza* ① ka·be·sa
headache *dolor de cabeza* ⓜ
do·lor de ka·be·sa
headlights *focos* ⓜ pl fo·kos
health *salud* ① sa·lood
health-food store *macrobiótica* ①
ma·kro·byo·tee·ka
hear *oír* o·eer
hearing aid *audífono* ⓜ ow·dee·fo·no
heart *corazón* ⓜ ko·ra·son
heart attack *ataque al corazón* ⓜ
a·ta·ke al ko·ra·son
heart condition *condición cardíaca* ①
kon·dee·syon kar·dee·a·ka
heat *calor* ⓜ ka·lor
heated *calentado/a* ⓜ/① ka·len·ta·do/a
heater *calentador* ⓜ ka·len·ta·dor
heating *calentamiento* ⓜ ka·len·ta·myen·to
heavy (weight) *pesado/a* ⓜ/① pe·sa·do/a
helmet *casco* ⓜ kas·ko
help *ayuda* ① a·yoo·da
help *v ayudar* a·yoo·dar
hepatitis *hepatitis* ① e·pa·tee·tees
her *ella* e·ya
her (possessive) *su* soo
herb *hierba* ① yer·ba
herbalist *hierbero/a* ⓜ/① yer·be·ro/a

here *aquí* a·kee
heroin *heroína* ① e·ro·ee·na
herring *arenque* ⓜ a·ren·ke
high (height) *alto/a* ⓜ/① al·to/a
highchair *silla de comer para niños* ①
see·ya de ko·mer pa·ra nee·nyos
high school *colegio* ⓜ ko·le·khyo
highway *autopista* ① ow·to·pees·ta
hike *caminar* ka·mee·nar
hiking *caminata* ① ka·mee·na·ta
hiking boots *botas para caminata* ①
bo·tas pa·ra ka·mee·na·ta
hiking route *sendero* ⓜ sen·de·ro
hill *loma* ① lo·ma
him *él* el
Hindu n&a *hindú* ⓜ&① een·doo
hire (rent) *alquilar* al·kee·lar
his *su* soo
historical *histórico/a* ⓜ/① ees·to·ree·ko/a
history *historia* ① ees·to·rya
hitchhike *pedir un aventón*
pe·deer oon a·ven·ton
HIV *VIH* ⓜ ve ee a·che
hockey *hockey* ⓜ o·kee
holiday *feriado* ⓜ fe·ree·a·do
holidays *vacación* ① va·ka·syon
home *hogar* ⓜ o·gar
homeless n&a *indigente* ⓜ&①
een·dee·khen·te
homeopathy *homeopatía* ①
o·me·o·pa·tee·a
homesick *nostálgico/a* ⓜ/①
nos·tal·khee·ko/a
homosexual n&a *homosexual* ⓜ&①
o·mo·sek·swal
honey *miel* ① myel
honeymoon *luna de miel* ① loo·na de myel
horoscope *horóscopo* ⓜ o·ros·ko·po
horse *caballo* ⓜ ka·ba·yo
horse racing *carreras de caballo* ① pl
ka·re·ras de ka·ba·yo
horse riding *equitación* ① e·kee·ta·syon
hospital *hospital* ⓜ os·pee·tal
hospitality *hospitalidad* ① os·pee·ta·lee·dad
hot *caliente* ⓜ&① ka·lyen·te
hot water *agua caliente* ① a·gwa ka·lyen·te
hotel *hotel* ⓜ o·tel
hour *hora* ① o·ra
house *casa* ① ka·sa

housework *trabajo de la casa* ⓜ
tra-*ba*-kho de la *ka*-sa
how *cómo* ko-mo
how many *cuántos/as* ⓜ/ⓕ *kwan*-tos/as
how much *cuánto/a* ⓜ/ⓕ *kwan*-to/a
hug *abrazar* a-bra-*sar*
huge *enorme* ⓜ&ⓕ e-*nor*-me
humanities *humanidades* ⓕ pl
oo-ma-nee-*da*-des
human resources *recursos humanos* ⓜ pl
re-*koor*-sos oo-*ma*-nos
human rights *derechos humanos* ⓜ pl
de-*re*-chos oo-*ma*-nos
hundred *cien* syen
hungry *hambriento/a* ⓜ/ⓕ
am-bree-*yen*-to/a
hunting *caza* ⓕ *ka*-sa
hurt (be painful) *doler* do-*ler*
hurt (cause pain) *lastimar* las-tee-*mar*
husband *esposo* ⓜ es-*po*-so

I

I *yo* yo
ice *hielo* ⓜ *ye*-lo
ice cream *helado* ⓜ e-*la*-do
ice-cream parlour *heladería* ⓕ e-la-de-*ree*-a
ice hockey *hockey sobre hielo* ⓜ
o-kee *so*-bre *ye*-lo
identification *identificación* ⓕ
ee-den-tee-fee-ka-*syon*
identification card (ID)
cédula de identificación ⓕ
se-doo-la de ee-den-tee-fee-ka-*syon*
idiot *idiota* ⓜ&ⓕ ee-*dyo*-ta
if *si* see
ill *enfermo/a* ⓜ/ⓕ en-*fer*-mo/a
immigration *migración* ⓕ mee-gra-*syon*
important *importante* ⓜ&ⓕ eem-por-*tan*-te
impossible *imposible* ⓜ&ⓕ eem-po-*see*-ble
in *en* en
in a hurry *apurado/a* ⓜ/ⓕ a-poo-*ra*-do/a
included *incluido/a* ⓜ/ⓕ een-kloo-ee-do/a
income tax *impuesto* ⓜ eem-*pwes*-to
indicator *indicador* ⓜ een-dee-ka-*dor*
indigestion *indigestión* ⓕ
een-dee-khes-*tyon*
indoor *adentro* a-*den*-tro
industry *industria* ⓕ een-*doos*-tree-a
infection *infección* ⓕ een-fek-*syon*

inflammation *inflamación* ⓕ
een-fla-ma-*syon*
influenza *gripe* ⓕ *gree*-pe
information *información* ⓕ een-for-ma-*syon*
in front of *en frente de* en *fren*-te de
ingredient *ingrediente* ⓜ een-gre-*dyen*-te
inject *inyectar* een-yek-*tar*
injection *inyección* ⓕ een-yek-*syon*
injured *lastimado/a* ⓜ/ⓕ las-tee-*ma*-do/a
injury *herida* ⓕ e-*ree*-da
inner tube (tyre) *tubo interno* ⓜ
too-bo een-*ter*-no
innocent *inocente* ⓜ&ⓕ ee-no-*sen*-te
insect *insecto* ⓜ een-*sek*-to
insect repellent *repelente* ⓜ re-pe-*len*-te
inside *dentro de* *den*-tro de
instructor *instructor/instructora* ⓜ/ⓕ
eens-trook-*tor*/eens-trook-*to*-ra
insurance *seguro* ⓜ se-*goo*-ro
interesting *interesante* ⓜ&ⓕ
een-te-re-*san*-te
intermission *intermedio* ⓜ een-ter-*me*-dyo
international *internacional* ⓜ&ⓕ
een-ter-na-syo-*nal*
Internet *internet* ⓜ een-ter-*net*
Internet café *café internet* ⓜ
ka-*fe* een-ter-*net*
interpreter *intérprete* ⓜ&ⓕ een-*ter*-pre-te
interview *entrevista* ⓕ en-tre-*vees*-ta
invite *invitar* een-vee-*tar*
Ireland *Irlanda* ⓕ eer-*lan*-da
iron (for clothes) *plancha* ⓕ *plan*-cha
island *isla* ⓕ *ees*-la
IT (information technology)
informática ⓕ een-for-*ma*-tee-ka
Italy *Italia* ⓕ ee-*ta*-lya
itch *picazón* ⓕ pee-ka-*son*
itemised *detallado/a* ⓜ/ⓕ de-ta-*ya*-do/a
itinerary *itinerario* ⓜ ee-tee-ne-*ra*-ryo
IUD *DIU* ⓜ de ee oo

J

jacket *jacket* ⓜ *cha*-ket
jail *cárcel* ⓕ *kar*-sel
jam *jalea* ⓕ kha-*le*-a
January *enero* ⓜ e-*ne*-ro
Japan *Japón* ⓜ kha-*pon*
jar *frasco* ⓜ *fras*-ko
jaw *mandíbula* ⓕ man-*dee*-boo-la
jealous *celoso/a* ⓜ/ⓕ se-*lo*-so/a

jeans *jeans* ⓜ yeens
jet lag *desfase de horario* ⓜ
  des·fa·se de o·ra·ryo
jewellery *joyas* ① pl kho·yas
Jewish *judío/a* ⓜ/① khoo·dee·o/a
job *trabajo* ⓜ tra·ba·kho
jogging *trotar* ⓜ tro·tar
joke *chiste* ⓜ chees·te
journalist *periodista* ⓜ&① pe·ree·o·dees·ta
journey *viaje* ⓜ vya·khe
judge *juez/jueza* ⓜ/① khwes/khwe·sa
juice *jugo* ⓜ khoo·go
July *julio* ⓜ khoo·lyo
jump *saltar* sal·tar
jumper (sweater) *suéter* ⓜ swe·ter
jumper leads *jumpers* ⓜ pl chom·pers
June *junio* ⓜ khoo·nyo

K

kayak *kayak* ⓜ ka·yak
ketchup *ketchup* ⓜ ke·choop
key (door etc) *llave* ① ya·ve
keyboard *teclado* ⓜ te·kla·do
kick *patear* pa·te·ar
kidney *riñón* ⓜ ree·nyon
kilogram *kilogramo* ⓜ kee·lo·gra·mo
kilometre *kilómetro* ⓜ kee·lo·me·tro
kind (nice) *amable* ⓜ&① a·ma·ble
kindergarten *kinder* ⓜ keen·der
king *rey* ⓜ ray
kiosk *quiosco* ⓜ kyos·ko
kiss *beso* ⓜ be·so
kiss v *besar* be·sar
kitchen *cocina* ① ko·see·na
knee *rodilla* ① ro·dee·ya
knife *cuchillo* ⓜ koo·chee·yo
know (someone) *conocer* ko·no·ser
know (something) *saber* sa·ber
kosher *kosher* ⓜ&① ko·sher

L

labourer *trabajador/trabajadora* ⓜ/①
  tra·ba·kha·dor/tra·ba·kha·do·ra
lake *lago* ⓜ la·go
lamb (meat) *cordero* ⓜ kor·de·ro
land *tierra* ① tye·ra
landlady *dueña* ① dwe·nya

landlord *dueño* ⓜ dwe·nyo
language *idioma* ⓜ ee·dyo·ma
laptop *laptop* ⓜ lap·top
large *grande* ⓜ&① gran·de
last (final) *último/a* ⓜ/① ool·tee·mo/a
last (previous) *pasado/a* ⓜ/① pa·sa·do/a
late adv *tarde* tar·de
later *más tarde* mas tar·de
laugh *reír* re·eer
launderette *lavandería* ① la·van·de·ree·a
laundry (clothes) *ropa* ① ro·pa
laundry (place) *lavandería* ① la·van·de·ree·a
law (legislation) *ley* ① lay
law (profession) *derecho* ⓜ de·re·cho
lawyer *abogado/a* ⓜ/① a·bo·ga·do/a
laxative *laxante* ⓜ lak·san·te
lazy *perezoso/a* ⓜ/① pe·re·so·so/a
leader *líder* ⓜ&① lee·der
leaf *hoja* ① o·kha
learn *aprender* a·pren·der
leather *cuero* ⓜ kwe·ro
lecturer *presentador/presentadora* ⓜ/①
  pre·sen·ta·dor/pre·sen·ta·do·ra
ledge *borde* ⓜ bor·de
left (direction) *izquierda* ① ees·kyer·da
left-luggage office *consigna* ① kon·seeg·na
left-wing *izquierdista* ⓜ&① ees·kyer·dees·ta
leg (body) *pierna* ① pyer·na
legal *legal* ⓜ&① le·gal
legislation *legislación* ① le·khee·sla·syon
legume *legumbre* ① le·goom·bre
lemon *limón* ⓜ lee·mon
lemonade *limonada* ① lee·mo·na·da
lens (camera) *objetivo* ⓜ ob·khe·tee·vo
lentil *lenteja* ① len·te·kha
lesbian n&a *lesbiana* ① les·bya·na
less *menos* me·nos
letter (mail) *carta* ① kar·ta
lettuce *lechuga* ① le·choo·ga
liar *mentiroso/a* ⓜ/① men·tee·ro·so/a
librarian *bibliotecario/a* ⓜ/①
  bee·blee·o·te·ka·ryo/a
library *biblioteca* ① bee·blee·o·te·ka
lice *piojos* ⓜ pl pyo·khos
licence *licencia* ① lee·sen·sya
license plate number *número de placa* ⓜ
  noo·me·ro de pla·ka
lie (not stand) *acostarse* a·kos·tar·se
lie (not tell the truth) *mentir* men·teer
life *vida* ① vee·da

life jacket *chaleco salvavidas* ⓜ
cha·*le*·ko sal·va·*vee*·das
lift (elevator) *ascensor* ⓜ a·sen·*sor*
light *luz* ⓕ lus
light (colour) *claro/a* ⓜ/ⓕ *kla*·ro/a
light (weight) *liviano/a* ⓜ/ⓕ lee·*vya*·no/a
light bulb *bombillo* ⓜ bom·*bee*·yo
lighter (cigarette) *encendedor* ⓜ
en·sen·de·*dor*
light meter *medidor de luz* ⓜ
me·dee·*dor* de lus
like v *gustar* goos·*tar*
lime (fruit) *limón* ⓜ lee·*mon*
linen (material) *lino* ⓜ *lee*·no
linen (sheets) *sábanas* ⓕ pl *sa*·ba·nas
linguist *lingüista* ⓜ&ⓕ leen·*gwees*·ta
lip balm *brillo* ⓜ *bree*·yo
lips *labios* ⓜ pl *la*·byos
lipstick *pintura de labios* ⓕ
peen·*too*·ra de *la*·byos
liquor store *licorera* ⓕ lee·ko·*re*·ra
listen *escuchar* es·koo·*char*
little (quantity) *poco/a* ⓜ/ⓕ *po*·ko/a
little (size) *pequeño/a* ⓜ/ⓕ pe·*ke*·nyo/a
live *vivir* vee·*veer*
liver *hígado* ⓜ *ee*·ga·do
lizard *lagartija* ⓕ la·gar·*tee*·kha
local *local* ⓜ&ⓕ lo·*kal*
lock *candado* ⓜ kan·*da*·do
lock v *cerrar con llave* se·*rar* kon *ya*·ve
locked *cerrado/a con llave* ⓜ/ⓕ
se·*ra*·do/a kon *ya*·ve
long *largo/a* ⓜ/ⓕ *lar*·go/a
look *ver* ver
look after *cuidar* kwee·*dar*
look for *buscar* boos·*kar*
lookout *mirador* ⓜ mee·ra·*dor*
loose *flojo/a* ⓜ/ⓕ *flo*·kho/a
loose change *menudo* ⓜ me·*noo*·do
lose *perder* per·*der*
lost *perdido/a* ⓜ/ⓕ per·*dee*·do/a
lost property office
oficina de objetos perdidos ⓕ
o·fee·*see*·na de ob·*khe*·tos per·*dee*·dos
(a) lot *mucho/a* ⓜ/ⓕ *moo*·cho/a
loud *ruidoso/a* ⓜ/ⓕ rwee·*do*·so/a
love *amor* ⓜ a·*mor*
love v *amar* a·*mar*
lover *amante* ⓜ&ⓕ a·*man*·te
low *bajo/a* ⓜ/ⓕ *ba*·kho/a

lubricant *lubricante* ⓜ loo·bree·*kan*·te
luck *suerte* ⓕ *swer*·te
lucky *afortunado/a* ⓜ/ⓕ a·for·too·*na*·do/a
luggage *equipaje* ⓜ e·kee·*pa*·khe
luggage tag *etiqueta del equipaje* ⓕ
e·tee·*ke*·ta del e·kee·*pa*·khe
lump *bulto* ⓜ *bool*·to
lunch *almuerzo* ⓜ al·*mwer*·so
lung *pulmón* ⓜ pool·*mon*
luxury *lujoso/a* ⓜ/ⓕ loo·*kho*·so/a

M

machine *máquina* ⓕ *ma*·kee·na
magazine *revista* ⓕ re·*vees*·ta
mail *correo* ⓜ ko·*re*·o
mail *enviar* en·*vyar*
mailbox *buzón* ⓜ boo·*son*
main *principal* ⓜ&ⓕ preen·see·*pal*
main road *calle principal* ⓕ
ka·ye preen·see·*pal*
make *hacer* a·*ser*
make-up *maquillaje* ⓜ ma·kee·*ya*·khe
malaria *malaria* ⓕ ma·*la*·rya
mammogram *mamografía* ⓕ
ma·mo·gra·*fee*·a
man *hombre* ⓜ *om*·bre
manager (business) *gerente* ⓜ&ⓕ
khe·*ren*·te
manager (sport) *director/directora* ⓜ/ⓕ
dee·rek·*tor*/dee·rek·*to*·ra
mandarin *mandarina* ⓕ man·da·*ree*·na
mango *mango* ⓜ *man*·go
mangrove *manglar* ⓜ man·*glar*
many *muchos/as* ⓜ/ⓕ pl *moo*·chos/as
map *mapa* ⓜ *ma*·pa
March *marzo* ⓜ *mar*·so
margarine *margarina* ⓕ mar·ga·*ree*·na
marijuana *marihuana* ⓕ ma·ree·*wa*·na
marital status *estado civil* ⓜ
es·*ta*·do see·*veel*
market *mercado* ⓜ mer·*ka*·do
marriage *matrimonio* ⓜ ma·tree·*mo*·nyo
married *casado/a* ⓜ/ⓕ ka·*sa*·do/a
marry *casarse* ka·*sar*·se
martial arts *artes marciales* ⓕ
ar·tes mar·*sya*·les
mass (Catholic) *misa* ⓕ *mee*·sa
massage *masaje* ⓜ ma·*sa*·khe

masseur *masajeador* ⓜ ma·sa·khe·a·*dor*

masseuse *masajeadora* ⓕ ma·sa·khe·a·*do*·ra

mat *colchoneta* ⓕ kol·cho·ne·ta

match (sports) *partido* ⓜ par·*tee*·do

matches (lighting) *fósforos* ⓜ pl *fos*·fo·ros

mattress *colchón* ⓜ kol·*chon*

May *mayo* ⓜ *ma*·yo

maybe *tal vez* tal ves

mayonnaise *mayonesa* ⓕ ma·yo·ne·sa

mayor *alcalde/alcaldesa* ⓜ/ⓕ
al·*kal*·de/al·kal·de·sa

me *mí* mee

meal *comida* ⓕ ko·*mee*·da

measles *sarampión* ⓜ sa·ram·*pyon*

meat *carne* ⓕ *kar*·ne

mechanic *mecánico/a* ⓜ/ⓕ me·ka·nee·ko/a

media *medios* ⓜ pl *me*·dyos

medicine (medication) *medicamento* ⓜ
me·dee·ka·*men*·to

medicine (profession) *medicina* ⓕ
me·dee·*see*·na

meditation *meditación* ⓕ me·dee·ta·*syon*

meet (first time) *conocerse* ko·no·*ser*·se

meet (get together) *encontrarse*
en·kon·*trar*·se

melon *melón* ⓜ me·*lon*

member *miembro/a* ⓜ/ⓕ *myem*·bro/a

memory card *tarjeta de memoria* ⓕ
tar·*khe*·ta de me·*mo*·rya

menstruation *regla* ⓕ *re*·gla

menu *menú* ⓜ me·*noo*

message *mensaje* ⓜ men·*sa*·khe

metal *metal* ⓜ me·*tal*

metre *metro* ⓜ *me*·tro

microwave oven *horno microondas* ⓜ
or·no mee·kro·on·das

midday *mediodía* ⓜ me·dyo·*dee*·a

midnight *medianoche* ⓕ me·dya·no·che

migraine *migraña* ⓕ mee·*gra*·nya

military *ejército* ⓜ e·*kher*·see·to

military service *servicio militar* ⓜ
ser·*vee*·syo mee·lee·*tar*

milk *leche* ⓕ *le*·che

millimetre *milímetro* ⓜ mee·*lee*·me·tro

million *millón* ⓜ mee·*yon*

mince *picadillo* ⓜ pee·ka·*dee*·yo

mineral water *agua mineral* ⓕ
a·gwa mee·ne·*ral*

minute *minuto* ⓜ mee·*noo*·to

mirror *espejo* ⓜ es·*pe*·kho

miscarriage *aborto natural* ⓜ
a·*bor*·to na·too·*ral*

miss (feel absence of) *extrañar* eks·tra·*nyar*

miss (lose) *perder* per·*der*

mistake *error* ⓜ e·*ror*

mix *mezclar* mes·*klar*

mobile phone *teléfono celular* ⓜ
te·*le*·fo·no se·loo·*lar*

modem *módem* ⓜ *mo*·dem

modern *moderno/a* ⓜ/ⓕ mo·*der*·no/a

moisturiser *humectante* ⓜ oo·mek·*tan*·te

monastery *monasterio* ⓜ mo·nas·*te*·ryo

Monday *lunes* ⓜ *loo*·nes

money *dinero* ⓜ dee·*ne*·ro

monk *monje* ⓜ *mon*·khe

monkey *mono* ⓜ *mo*·no

month *mes* ⓜ mes

monument *monumento* ⓜ mo·noo·*men*·to

moon *luna* ⓕ *loo*·na

more *más* mas

morning *mañana* ⓕ ma·*nya*·na

morning sickness *achaques* ⓜ pl a·*cha*·kes

mosque *mezquita* ⓕ mes·*kee*·ta

mosquito *zancudo* ⓜ san·*koo*·do

mosquito coil *espiral para mosquitos* ⓜ
es·pee·*ral* pa·ra mos·*kee*·tos

mosquito net *mosquitero* ⓜ mos·kee·*te*·ro

motel *motel* ⓜ mo·*tel*

mother *madre* ⓕ *ma*·dre

mother-in-law *suegra* ⓕ *swe*·gra

motorbike *moto* ⓕ *mo*·to

motorboat *lancha* ⓕ *lan*·cha

motorcycle *moto* ⓕ *mo*·to

motorway (tollway) *autopista* ⓕ
ow·to·*pees*·ta

mountain *montaña* ⓕ mon·*ta*·nya

mountain bike *bicicleta montañera* ⓕ
bee·see·*kle*·ta mon·ta·*nye*·ra

mountaineering *montañismo* ⓜ
mon·ta·*nyees*·mo

mountain path *camino de montaña* ⓜ
ka·*mee*·no de mon·ta·nya

mountain range *cordillera* ⓕ kor·dee·*ye*·ra

mouse (animal) *ratón* ⓜ ra·*ton*

mouse (computer) *mouse* ⓜ mows

mouth *boca* ⓕ *bo*·ka

movie *película* ⓕ pe·*lee*·koo·la

mud *barro* ⓜ *ba*·ro

muesli *granola* ⓕ gra·*no*·la

mumps *paperas* ⓕ pl pa·*pe*·ras

murder *asesinato* ⓜ a·se·see·*na*·to

murder v *asesinar* a·se·see·*nar*

muscle *músculo* ⓜ *moos*·koo·lo

museum *museo* ⓜ moo·*se*·o

mushroom *hongo* ⓜ *on*·go

music *música* ⓕ *moo*·see·ka

music shop *tienda de música* ⓕ
  tyen·da de *moo*·see·ka

musician *músico/a* ⓜ/ⓕ *moo*·see·ko/a

Muslim *musulmán/musulmana* ⓜ/ⓕ
  moo·sool·*man*/moo·sool·*ma*·na

mussel *mejillón* ⓜ me·khee·*yon*

mustard *mostaza* ⓕ mos·*ta*·sa

mute *mudo/a* ⓜ/ⓕ *moo*·do/a

my *mi* mee

N

nail clippers *cortauñas* ⓕ kor·ta·*oo*·nyas

name *nombre* ⓜ *nom*·bre

napkin *servilleta* ⓕ ser·vee·*ye*·ta

nappy *pañal* ⓜ pa·*nyal*

nappy rash *salpullido* ⓜ sal·poo·*yee*·do

nationality *nacionalidad* ⓕ
  na·syo·na·lee·*dad*

national park *parque nacional* ⓜ
  par·ke na·syo·*nal*

nature *naturaleza* ⓕ na·too·ra·*le*·sa

naturopathy *neuropatía* ⓕ ne·oo·ro·pa·*tee*·a

nausea *náuseas* ⓕ pl *now*·se·as

near *cerca de* *ser*·ka de

nearby *cerca* *ser*·ka

nearest *más cerca* mas *ser*·ka

necessary *necesario/a* ⓜ/ⓕ ne·se·*sa*·ryo/a

neck *cuello* ⓜ *kwe*·yo

necklace *cadena* ⓕ ka·*de*·na

nectarine *nectarina* ⓕ nek·ta·*ree*·na

need *necesitar* ne·se·see·*tar*

needle (sewing) *aguja* ⓕ a·*goo*·kha

needle (syringe) *jeringa* ⓕ khe·*reen*·ga

negative *negativo/a* ⓜ/ⓕ ne·ga·*tee*·vo/a

negatives (photos) *negativos* ⓜ pl
  ne·ga·*tee*·vos

neither *ninguno/a* ⓜ/ⓕ neen·*goo*·no/a

net *red* ⓕ red

Netherlands *Holanda* ⓕ o·*lan*·da

network (phone/Internet) *red* ⓕ red

never *nunca* *noon*·ka

new *nuevo/a* ⓜ/ⓕ *nwe*·vo/a

news *noticias* ⓕ pl no·*tee*·syas

newsagency *agencia de noticias* ⓕ
  a·*khen*·sya de no·*tee*·syas

newspaper *periódico* ⓜ pe·ryo·dee·ko

newsstand *venta de periódicos* ⓕ
  ven·ta de pe·ryo·*dee*·kos

New Year's Day *día de Año Nuevo* ⓜ
  dee·a de *a*·nyo *nwe*·vo

New Year's Eve *víspera de Año Nuevo* ⓕ
  vees·pe·ra de *a*·nyo *nwe*·vo

New Zealand *Nueva Zelanda* ⓕ
  nwe·va se·*lan*·da

next (following) *próximo/a* ⓜ/ⓕ
  prok·see·mo/a

next to *junto a* *khoon*·to a

nice *bueno/a* ⓜ/ⓕ *bwe*·no/a

Nicaragua *Nicaragua* ⓕ nee·ka·*ra*·gwa

nickname *apodo* ⓜ a·*po*·do

night *noche* ⓕ *no*·che

nightclub *club nocturno* ⓜ
  kloob nok·*toor*·no

night out *salida de noche* ⓕ
  sa·*lee*·da de *no*·che

no *no* no

noisy *ruidoso/a* ⓜ/ⓕ rwee·*do*·so/a

none *ninguno/a* ⓜ/ⓕ neen·*goo*·no/a

nonsmoking *no fumado* no foo·*ma*·do

noodles *fideos* ⓜ pl fee·*de*·os

noon *mediodía* ⓜ me·dyo·*dee*·a

north *norte* ⓜ *nor*·te

Norway *Noruega* ⓕ no·*rwe*·ga

nose *nariz* ⓕ na·*rees*

not *no* no

notebook *cuaderno* ⓜ kwa·*der*·no

nothing *nada* *na*·da

November *noviembre* ⓜ no·*vyem*·bre

now *ahora* a·*o*·ra

nuclear energy *energía nuclear* ⓕ
  e·ner·*khee*·a noo·kle·*ar*

nuclear testing *pruebas nucleares* ⓕ pl
  prwe·bas noo·kle·*a*·res

nuclear waste *desechos nucleares* ⓜ pl
  de·*se*·chos noo·kle·*a*·res

number *número* ⓜ *noo*·me·ro

numberplate *placa* ⓕ *pla*·ka

nun *monja* ⓕ *mon*·kha

nurse *enfermero/a* ⓜ/ⓕ en·fer·*me*·ro/a

nut (food) *nuez* ⓕ nwes

O

oats *avena* ⓕ a·ve·na
ocean *océano* ⓜ o·se·a·no
October *octubre* ⓜ ok·too·bre
off (power) *apagado/a* ⓜ/ⓕ a·pa·ga·do/a
off (spoilt) *malo/a* ⓜ/ⓕ ma·lo/a
office *oficina* ⓕ o·fee·see·na
office worker *trabajador de oficina* ⓜ
  tra·ba·kha·dor de o·fee·see·na
often *a menudo* a me·noo·do
oil (cooking) *aceite* ⓜ a·say·te
oil (petrol) *petróleo* ⓜ pe·tro·le·o
old (age) *viejo/a* ⓜ/ⓕ vye·kho/a
olive *aceituna* ⓕ a·say·too·na
olive oil *aceite de oliva* ⓜ a·say·te de o·lee·va
Olympic Games *Juegos Olímpicos* ⓜ pl
  khwe·gos o·leem·pee·kos
omelette *omelet* ⓕ o·me·let
on *sobre* so·bre
on (power) *encendido/a* ⓜ/ⓕ
  en·sen·dee·do/a
once *una vez* oo·na ves
one *uno/a* ⓜ/ⓕ oo·no/a
one-way ticket *tiquete de ida* ⓕ
  tee·ke·te de ee·da
onion *cebolla* ⓕ se·bo·ya
only *sólo* so·lo
on time *a tiempo* a tyem·po
open *abrir* a·breer
open (business) *abierto/a* ⓜ/ⓕ a·byer·to/a
opening hours *horario* ⓜ o·ra·ryo
opera *ópera* ⓕ o·pe·ra
operation (medical) *operación* ⓕ
  o·pe·ra·syon
operator (telephone) *operador/operadora*
  ⓜ/ⓕ o·pe·ra·dor/o·pe·ra·do·ra
opinion *opinión* ⓕ o·pee·nyon
opposite *opuesto* o·pwes·to
optometrist *optometrista* ⓜ&ⓕ
  op·to·me·trees·ta
or *o* o
orange (colour) *anaranjado/a* ⓜ/ⓕ
  a·na·ran·kha·do/a
orange (fruit) *naranja* ⓕ na·ran·kha
orange juice *jugo de naranja* ⓜ
  khoo·go de na·ran·kha
orchestra *orquesta* ⓕ or·kes·ta
order (food) *pedido* ⓜ pe·dee·do

order *orden* ⓜ or·den
order v *ordenar* or·de·nar
ordinary *ordinario/a* ⓜ/ⓕ or·dee·na·ryo/a
orgasm *orgasmo* ⓜ or·gas·mo
original *original* ⓜ&ⓕ o·ree·khee·nal
other *otro/a* ⓜ/ⓕ o·tro/a
our *nuestro/a* ⓜ/ⓕ nwes·tro/a
out of order *fuera de servicio*
  fwe·ra de ser·vee·syo
outside *fuera de* fwe·ra de
ovarian cyst *quiste en los ovarios* ⓜ
  kees·te en los o·va·ryos
ovary *ovario* ⓜ o·va·ryo
oven *horno* ⓜ or·no
overcoat *abrigo* ⓜ a·bree·go
overdose *sobredosis* ⓕ so·bre·do·sees
overnight *por a noche* por a no·che
overseas *extranjero/a* ⓜ/ⓕ
  eks·tran·khe·ro/a
owe *deber* de·ber
owner *dueño/a* ⓜ/ⓕ dwe·nyo/a
oxygen *oxígeno* ⓜ ok·see·khe·no
oyster *ostra* ⓕ os·tra
ozone layer *capa de ozono* ⓕ
  ka·pa de o·so·no

P

pacemaker *marcapasos* ⓜ mar·ka·pa·sos
Pacific Ocean *Océano Pacífico* ⓜ
  o·se·a·no pa·see·fee·ko
pacifier (dummy) *chupeta* ⓕ choo·pe·ta
package *paquete* ⓜ pa·ke·te
packet *paquete* ⓜ pa·ke·te
padlock *candado* ⓜ kan·da·do
page *página* ⓕ pa·khee·na
pain *dolor* ⓜ do·lor
painful *doloroso/a* ⓜ/ⓕ do·lo·ro·so/a
painkiller *pastilla para el dolor* ⓕ
  pas·tee·ya pa·ra el do·lor
painter *pintor/pintora* ⓜ/ⓕ
  peen·tor/peen·to·ra
painting (artwork) *cuadro* ⓜ kwa·dro
painting (technique) *pintura* ⓕ peen·too·ra
pair (couple) *pareja* ⓕ pa·re·kha
palace *palacio* ⓜ pa·la·syo
pan *sartén* ⓜ sar·ten
Panama *Panamá* ⓕ pa·na·ma

pants (trousers) *pantalones* ⓜ pl
  pan·ta·*lo*·nes
pantyhose *pantys* ① pl *pan*·tees
panty liners *protectores* ⓜ pl pro·tek·*to*·res
paper *papel* ⓜ pa·*pel*
paperwork *papeleo* ⓜ pa·pe·*le*·o
pap smear *papanicolau* ⓜ pa·pa·nee·ko·*low*
paraplegic *parapléjico/a* ⓜ/①
  pa·ra·*ple*·khee·ko/a
parcel *parcela* ① par·*se*·la
parents *papás* ⓜ pl pa·*pas*
park *parque* ⓜ *par*·ke
park (vehicle) *parquear* par·ke·*ar*
parliament *parlamento* ⓜ par·la·*men*·to
parrot *loro/a* ⓜ/① *lo*·ro/a
part (component) *parte* ① *par*·te
part-time *tiempo parcial* ⓜ *tyem*·po par·*syal*
party (night out) *fiesta* ① *fyes*·ta
party (politics) *partido* ⓜ par·*tee*·do
pass *pasar* pa·*sar*
passenger *pasajero/a* ⓜ/① pa·sa·*khe*·ro/a
passionfruit *maracuyá* ① ma·ra·koo·*ya*
passport *pasaporte* ⓜ pa·sa·*por*·te
passport number *número de pasaporte* ⓜ
  noo·me·ro de pa·sa·*por*·te
past *pasado* ⓜ pa·*sa*·do
pasta *pasta* ① *pas*·ta
pastry *pastel* ⓜ pas·*tel*
path *camino* ⓜ ka·*mee*·no
pay *pagar* pa·*gar*
payment *pago* ⓜ *pa*·go
pea *petipoa* ① pe·tee·*po*·a
peace *paz* ① pas
peach *melocotón* me·lo·ko·*ton*
peak (mountain) *cima* ① *see*·ma
peanut *maní* ① ma·*nee*
pear *pera* ① *pe*·ra
pedal *pedal* ⓜ pe·*dal*
pedestrian *peatón* ⓜ pe·a·*ton*
pen (ballpoint) *lapicero* ⓜ la·pee·*se*·ro
pencil *lápiz* ⓜ *la*·pees
penis *pene* ⓜ *pe*·ne
penknife *navaja* ① na·*va*·kha
pensioner *pensionado/a* ⓜ/①
  pen·syo·na·do/a
people *gente* ① *khen*·te
pepper (bell) *pimentón* ⓜ pee·men·*ton*
pepper (spice) *pimienta* ① pee·*myen*·ta
per (day) *por (día)* por (*dee*·a)
per cent *porcentaje* ⓜ por·sen·*ta*·khe

perfect *perfecto/a* ⓜ/① per·*fek*·to/a
performance *presentación* ①
  pre·sen·ta·*syon*
perfume *perfume* ⓜ per·*foo*·me
period pain *dolores menstruales* ⓜ pl
  do·lo·res mens·*trwa*·les
permission *permiso* ⓜ per·*mee*·so
permit *permiso* ⓜ per·*mee*·so
person *persona* ① per·*so*·na
petition *petición* ① pe·tee·*syon*
petrol *gasolina* ① ga·so·*lee*·na
petrol station *bomba* ① *bom*·ba
pharmacist *farmacéutico/a* ⓜ/①
  far·ma·*se*·oo·tee·ko/a
pharmacy *farmacia* ① far·*ma*·sya
phone book *guía telefónica* ①
  gee·a te·le·*fo*·nee·ka
phone box *casetilla de teléfono* ①
  ka·se·*tee*·ya de te·*le*·fo·no
phone card *tarjeta de teléfono* ①
  tar·*khe*·ta de te·*le*·fo·no
photo *foto* ① *fo*·to
photograph v *fotografiar* fo·to·gra·*fyar*
photographer *fotógrafo/a* ⓜ/①
  fo·*to*·gra·fo/a
photography *fotografía* ① fo·to·gra·*fee*·a
phrasebook *libro de frases* ⓜ
  lee·bro de *fra*·ses
piano *piano* ⓜ pee·*a*·no
pickaxe *pico* ⓜ *pee*·ko
pickles *pepinillos* ⓜ pl pe·pee·*nee*·yos
picnic *picnic* ⓜ *peek*·neek
pie *pastel* ⓜ pas·*tel*
piece *pedazo* ⓜ pe·*da*·so
pig *cerdo* ⓜ • *chancho* ⓜ *ser*·do • *chan*·cho
pill *pastilla* ① pas·*tee*·ya
the pill *pastilla anticonceptiva* ①
  pas·*tee*·ya an·tee·kon·sep·*tee*·va
pillow *almohada* ① al·mo·*a*·da
pillowcase *funda* ① *foon*·da
pineapple *piña* ① *pee*·nya
pink *rosado/a* ⓜ/① ro·*sa*·do/a
pistachio *pistacho* ⓜ pees·*ta*·cho
place *lugar* ⓜ loo·*gar*
place of birth *lugar de nacimiento* ⓜ
  loo·*gar* de na·see·*myen*·to
plane *avión* ⓜ a·*vyon*
planet *planeta* ⓜ pla·*ne*·ta
plant *mata* ① *ma*·ta
plastic *plástico* ⓜ *plas*·tee·ko

plate *plato* ⓜ *pla*·to
plateau *meseta* ⓕ me·*se*·ta
platform *plataforma* ⓕ pla·ta·*for*·ma
play (cards, etc) *jugar* khoo·*gar*
play (instrument) *tocar* to·*kar*
play (theatre) *obra de teatro* ⓕ
  o·bra de te·*a*·tro
plug (bath) *tapón* ⓜ ta·*pon*
plug (electricity) *enchufe* ⓜ en·*choo*·fe
plum *ciruela* ⓕ see·*rwe*·la
plumber *plomero* ⓜ plo·*me*·ro
pocket *bolsillo* ⓜ bol·*see*·yo
pocketknife *cuchilla* ⓕ koo·*chee*·ya
poetry *poesía* ⓕ po·e·*see*·a
point *señalar* se·nya·*lar*
poisonous *venenoso/a* ⓜ/ⓕ ve·ne·*no*·so/a
police *policía* ⓕ po·lee·*see*·a
police officer (city) *policía* ⓜ&ⓕ
  po·lee·*see*·a
police officer (country) *guarda rural* ⓜ&ⓕ
  gwar·da roo·*ral*
police station *estación de policía* ⓕ
  es·ta·*syon* de po·lee·*see*·a
policy *política* ⓕ po·*lee*·tee·ka
politician *político* po·*lee*·tee·ko
politics *política* ⓕ po·*lee*·tee·ka
pollen *polen* ⓜ *po*·len
pollution *contaminación* ⓕ
  kon·ta·mee·na·*syon*
pool (game) *pool* ⓜ pool
pool (swimming) *piscina* ⓕ pee·*see*·na
poor *pobre* ⓜ&ⓕ *po*·bre
popular *popular* ⓜ&ⓕ po·poo·*lar*
pork *cerdo* ⓜ · *chancho* ⓜ *ser*·do · *chan*·cho
port (harbour) *puerto* ⓜ *pwer*·to
positive *positivo/a* ⓜ/ⓕ po·see·*tee*·vo/a
possible *posible* ⓜ&ⓕ po·*see*·ble
post *mandar* man·*dar*
postage *franqueo* ⓜ fran·*ke*·o
postcard *postal* ⓕ pos·*tal*
poster *póster* ⓜ *pos*·ter
postcode *código postal* ⓜ *ko*·dee·go pos·*tal*
post office *correo* ⓜ ko·*re*·o
pot (ceramics) *vasija* ⓕ va·*see*·kha
pot (cooking) *olla* ⓕ *o*·ya
potato *papa* ⓕ *pa*·pa
pottery *alfarería* ⓕ al·fa·re·*ree*·a
pound (currency/weight) *libra* ⓕ *lee*·bra
poverty *pobreza* ⓕ po·*bre*·sa
powder *polvo* ⓜ *pol*·vo

power *poder* ⓜ po·*der*
prawn *gamba* ⓕ *gam*·ba
prayer *oración* ⓕ o·ra·*syon*
prayer book *libro de oraciones* ⓜ
  lee·bro de o·ra·*syo*·nes
prefer *preferir* pre·fe·*reer*
pregnancy test kit *prueba de embarazo* ⓕ
  prwe·ba de em·ba·*ra*·so
pregnant *embarazada* ⓕ em·ba·ra·*sa*·da
premenstrual tension *tensión*
  premenstrual ⓕ ten·*syon* pre·mens·*trwal*
prepare *preparar* pre·pa·*rar*
prescription (medical) *receta* ⓕ re·*se*·ta
present (gift) *regalo* ⓜ re·*ga*·lo
present (time) *presente* ⓜ pre·*sen*·te
president *presidente* ⓜ&ⓕ pre·see·*den*·te
pressure (tyre) *presión* ⓕ pre·*syon*
pretty *bonito/a* ⓜ/ⓕ bo·*nee*·to/a
price *precio* ⓜ *pre*·syo
priest *cura* ⓜ *koo*·ra
prime minister *primer ministro/primera*
  ministra ⓜ/ⓕ pree·*mer* mee·*nees*·tro/
  pree·*me*·ra mee·*nees*·tra
printer (computer) *impresora* ⓕ
  eem·pre·*so*·ra
prison *cárcel* ⓕ *kar*·sel
prisoner *reo/a* ⓜ/ⓕ *re*·o/a
private *privado/a* ⓜ/ⓕ pree·*va*·do/a
produce *producir* pro·doo·*seer*
profit *lucrar* loo·*krar*
program *programa* ⓜ pro·*gra*·ma
projector *proyector* ⓜ pro·yek·*tor*
promise *prometer* pro·me·*ter*
prostitute *prostituto/a* ⓜ/ⓕ
  pros·tee·*too*·to/a
protect *proteger* pro·te·*kher*
protected *protegido/a* ⓜ/ⓕ
  pro·te·*khee*·do/a
protest *protesta* ⓕ pro·*tes*·ta
protest v *protestar* pro·tes·*tar*
provisions *provisiones* ⓕ pl pro·vee·*syo*·nes
public gardens *jardines públicos* ⓜ pl
  khar·*dee*·nes poo·*blee*·kos
public phone *teléfono público* ⓜ
  te·*le*·fo·no poo·*blee*·ko
public relations *relaciones públicas* ⓕ pl
  re·la·*syo*·nes poo·*blee*·kas
public toilet *baño público* ⓜ
  ba·nyo poo·*blee*·ko
pull *halar* a·*lar*

pump *bomba* ① bom·ba
pumpkin *calabaza* ① ka·la·ba·sa
puncture v *estallar* es·ta·yar
pure *puro/a* ⓜ/① poo·ro/a
purple *morado/a* ⓜ/① mo·ra·do/a
purse *cartera* ① kar·te·ra
push *empujar* em·poo·khar
put *poner* po·ner

Q

quadriplegic *cuadrapléjico/a* ⓜ/①
kwa·dra·*ple*·khee·ko/a
qualifications *cualidades* ① pl
kwa·lee·da·des
quality *calidad* ① ka·lee·*dad*
quarantine *cuarentena* ① kwa·ren·te·na
quarter *cuarto* ⓜ *kwar*·to
queen *reina* ① *ray*·na
question *pregunta* ① pre·*goon*·ta
queue *fila* ① *fee*·la
quick *rápido/a* ⓜ/① ra·pee·do/a
quiet *callado/a* ⓜ/① ka·ya·do/a
quit *darse por vencido/a* ⓜ/①
dar·se por ven·*see*·do/a

R

rabbit *conejo* ⓜ ko·*ne*·kho
rabies *rabia* ① ra·bya
race (sport) *carrera* ① ka·re·ra
racetrack *pista* ① pees·ta
racing bike *bicicleta de carreras* ①
bee·see·*kle*·ta de ka·re·ras
racism *racismo* ⓜ ra·sees·mo
racquet *raqueta* ① ra·ke·ta
radiator *radiador* ⓜ ra·dya·dor
radio *radio* ① ra·dyo
radish *rábano* ⓜ ra·ba·no
railway station *estación de tren* ①
es·ta·syon de tren
rain *lluvia* ① yoo·vya
raincoat *capa* ① ka·pa
rainforest *bosque lluvioso* ⓜ
bos·ke yoo·vyo·so
raisin *pasa* ① pa·sa
rally (protest) *protesta* ① pro·tes·ta
rape *violación* ① vyo·la·syon
rape v *violar* vyo·lar

rare (steak) *poco cocido/a* po·ko ko·see·do/a
rare (uncommon) *raro/a* ⓜ/① ra·ro/a
rash *salpullido* ⓜ sal·poo·yee·do
raspberry *frambuesa* ① fram·bwe·sa
rat *rata* ① ra·ta
rave (party) *rave* ⓜ ra·ve
raw *crudo/a* ⓜ/① kroo·do/a
razor *rasuradora* ① ra·soo·ra·do·ra
razor blade *navajilla* ① na·va·khee·ya
read *leer* le·er
reading *lectura* ① lek·too·ra
ready *listo/a* ⓜ/① lees·to/a
real estate agent *agente de bienes raíces* ⓜ
a·*khen*·te de *bye*·nes ra·ee·ses
realistic *realista* ⓜ&① re·a·lees·ta
rear (location) *atrás* a·tras
reason *razón* ① ra·son
receipt *recibo* ⓜ re·see·bo
recently *recientemente* re·syen·te·*men*·te
recommend *recomendar* re·ko·men·dar
record *grabar* gra·bar
recording *grabación* ① gra·ba·syon
recyclable *reciclable* ⓜ&① re·see·*kla*·ble
recycle *reciclar* re·see·klar
red *rojo/a* ⓜ/① ro·kho/a
red wine *vino tinto* ⓜ vee·no teen·to
referee *árbitro* ⓜ ar·bee·tro
reference *referencia* ① re·fe·ren·sya
reflexology *reflexología* ①
re·flek·so·lo·khee·a
refrigerator *refri* ⓜ re·free
refugee *refugiado/a* ⓜ/① re·foo·khya·do/a
refund *reintegro* ⓜ re·een·te·gro
refuse *negar* ne·gar
regional *regional* ⓜ&① re·khyo·nal
registered mail *correo certificado* ⓜ
ko·re·o ser·tee·fee·ka·do
rehydration salts *sales para rehidratación*
① pl sa·les pa·ra re·ee·dra·ta·syon
relationship *relación* ① re·la·syon
relax *relajarse* re·la·khar·se
relic *reliquia* ① re·lee·kya
religion *religión* ① re·lee·khyon
religious *religioso/a* ⓜ/① re·lee·khyo·so/a
remote *remoto/a* ⓜ/① re·mo·to/a
remote control *control remoto* ⓜ
kon·*trol* re·mo·to
rent *alquilar* al·kee·lar
repair *reparar* re·pa·rar
republic *república* ① re·poo·blee·ka

reservation (booking) *reservación* ⓕ
re·ser·va·*syon*

rest *descansar* des·kan·*sar*

restaurant *restaurante* ⓜ re·stow·*ran*·te

résumé (CV) *currículum* ⓜ koo·ree·koo·loom

retired *retirado/a* ⓜ/ⓕ re·tee·*ra*·do/a

return *volver* vol·*ver*

return ticket *tiquete de ida y vuelta* ⓜ
tee·*ke*·te de *ee*·da ee *vwel*·ta

review *revisión* ⓕ re·vee·*syon*

rhythm *ritmo* ⓜ *reet*·mo

rib (body) *costilla* ⓕ kos·*tee*·ya

rice *arroz* ⓜ a·*ros*

rich *rico/a* ⓜ/ⓕ *ree*·ko/a

ride *aventón* a·ven·*ton*

ride (bike, horse) *andar* an·*dar*

right (correct) *correcto/a* ⓜ/ⓕ ko·*rek*·to/a

right (direction) *derecha* ⓕ de·*re*·cha

right-wing *derechista* ⓜ&ⓕ de·re·*chees*·ta

ring (jewellry) *anillo* ⓜ a·*nee*·yo

ring (phone) *timbre* ⓜ *teem*·bre

rip-off *robo* ⓜ *ro*·bo

risk *riesgo* ⓜ *ryes*·go

river *río* ⓜ *ree*·o

road *calle* ⓕ *ka*·ye

road map *mapa de calles* ⓜ
ma·pa de *ka*·yes

rob *robar* ro·*bar*

rock (music) *rock* ⓜ rok

rock (stone) *piedra* ⓕ *pye*·dra

rock climbing *escalada* ⓕ es·ka·*la*·da

rock group *grupo de rock* ⓜ *groo*·po de rok

roll (bread) *bollo (de pan)* ⓜ *bo*·yo (de pan)

rollerblading *patinaje sobre ruedas* ⓜ
pa·tee·*na*·khe so·bre *rwe*·das

romantic n&a *romántico/a* ⓜ/ⓕ
ro·man·*tee*·ko/a

room *habitación* ⓕ a·bee·ta·*syon*

room number *número de habitación* ⓜ
noo·me·ro de a·bee·ta·*syon*

rope *cuerda* ⓕ *kwer*·da

round (drinks) *ronda* ⓕ *ron*·da

round (shape) *redondo/a* ⓜ/ⓕ re·*don*·do/a

roundabout *rotonda* ⓕ ro·*ton*·da

route *ruta* ⓕ *roo*·ta

rowing *remo* ⓜ *re*·mo

rubbish *basura* ⓕ ba·*soo*·ra

rubella *rubéola* ⓕ roo·be·*o*·la

rug *alfombra* ⓕ al·*fom*·bra

ruins *ruinas* ⓕ pl *rwee*·nas

rule *regla* ⓕ *re*·gla

rum *ron* ⓜ ron

run *correr* ko·*rer*

running *corriendo* ⓜ ko·*ryen*·do

runny nose *moquera* ⓕ mo·*ke*·ra

S

sad *triste* ⓜ&ⓕ *trees*·te

saddle *montura* ⓕ mon·*too*·ra

safe *seguro/a* ⓜ/ⓕ se·*goo*·ro/a

safe (for valuables) *caja fuerte* ⓕ
ka·kha *fwer*·te

safe sex *sexo seguro* ⓜ *sek*·so se·*goo*·ro

sailboarding *windsurf* ⓜ *weend*·soorf

saint *santo/a* ⓜ/ⓕ *san*·to/a

salad *ensalada* ⓕ en·sa·*la*·da

salami *salami* ⓜ sa·*la*·mee

salary *salario* ⓜ sa·*la*·ryo

sale *promoción* ⓕ pro·mo·*syon*

sales assistant *asistente de ventas* ⓜ&ⓕ
a·sees·*ten*·te de *ven*·tas

sales tax *impuesto de ventas* ⓜ
eem·*pwes*·to de *ven*·tas

salmon *salmón* ⓜ sal·*mon*

salt *sal* ⓕ sal

same *mismo/a* ⓜ/ⓕ *mees*·mo/a

sand *arena* ⓕ a·*re*·na

sandals *chancletas* ⓕ pl chan·*kle*·tas

sanitary napkin *toalla sanitaria* ⓕ
to·a·ya sa·nee·*ta*·rya

sardine *sardina* ⓕ sar·*dee*·na

Saturday *sábado* ⓜ *sa*·ba·do

sauce *salsa* ⓕ *sal*·sa

saucepan *olla* ⓕ *o*·ya

sauna *sauna* ⓕ *sow*·na

sausage *chorizo* ⓜ cho·*ree*·so

saxophone *saxofón* ⓜ sak·so·*fon*

say *decir* de·*seer*

scalp *cuero cabelludo* ⓜ *kwe*·ro ka·be·*yoo*·do

scarf *bufanda* ⓕ boo·*fan*·da

school *escuela* ⓕ es·*kwe*·la

science *ciencia* ⓕ *syen*·sya

scientist *científico/a* ⓜ/ⓕ syen·*tee*·fee·ko/a

scissors *tijeras* ⓕ pl tee·*khe*·ras

score *anotar* a·no·*tar*

scoreboard *marcador* ⓜ mar·ka·*dor*

Scotland *Escocia* ⓕ es·*ko*·sya

scrambled (eggs) *revuelto/a* ⓜ/ⓕ
re·*vwel*·to/a

sculpture *escultura* ⓕ es·kool·*too*·ra

sea *mar* ⓜ mar

seasick *mareado/a* ⓜ/ⓕ ma·re·a·do/a

seaside *costa* ⓕ *kos*·ta

season *temporada* ⓕ tem·po·*ra*·da

seat (place) *asiento* ⓜ a·*syen*·to

seatbelt *cinturón* ⓜ seen·too·ron

second (time unit) *segundo* ⓜ se·*goon*·do

second (number) *segundo/a* ⓜ/ⓕ
se·*goon*·do/a

second class *segunda clase* ⓕ
se·*goon*·da *kla*·se

secondhand *usado/a* ⓜ/ⓕ oo·*sa*·do/a

secondhand shop *tienda de artículos usados*
ⓕ *tyen*·da de ar·*tee*·koo·los oo·*sa*·dos

secretary *secretario/a* ⓜ/ⓕ se·kre·*ta*·ryo/a

see *ver* ver

self-employed *tener su propio negocio*
te·*ner* soo pro·pyo ne·*go*·syo

selfish *egoísta* ⓜ&ⓕ e·go·*ees*·ta

self-service ⓜ *auto servicio* ow·to ser·*vee*·syo

sell *vender* ven·*der*

send *enviar* en·*vyar*

sensible *sensible* ⓜ&ⓕ sen·*see*·ble

sensual *sensual* ⓜ&ⓕ sen·*swal*

separate *separado/a* ⓜ/ⓕ se·pa·*ra*·do/a

September *septiembre* ⓜ sep·*tyem*·bre

serious *serio/a* ⓜ/ⓕ se·ryo/a

service *servicio* ⓜ ser·*vee*·syo

service charge *servicio* ⓜ ser·*vee*·syo

service station *bomba* ⓕ *bom*·ba

serviette *servilleta* ⓕ ser·vee·*ye*·ta

several *varios/as* ⓜ/ⓕ pl *va*·ryos/as

sew *coser* ko·*ser*

sex *sexo* ⓜ *sek*·so

sexism *sexismo* ⓜ sek·*sees*·mo

shade *sombra* ⓕ *som*·bra

shadow *sombra* ⓕ *som*·bra

shampoo *champú* ⓜ cham·*poo*

shape *forma* ⓕ *for*·ma

share (with) *compartir (con)*
kom·par·*teer* (kon)

shave *rasurar* ra·soo·*rar*

shaving cream *espuma de afeitar* ⓕ
es·*poo*·ma de a·*fay*·tar

she *ella* e·ya

sheep *oveja* ⓕ o·ve·kha

sheet (bed) *sábana* ⓕ *sa*·ba·na

shelf *repisa* ⓕ re·*pee*·sa

shingles (illness) *herpes* ⓜ er·pes

ship *barco* ⓜ bar·ko

shirt *camisa* ⓕ ka·*mee*·sa

shoe *zapato* ⓜ sa·*pa*·to

shoelace *cordón de zapato* ⓜ
kor·*don* de sa·*pa*·to

shoe shop *zapatería* ⓕ sa·pa·te·*ree*·a

shoot *disparar* dees·pa·*rar*

shop *tienda* ⓕ *tyen*·da

shop v *ir de compras* eer de *kom*·pras

shopping *compras* ⓕ pl *kom*·pras

shopping centre *centro comercial* ⓜ
sen·tro ko·mer·*syal*

short (height) *bajo/a* ⓜ/ⓕ *ba*·kho/a

short (length) *corto/a* ⓜ/ⓕ *kor*·to/a

shortage *escasez* ⓕ es·ka·*ses*

shorts *chores* ⓜ pl *cho*·res

shoulder *hombro* ⓜ *om*·bro

shout *gritar* gree·*tar*

show *espectáculo* ⓜ es·pek·*ta*·koo·lo

show v *enseñar* en·se·*nyar*

shower (bath) *ducha* ⓕ *doo*·cha

shrine *santuario* ⓜ san·too·a·ryo

shut *cerrado/a* ⓜ/ⓕ se·*ra*·do/a

shy *tímido/a* ⓜ/ⓕ *tee*·mee·do/a

sick *enfermo/a* ⓜ/ⓕ en·*fer*·mo/a

side *lado* ⓜ *la*·do

sign *señal* ⓕ se·*nyal*

sign (one's name) v *firmar* feer·*mar*

signature *firma* ⓕ *feer*·ma

silk *seda* ⓕ se·da

silver *plata* ⓕ *pla*·ta

SIM card *tarjeta SIM* ⓕ tar·*khe*·ta seem

similar *similar* ⓜ&ⓕ see·mee·*lar*

simple *sencillo/a* ⓜ/ⓕ sen·*see*·yo/a

since (time) *desde* des·de

sing *cantar* kan·*tar*

singer *cantante* ⓜ&ⓕ kan·*tan*·te

single (person) *soltero/a* ⓜ/ⓕ sol·*te*·ro/a

single room *habitación sencilla* ⓕ
a·bee·ta·*syon* sen·*see*·ya

sister *hermana* ⓕ er·*ma*·na

sit *sentarse* sen·*tar*·se

size (clothes) *talla* ⓕ *ta*·ya

size (general) *tamaño* ⓜ ta·*ma*·nyo

skate *patinar* pa·tee·*nar*

skateboarding *andar en patineta* ⓜ
an·*dar* en pa·tee·ne·ta

ski *esquiar* es·*kyar*

skiing *esquí* ⓜ es·*kee*

skim milk *leche descremada* ⓕ *le*·che des·kre·*ma*·da

skin *piel* ⓕ pyel

skirt *enagua* ⓕ e·*na*·gwa

skull *cráneo* ⓜ *kra*·ne·o

sky *cielo* ⓜ *sye*·lo

sleep *sueño* ⓜ *swe*·nyo

sleep *dormir* dor·*meer*

sleeping bag *saco de dormir* ⓜ *sa*·ko de dor·*meer*

sleeping berth *litera* ⓕ lee·*te*·ra

sleeping pills *pastillas para dormir* ⓕ pl pas·*tee*·yas *pa*·ra dor·*meer*

slice *tajada* ⓕ ta·*kha*·da

slide (film) *diapositivas* ⓕ pl dya·po·se·*tee*·vas

slow *lento/a* ⓜ/ⓕ *len*·to/a

slowly *despacio* des·*pa*·syo

small *pequeño/a* ⓜ/ⓕ pe·*ke*·nyo/a

smaller *más pequeño/a* ⓜ/ⓕ mas pe·*ke*·nyo/a

(the) smallest *el/la más pequeño/a* ⓜ/ⓕ el/la mas pe·*ke*·nyo/a

smell *olor* ⓜ o·*lor*

smile *sonreír* son·re·*eer*

smoke (cigarettes) *fumar* foo·*mar*

snack *merienda* ⓕ me·*ryen*·da

snail *caracol* ⓜ ka·ra·*kol*

snake *culebra* ⓕ koo·*le*·bra

snorkelling *esnorclear* ⓜ es·nor·kle·*ar*

snow *nieve* ⓕ *nye*·ve

snowboarding *snowboarding* ⓜ es·*no*·bor·deen

snow pea *vainica china* ⓕ vai·*nee*·ka *chee*·na

soap *jabón* ⓜ kha·*bon*

soap opera *novela* ⓕ no·*ve*·la

soccer *fútbol* ⓜ *foot*·bal

socialist n&a *socialista* ⓜ&ⓕ so·sya·*lees*·ta

social welfare *bienestar social* ⓜ byen·es·*tar* so·*syal*

socks *medias* ⓕ pl *me*·dyas

soft-boiled (eggs) *tierno/a* ⓜ/ⓕ *tyer*·no/a

soft drink *refresco* ⓜ re·*fres*·ko

soldier *soldado* ⓜ sol·*da*·do

some *algún/alguna* ⓜ/ⓕ al·*goon*/al·*goo*·na

someone *alguien* al·gyen

something *algo* al·go

sometimes *a veces* a *ve*·ses

son *hijo* ⓜ *ee*·kho

song *canción* ⓕ kan·*syon*

soon *pronto* ⓜ *pron*·to

sore *adolorido/a* ⓜ/ⓕ a·do·lo·*ree*·do/a

soup *sopa* ⓕ *so*·pa

sour cream *natilla* ⓕ na·*tee*·ya

south *sur* ⓜ soor

souvenir *recuerdo* ⓜ re·*kwer*·do

souvenir shop *tienda de recuerdos* ⓕ *tyen*·da de re·*kwer*·dos

soy milk *leche de soya* ⓕ *le*·che de *so*·ya

soy sauce *salsa de soya* ⓕ *sal*·sa de *so*·ya

space (room) *campo* ⓜ *kam*·po

Spain *España* ⓕ es·*pa*·nya

Spanish (language) *castellano · español* ka·ste·*ya*·no · es·pa·*nyol*

sparkling wine *vino espumante* ⓜ *vee*·no es·poo·*man*·te

speak *hablar* a·*blar*

special *especial* ⓜ&ⓕ es·pe·*syal*

specialist *especialista* ⓜ&ⓕ es·pe·sya·*lees*·ta

speed (drug) *anfetamina* ⓕ an·fe·ta·*mee*·na

speed (travel) *velocidad* ⓕ ve·lo·see·*dad*

speed limit *límite de velocidad* ⓜ *lee*·mee·te de ve·lo·see·*dad*

speedometer *velocímetro* ⓜ ve·lo·*see*·me·tro

spider *araña* ⓕ a·*ra*·nya

spinach *espinaca* ⓕ es·pee·*na*·ka

spoilt (food) *podrido/a* ⓜ/ⓕ po·*dree*·do/a

spoilt (person) *chineado/a* ⓜ/ⓕ chee·ne·*a*·do/a

spoke (wheel) *radio* ⓜ *ra*·dyo

spoon *cuchara* ⓕ koo·*cha*·ra

sport *deporte* ⓜ de·*por*·te

sportsperson *deportista* ⓜ&ⓕ de·por·*tees*·ta

sports store *tienda deportiva* ⓕ *tyen*·da de·por·*tee*·va

sprain *esguince* ⓜ es·*geen*·se

spring (coil) *resorte* ⓜ re·*sor*·te

spring (season) *primavera* ⓕ pree·ma·*ve*·ra

square (town) *plaza* ⓕ *pla*·sa

stadium *estadio* ⓜ es·*ta*·dyo

stairway *escaleras* ⓕ pl es·ka·*le*·ras

stale *rancio/a* ⓜ/ⓕ *ran*·syo/a

stamp (postage) *estampilla* ⓕ es·tam·*pee*·ya

stand-by ticket *tiquete de stand-by* ⓜ *tee*·*ke*·te de stan·*bai*

star estrella ① es·tre·ya
(four-)star (cuatro) estrellas
(kwa·tro) es·tre·yas
start inicio ⓜ ee·nee·syo
start empezar em·pe·sar
station estación ① es·ta·syon
stationer librería ① lee·bre·ree·a
statue estatua ① es·ta·twa
stay quedarse ke·dar·se
steak (beef) bistec ⓜ bee·stek
steal robar ro·bar
steep empinado/a ⓜ/① em·pee·na·do/a
step grada ① gra·da
stereo equipo de sonido ⓜ
e·kee·po de so·nee·do
still water agua sin gas ① a·gwa seen gas
stockings calcetines ⓜ pl kal·se·tee·nes
stolen robado/a ⓜ/① ro·ba·do/a
stomach estómago ⓜ es·to·ma·go
stomachache dolor de estómago ⓜ
do·lor de es·to·ma·go
stone piedra ① pye·dra
stoned (drugged) pijiado/a ⓜ/①
pee·khya·do/a
stop (bus, tram) parada ① pa·ra·da
stop (cease) parar pa·rar
stop (prevent) prevenir pre·ve·neer
storm tormenta ① tor·men·ta
story cuento ⓜ kwen·to
stove cocina ① ko·see·na
straight recto/a ⓜ/① rek·to/a
strange raro/a ⓜ/① ra·ro/a
stranger desconocido/a ⓜ/①
des·ko·no·see·do/a
strawberry fresa ① fre·sa
stream arrollo ⓜ a·ro·yo
street calle ① ka·ye
street market mercado callejero ⓜ
mer·ka·do ka·ye·khe·ro
strike (hit) golpe ⓜ gol·pe
strike (stoppage) huelga ① wel·ga
string hilo ⓜ ee·lo
stroke (health) derrame ⓜ de·ra·me
stroller coche ⓜ ko·che
strong fuerte ⓜ&① fwer·te
stubborn terco/a ⓜ/① ter·ko/a
student estudiante ⓜ&① es·too·dyan·te
studio estudio ⓜ es·too·dyo
stupid estúpido/a ⓜ/① es·too·pee·do/a
style estilo ⓜ es·tee·lo

subtitles subtítulos ⓜ pl soob·tee·too·los
suburb suburbio ⓜ soo·boor·byo
sugar azúcar ⓜ a·soo·kar
suitcase maleta ① ma·le·ta
summer verano ⓜ ve·ra·no
sun sol ⓜ sol
sunblock bloqueador ⓜ blo·ke·a·dor
sunburn quemadura de sol ①
ke·ma·doo·ra de sol
Sunday domingo ⓜ do·meen·go
sunglasses anteojos de sol ⓜ pl
an·te·o·khos de sol
sunny soleado/a ⓜ/① so·le·a·do/a
sunrise amanecer ⓜ a·ma·ne·ser
sunset atardecer ⓜ a·tar·de·ser
sunstroke insolación ① een·so·la·syon
supermarket supermercado ⓜ
soo·per·mer·ka·do
superstition superstición ①
soo·pers·tee·syon
supporter (politics) partidario/a ⓜ/①
par·tee·da·ryo/a
supporter (sport) aficionado/a ⓜ/①
a·fee·syo·na·do/a
surfing surf ⓜ soorf
surf v surfear soor·fe·ar
surface mail (land) correo por tierra ⓜ
ko·re·o por tye·ra
surface mail (sea) correo por mar ⓜ
ko·re·o por mar
surfboard tabla de surf ① ta·bla de soorf
surfing surf ⓜ soorf
surname apellido ⓜ a·pe·yee·do
surprise sorpresa ① sor·pre·sa
sweater suéter ⓜ swe·ter
Sweden Suecia ① swe·sya
sweet dulce ⓜ&① dool·se
sweets dulces ⓜ pl dool·ses
swelling hinchazón ① een·cha·son
swim nadar na·dar
swimming nado ⓜ na·do
swimming pool piscina ① pee·see·na
swimsuit vestido de baño ⓜ
ves·tee·do de ba·nyo
Switzerland Suiza ① swee·sa
synagogue sinagoga ① see·na·go·ga
synthetic sintético/a ⓜ/① seen·te·tee·ko/a
syringe jeringa ① khe·reen·ga

T

table *mesa* ⓕ *me*·sa
tablecloth *mantel* ⓜ man·*tel*
table tennis *tenis de mesa* ⓜ
  te·nees de *me*·sa
tail *cola* ⓕ *ko*·la
tailor *sastre* ⓜ *sas*·tre
take *llevar* ye·*var*
take a photo *tomar una foto*
  to·*mar* oo·na *fo*·to
talk *hablar* a·*blar*
tall *alto/a* ⓜ/ⓕ *al*·to/a
tampon *tampón* ⓜ tam·*pon*
tanning lotion *bronceador* ⓜ bron·se·a·*dor*
tap (sink) *tubo* ⓜ *too*·bo
tap water *agua de tubo* ⓕ *a*·gwa de *too*·bo
tasty *rico/a* ⓜ/ⓕ *ree*·ko/a
tax *impuesto* ⓜ eem·*pwes*·to
taxi *taxi* ⓜ *tak*·see
taxi stand *parada de taxis* ⓕ
  pa·*ra*·da de *tak*·sees
tea *té* ⓜ te
teacher *maestro/a* ⓜ/ⓕ ma·*es*·tro/a
team *equipo* ⓜ e·*kee*·po
teaspoon *cucharita* ⓕ koo·cha·*ree*·ta
technique *técnica* ⓕ *tek*·nee·ka
teeth *dientes* ⓜ pl *dyen*·tes
telegram *telegrama* ⓜ te·le·*gra*·ma
telephone *teléfono* ⓜ te·*le*·fo·no
telephone *llamar* ya·*mar*
telephone centre *central telefónica* ⓕ
  sen·*tral* te·le·fo·*nee*·ka
telescope *telescopio* ⓜ te·les·*ko*·pyo
television *televisión* ⓕ te·le·vee·*syon*
tell *decir* de·*seer*
temperature (fever) *fiebre* ⓕ *fye*·bre
temperature (weather) *temperatura* ⓕ
  tem·pe·ra·*too*·ra
temple (building) *templo* ⓜ *tem*·plo
tennis *tenis* ⓜ *te*·nees
tennis court *cancha de tenis* ⓕ
  kan·cha de *te*·nees
tent *tienda de campaña* ⓕ
  tyen·da de kam·*pa*·nya
tent peg *clavija* ⓕ kla·*vee*·kha
terrible *terrible* ⓜ&ⓕ te·*ree*·ble
terrorism *terrorismo* ⓜ te·ro·*rees*·mo
test *prueba* ⓕ *prwe*·ba

thank *agradecer* a·gra·de·*ser*
that *a* *ese/a* ⓜ/ⓕ e·se/a
theatre *teatro* ⓜ te·*a*·tro
their *su* soo
there *ahí* a·*ee*
they *ellos/as* ⓜ/ⓕ pl e·yos/as
thick *grueso/a* ⓜ/ⓕ grwe·so/a
thief *ladrón/ladrona* ⓜ/ⓕ la·*dron*/la·*dro*·na
thin *delgado/a* ⓜ/ⓕ del·*ga*·do/a
think *pensar* pen·*sar*
third *tercero/a* ⓜ/ⓕ ter·*se*·ro/a
this *a* *este/a* ⓜ/ⓕ *es*·te/a
thread *hilo* ⓜ *ee*·lo
throat *garganta* ⓕ gar·*gan*·ta
thrush (health) *zorzal* ⓜ sor·*sal*
thunderstorm *tormenta eléctrica* ⓕ
  tor·*men*·ta e·*lek*·tree·ka
Thursday *jueves* ⓜ *khwe*·ves
ticket *tiquete* ⓜ tee·*ke*·te
ticket collector *colector de tiquetes* ⓜ
  ko·lek·*tor* de tee·*ke*·tes
ticket machine *máquina de tiquetes* ⓕ
  ma·kee·na de tee·*ke*·tes
ticket office *ventanilla* ⓕ ven·ta·*nee*·ya
tide *marea* ⓕ ma·*re*·a
tight *socado/a* ⓜ/ⓕ so·*ka*·do/a
time *tiempo* ⓜ *tyem*·po
time difference *diferencia de hora* ⓕ
  dee·fe·*ren*·sya de *o*·ra
timetable *itinerario* ⓜ ee·tee·ne·*ra*·ryo
tin (can) *lata* ⓕ *la*·ta
tin opener *abrelatas* ⓜ a·bre·*la*·tas
tiny *diminuto/a* ⓜ/ⓕ dee·mee·*noo*·to/a
tip (gratuity) *propina* ⓕ pro·*pee*·na
tire *llanta* ⓕ *yan*·ta
tired *cansado/a* ⓜ/ⓕ kan·*sa*·do/a
tissues *klíneks* ⓜ pl *klee*·neks
to *a* a
toast (food) *tostada* ⓕ tos·*ta*·da
toaster *tostador* ⓜ tos·ta·*dor*
tobacco *tabaco* ⓜ ta·*ba*·ko
tobacconist *tabaquería* ⓕ ta·ba·ke·*ree*·a
today *hoy* oi
toe *dedo del pie* ⓜ *de*·do del pye
together *juntos/as* ⓜ/ⓕ pl *khoon*·tos/as
toilet *baño* ⓜ *ba*·nyo
toilet paper *papel higiénico* ⓜ
  pa·*pel* ee·khye·*nee*·ko
tomato *tomate* ⓜ to·*ma*·te

U

tomato sauce *salsa de tomate* ①
sal·sa de to·ma·te

tomorrow *mañana* ma·nya·na

tonight *esta noche* es·ta no·che

too (much) *demasiado* de·ma·sya·do

too (also) *también* tam·byen

tooth *diente* ⓜ dyen·te

toothache *dolor de diente* ⓜ
do·lor de dyen·te

toothbrush *cepillo de dientes* ⓜ
se·pee·yo de dyen·tes

toothpaste *pasta de dientes* ①
pas·ta de dyen·tes

toothpick *palillo de dientes* ⓜ
pa·lee·yo de dyen·tes

torch (flashlight) *foco* ⓜ fo·ko

touch *tocar* to·kar

tour *tour* ⓜ toor

tourist *turista* ⓜ&① too·rees·ta

tourist office *oficina de turismo* ①
o·fee·see·na de too·rees·mo

towards *hacia* a·see·a

towel *paño* ⓜ pa·nyo

tower *torre* ① to·re

toxic waste *desecho tóxico* ⓜ
de·se·cho tok·see·ko

toy shop *juguetería* ① khoo·ge·te·ree·a

track (path) *camino* ⓜ ka·mee·no

track (sport) *pista* ① pees·ta

trade *comercio* ⓜ ko·mer·syo

tradesperson *comerciante* ⓜ&①
ko·mer·syan·te

traffic *tránsito* ⓜ tran·see·to

traffic light *semáforo* ⓜ se·ma·fo·ro

trail *camino* ⓜ ka·mee·no

train *tren* ⓜ tren

train station *estación de tren* ①
es·ta·syon de tren

tram *tranvía* ⓜ tran·vee·a

translate *traducir* tra·doo·seer

translator *traductor/traductora* ⓜ/①
tra·dook·tor/tra·dook·to·ra

transport *transporte* ⓜ trans·por·te

travel *viajar* vya·khar

travel agency *agencia de viajes* ①
a·khen·sya de vya·khes

travellers cheque *cheque de viajero* ⓜ
che·ke de vya·khe·ro

travel sickness *enfermedad del viajero* ①
en·fer·me·dad del vya·khe·ro

tree *árbol* ⓜ ar·bol

trip (journey) *viaje* ⓜ vya·khe

tropical plains *llanuras* ① pl ya·noo·ras

trousers *pantalones* ⓜ pl pan·ta·lo·nes

truck *camión* ⓜ ka·myon

trumpet *trompeta* ① trom·pe·ta

trust *confiar* kon·fyar

try (attempt) *tratar* tra·tar

T-shirt *camiseta* ① ka·mee·se·ta

tube (tyre) *neumático* ⓜ ne·oo·ma·tee·ko

Tuesday *martes* ⓜ mar·tes

tumour *tumor* ⓜ too·mor

tuna *atún* ⓜ a·toon

tune *melodía* ① me·lo·dee·a

turkey *pavo* ⓜ pa·vo

turn *dar vuelta* dar vwel·ta

TV *televisor* ⓜ te·le·vee·sor

tweezers *pinzas* ① pl peen·sas

twice *dos veces* dos ve·ses

twin beds *camas sencillas* ① pl
ka·mas sen·see·yas

twins *gemelos/as* ⓜ/① pl khe·me·los/as

two *dos* dos

type *tipo* ⓜ tee·po

typhoid *tifoidea* ① tee·foy·de·a

typical *típico/a* ⓜ/① tee·pee·ko/a

tyre *llanta* ① yan·ta

U

ultrasound *ultrasonido* ⓜ ool·tra·so·nee·do

umbrella *sombrilla* ① som·bree·ya

uncomfortable *incómodo/a* ⓜ/①
een·ko·mo·do/a

understand *entender* en·ten·der

underwear *ropa interior* ① ro·pa een·te·ryor

unemployed *desempleado/a* ⓜ/①
de·sem·ple·a·do/a

unfair *injusto/a* ⓜ/① een·khoos·to/a

uniform *uniforme* ⓜ oo·nee·for·me

universe *universo* ⓜ oo·nee·ver·so

university *universidad* ① oo·nee·ver·see·dad

unleaded (petrol) *sin plomo* seen plo·mo

unsafe *inseguro/a* ⓜ/① een·se·goo·ro/a

until *hasta* as·ta

unusual *raro/a* ⓜ/① ra·ro/a

up *arriba* a·ree·ba

uphill *cuesta arriba* kwes·ta a·ree·ba

urgent *urgente* ⓜ&① oor·khen·te

urinary infection *infección urinaria* ①
een·fek·*syon* oo·ree·na·rya
USA *Estados Unidos* ⓜ pl
es·*ta*·dos oo·*nee*·dos
useful *útil* ⓜ&① oo·teel

V

vacancy *espacio disponible* ⓜ
es·*pa*·syo dees·po·*nee*·ble
vacant *vacío/a* ⓜ/① va·*see*·o/a
vacation *vacación* ① va·ka·*syon*
vaccination *vacunación* ① va·koo·na·*syon*
vagina *vagina* ① va·*khee*·na
validate *validar* va·lee·*dar*
valley *valle* ⓜ *va*·ye
valuable *valioso/a* ⓜ/① va·*lyo*·so/a
value (price) *valor* ⓜ va·*lor*
van *van* ⓜ van
veal *ternera* ① ter·*ne*·ra
vegetable *vegetal* ⓜ ve·khe·*tal*
vegetarian n&a *vegetariano/a* ⓜ/①
ve·khe·ta·*rya*·no/a
vein *vena* ① *ve*·na
venereal disease *enfermedad venérea* ①
en·fer·me·*dad* ve·*ne*·re·a
venue *lugar* ⓜ loo·*gar*
very *muy* mooy
video camera *cámara de video* ①
ka·ma·ra de *vee·de*·o
video recorder *video* ⓜ *vee·de*·o
video tape *cinta de video* ①
seen·ta de *vee·de*·o
view *vista* ① *vees*·ta
village *pueblo* ⓜ *pwe*·blo
vine *vid* ① veed
vinegar *vinagre* ⓜ vee·*na*·gre
vineyard *viñedo* ⓜ vee·*nye*·do
violin *violín* ⓜ vee·o·*leen*
virus *virus* ⓜ *vee*·roos
visa *visa* ① *vee*·sa
visit *visita* ① vee·*see*·ta
vitamins *vitaminas* ① pl vee·ta·*mee*·nas
visually impaired *discapacitado/a visual*
ⓜ/① dees·ka·pa·see·*ta*·do/a va vee·*swal*
voice *voz* ⓜ vos
volcano *volcán* ⓜ vol·*kan*
volleyball *volibol* ⓜ vo·lee·*bol*
volume *volumen* ⓜ vo·*loo*·men
vote *votar* vo·*tar*

W

wage *salario* ⓜ sa·*la*·ryo
wait *esperar* es·pe·*rar*
waiter *mesero/a* ⓜ/① me·*se*·ro/a
waiting room *sala de espera* ①
sa·la de es·*pe*·ra
wake (someone) up *despertar* des·per·*tar*
walk *caminar* ka·mee·*nar*
wall *pared* ① pa·*red*
want *querer* ke·*rer*
war *guerra* ① *ge*·ra
wardrobe *armario* ⓜ ar·*ma*·ryo
warm *caliente* ⓜ&① ka·*lyen*·te
warn *advertir* ad·ver·*teer*
wash (oneself) *lavarse* la·*var*·se
wash (something) *lavar* la·*var*
wash cloth (flannel) *toallita* ① to·a·*yee*·ta
washing machine *lavadora* ① la·va·*do*·ra
wasp *avispa* ① a·*vees*·pa
watch (clock) *reloj* ⓜ re·*lokh*
watch *observar* ob·ser·*var*
water *agua* ① *a*·gwa
water bottle *botella de agua* ①
bo·*te*·ya de *a*·gwa
water bottle (hot) *termo* ⓜ *ter*·mo
waterfall *catarata* ① ka·ta·*ra*·ta
watermelon *sandía* ① san·*dee*·a
waterproof *contra agua* kon·tra *a*·gwa
water-skiing *esquí acuático* ⓜ
es·*kee* a·*kwa*·tee·ko
wave (beach) *ola* ① *o*·la
way *camino* ⓜ ka·*mee*·no
we *nosotros/as* ⓜ/① pl no·*so*·tros/as
weak *débil* ⓜ&① *de*·beel
wealthy *rico/a* ⓜ/① *ree*·ko/a
wear *ponerse* po·*ner*·se
weather *tiempo* ⓜ *tyem*·po
wedding *boda* ① *bo*·da
wedding cake *queque de bodas* ⓜ
ke·ke de *bo*·das
wedding present *regalo de bodas* ⓜ
re·*ga*·lo de *bo*·das
Wednesday *miércoles* ⓜ *myer*·ko·les
week *semana* ① se·*ma*·na
weekend *fin de semana* ⓜ feen de se·*ma*·na
weigh *pesar* pe·*sar*
weight *peso* ⓜ *pe*·so
weights *pesas* ① pl *pe*·sas

welcome *dar la bienvenida*
  dar la byen·ve·nee·da
welfare *bienestar* ⓜ byen·es·tar
well *bien* byen
west *oeste* ⓜ o·es·te
wet *mojado/a* ⓜ/ⓕ mo·kha·do/a
what *qué* ke
wheel *rueda* ⓕ rwe·da
wheelchair *silla de ruedas* ⓕ
  see·ya de rwe·das
when *cuándo* kwan·do
where *dónde* don·de
which *cuál* kwal
white *blanco/a* ⓜ/ⓕ blan·ko/a
white wine *vino blanco* ⓜ vee·no blan·ko
who *quién* kyen
wholemeal bread *pan integral* ⓜ
  pan een·te·gral
why *por qué* por ke
wide *ancho/a* ⓜ/ⓕ an·cho/a
wife *esposa* ⓕ es·po·sa
wildlife *flora y fauna silvestre* ⓕ
  flo·ra ee fow·na seel·ves·tre
win *ganar* ga·nar
wind *viento* ⓜ vyen·to
window *ventana* ⓕ ven·ta·na
windscreen *parabrisas* ⓜ pa·ra·bree·sas
wine *vino* ⓜ vee·no
wings *alas* ⓕ pl a·las
winner *ganador/ganadora* ⓜ/ⓕ
  ga·na·dor/ga·na·do·ra
winter *invierno* ⓜ een·vyer·no
wire *alambre* ⓜ a·lam·bre
wish *desear* de·se·ar
with *con* kon
within (time) *dentro de* den·tro de
without *sin* seen
woman *mujer* ⓕ moo·kher
wonderful *maravilloso/a* ⓜ/ⓕ
  ma·ra·vee·yo·so/a
wood (food) *madera* ⓕ ma·de·ra
wool *lana* ⓕ la·na
word *palabra* ⓕ pa·la·bra
work *trabajo* ⓜ tra·ba·kho

work (function) *funcionar* foon·syo·nar
work (job) *trabajar* tra·ba·khar
work experience *experiencia laboral* ⓕ
  eks·pe·ryen·sya la·bo·ral
workout *sesión de ejercicios* ⓕ
  se·syon de e·kher·see·syos
work permit *permiso de trabajo* ⓜ
  per·mee·so de tra·ba·kho
workshop *taller* ⓜ ta·yer
world *mundo* ⓜ moon·do
World Cup *Mundial* ⓜ moon·dyal
worms (intestinal) *lombrices* ⓕ pl
  lom·bree·ses
worried *preocupado/a* ⓜ/ⓕ
  pre·o·koo·pa·do/a
worship *adorar* a·do·rar
wrist *muñeca* ⓕ moo·nye·ka
write *escribir* es·kree·beer
writer *autor* ⓜ ow·tor
wrong *equivocado/n* ⓜ/ⓕ e·kee·vo·ka·do/a

Y

year *año* ⓜ a·nyo
yellow *amarillo/a* ⓜ/ⓕ a·ma·ree·yo/a
yes *sí* see
yesterday *ayer* a·yer
(not) yet *todavía (no)* to·da·vee·a (no)
you sg inf *tú* • *vos* too • vos
you sg pol *usted* oos·ted
you pl *ustedes* oos·te·des
young *joven* ⓜ&ⓕ kho·ven
your sg inf *tu* too
your sg pol&pl *su* so
youth hostel *albergue juvenil* ⓜ
  al·ber·ge khoo·ve·neel

Z

zip(per) *zipper* ⓜ see·per
zodiac *zodíaco* ⓜ so·dee·a·ko
zoo *zoológico* ⓜ so·o·lo·khee·ko
zoom lens *lente zoom* ⓜ len·te soom

The words in this dictionary are listed in Spanish alphabetical order (see the box **spanish alphabet**, page 13). Spanish nouns have their gender indicated with ⓜ (masculine) and ⓕ (feminine). If adjectives and nouns have just one form for both genders, it's marked as ⓜ&ⓕ. Where adjectives and nouns have separate masculine and feminine forms, the endings are divided by a slash (eg *bello/a* ⓜ/ⓕ). Where the letter *a* is added onto a masculine form to make a feminine form, the added ending is in brackets (eg *director(a)* ⓜ/ⓕ). See the **phrasebuilder** for more on gender. Words are also marked as n (noun), a (adjective), adv (adverb), v (verb), pl (plural), sg (singular), inf (informal) and pol (polite) where necessary. Verbs are given in the infinitive – for details on how to change verbs for use in a sentence, see the **phrasebuilder**, page 28.

A

a *a* to
— **bordo** *bor*·do aboard
— **menudo** me·*noo*·do often
— **tiempo** *tyem*·po on time
— **través** tra·*ves* across
— **veces** *ve*·ses sometimes
abajo a·*ba*·kho down
abeja ⓕ a·*be*·kha bee
abierto/a ⓜ/ⓕ a·*byer*·to/a open (business)
abogado/a ⓜ/ⓕ a·bo·*ga*·do/a lawyer
abordar a·bor·*dar* board (plane, ship)
aborto ⓜ a·*bor*·to abortion
— **natural** na·too·*ral* miscarriage
abrazar a·bra·*sar* hug
abrelatas ⓜ a·bre·*la*·tas can opener
abridor ⓜ a·bree·*dor* bottle opener
abrigo ⓜ a·*bree*·go coat
abril ⓜ a·*breel* April
abrir a·*breer* open v
abuela ⓕ a·*bwe*·la grandmother
abuelo ⓜ a·*bwe*·lo grandfather
aburrido/a ⓜ/ⓕ a·boo·*ree*·do/a
bored • boring
acampar a·kam·*par* camp v
accidente ⓜ ak·see·*den*·te accident
aceite ⓜ a·*say*·te oil (cooking)
achaques ⓜ pl a·*cha*·kes morning sickness
ácido ⓜ *a*·see·do acid
acondicionador ⓜ a·kon·dee·syo·na·*dor*
hair conditioner
acoso ⓜ a·*ko*·so harassment
acostarse a·kos·*tar*·se lie (not stand)
activista ⓜ&ⓕ ak·tee·*vees*·ta activist

actualidad ⓕ ak·twa·lee·*dad* current affairs
acupuntura ⓕ a·koo·poon·*too*·ra
acupuncture
adaptador ⓜ a·dap·ta·*dor* adaptor
adelante a·de·*lan*·te ahead
adentro a·*den*·tro indoor
adicción ⓕ a·deek·*syon* addiction
adiós a·*dyos* goodbye
adivinar a·dee·vee·*nar* guess
adivino/a ⓜ/ⓕ a·dee·*vee*·no/a fortune teller
administración ⓕ ad·mee·nees·tra·*syon*
administration
admisión ⓕ ad·mee·*syon* admission (price)
admitir ad·mee·*teer* admit
adolorido/a ⓜ/ⓕ a·do·lo·*ree*·do/a sore
adorar a·do·*rar* worship v
aduana ⓕ a·*dwa*·na customs (immigration)
adulto/a ⓜ/ⓕ a·*dool*·to/a adult n&a
advertir ad·ver·*teer* warn
aeróbicos ⓜ pl a·e·ro·*bee*·kos aerobics
aerolínea ⓕ a·e·ro·*lee*·ne·a airline
aeropuerto ⓜ a·e·ro·*pwer*·to airport
aficionado/a ⓜ/ⓕ a·fee·syo·*na*·do/a
fan (sport, etc)
afortunado/a ⓜ/ⓕ a·for·too·*na*·do/a lucky
afuera a·*fwe*·ra outside
agencia ⓕ a·*khen*·sya agency
— **de noticias** de no·*tee*·syas newsagency
— **de viajes** de *vya*·khes travel agency
agenda ⓕ a·*khen*·da diary
agente de bienes raíces ⓜ a·*khen*·te de
bye·nes ra·e·*ses* real estate agent
agosto ⓜ a·*gos*·to August
agradecer a·gra·de·*ser* thank

A

agradecido/a ⓜ/① a·gra·de·*see*·do/a *grateful*

agricultura ① a·gree·kool·*too*·ra *agriculture*

agua ① *a*·gwa *water*

aguja ① a·*goo*·kha *needle (sewing)*

ahí a·*ee there*

ahora a·*o*·ra *now*

aire ⓜ *ai*·re *air*
— **acondicionado** a·kon·dee·syo·*na*·do *air conditioning*

alas ① pl *a*·las *wings*

albergue juvenil ⓜ al·*ber*·ge khoo·ve·*neel youth hostel*

alcalde(sa) ⓜ/① al·*kal*·de/al·kal·de·sa *mayor*

alcohol ⓜ al·*kol alcohol*

alemán a·le·*man German (language)*

alergia ① a·*ler*·khee·a *allergy*

alfarería ① al·fa·re·*ree*·a *pottery*

alfombra ① al·*fom*·bra *rug*

algo *al*·go *something*

algodón ⓜ al·go·*don cotton*

alguien al·*gyen someone*

algún/alguna ⓜ/① al·*goon*/al·*goo*·na *some*

almohada ① al·mo·*a*·da *pillow*

almuerzo ⓜ al·*mwer*·so *lunch*

alojamiento ⓜ a·lo·kha·*myen*·to *accommodation*

alquilar al·kee·*lar rent* v

alquiler de carros ⓜ al·kee·*ler* de *ka*·ros *car hire*

altar ⓜ al·*tar altar*

alto/a ⓜ/① *al*·to/a *high • tall*

altura ① al·*too*·ra *altitude*

amable ⓜ&① a·*ma*·ble *kind • nice*

amanecer ⓜ a·ma·ne·*ser dawn • sunrise*

amante ⓜ&① a·*man*·te *lover*

amar a·*mar love* v

amargo/a ⓜ/① a·*mar*·go/a *bitter*

amarillo/a ⓜ/① a·ma·*ree*·yo/a *yellow*

ambos/as ⓜ/① pl *am*·bos/am·bas *both*

ambulancia ① am·boo·*lan*·sya *ambulance*

amigo/a ⓜ/① a·*mee*·go/a *friend*

amor ⓜ a·*mor love*

ampolla ① am·*po*·ya *blister*

anaranjado/a ⓜ/① a·na·ran·*kha*·do/a *orange (colour)*

anarquista ⓜ&① a·nar·*kees*·ta *anarchist* n&a

ancho/a ⓜ/① *an*·cho/a *wide*

andar an·*dar ride (bike, horse)*
— **en bicicleta** en bee·see·*kle*·ta *cycle* v
— **en patineta** en pa·tee·ne·ta *skateboard* v

anemia ① a·*ne*·mya *anaemia*

anillo ⓜ a·*nee*·yo *ring (jewellery)*

animal ⓜ a·nee·*mal animal*

anotar a·no·*tar score* v

anteayer ⓜ an·te·a·*yer day before yesterday*

anteojos ⓜ pl an·te·*o*·khos *glasses*
— **de sol** de sol *sunglasses*

anterior ⓜ&① an·te·*ryor last (previous)*

antes *an*·tes *before*

antibióticos ⓜ pl an·tee·*byo*·tee·kos *antibiotics*

anticonceptivos ⓜ pl an·tee·kon·sep·*tee*·vos *contraceptives*

antigüedad ① an·tee·gwe·*dad antique*

antiguo/a ⓜ/① an·*tee*·gwo/a *ancient*

antiséptico ⓜ an·tee·*sep*·tee·ko *antiseptic*

anuncio ⓜ a·*noon*·syo *advertisement*

año ⓜ *a*·nyo *year*

Año Nuevo ⓜ *a*·nyo *nwe*·vo *New Year*

apagado/a ⓜ/① a·pa·*ga*·do/a *off (power)*

apartamento ⓜ a·par·ta·*men*·to *apartment • flat*

apellido ⓜ a·pe·*yee*·do *surname*

apéndice ⓜ a·*pen*·dee·se *appendix (body)*

aplicadores ⓜ pl a·plee·ka·*do*·res *cotton buds (swabs)*

apodo ⓜ a·*po*·do *nickname*

apostar a·pos·*tar bet* v

aprender a·pren·*der learn*

apuesta ① a·*pwes*·ta *bet*

apurado/a ⓜ/① a·poo·*ra*·do/a *in a hurry*

aquí a·*kee here*

araña ① a·*ra*·nya *spider*

árbitro ⓜ *ar*·bee·tro *referee*

árbol ⓜ *ar*·bol *tree*

área de acampar ① *a*·re·a de a·kam·*par camping ground*

arena ① a·*re*·na *sand*

aretes ⓜ pl a·*re*·tes *earrings*

argumentar ar·goo·men·*tar argue*

armario ⓜ ar·*ma*·ryo *cupboard • wardrobe*

aromaterapia ① a·ro·ma·te·*ra*·pya *aromatherapy*

arqueológico/a ⓜ/① ar·ke·o·*lo*·khee·ko/a *archaeological*

arquitecto/a ⓜ/① ar·kee·*tek*·to/a *architect*

arquitectura ① ar·kee·tek·*too*·ra *architecture*

arrestar a·res·*tar arrest* v

arriba a·*ree*·ba *up*

arrollo ⓜ a·*ro*·yo *stream*

arte ⓜ *ar*·te *art*

artesanías ① pl ar·te·sa·*nee*·as *handicraft*

artesano/a ⓜ/① ar·te·*sa*·no/a *craftsman/woman*

artes marciales ① pl *ar*·tes mar·*sya*·les *martial arts*

artista ⓜ&① ar·*tees*·ta *artist*
— **callejero** ka·ye·*khe*·ro *busker*

asa ⓜ *a·sa* film speed
ascensor ⓜ *a·sen·sor* elevator (lift)
asesinar *a·se·see·nar* murder v
asesinato ⓜ *a·se·see·na·to* murder
asiento ⓜ *a·syen·to* seat (place)
asistente de ventas ⓜ&ⓕ
  a·sees·ten·te de ven·tas sales assistant
asma ⓕ *as·ma* asthma
aspirina ⓕ *as·pee·ree·na* aspirin
ataque al corazón ⓜ *a·ta·ke al ko·ra·son*
  heart attack
atardecer ⓜ *a·tar·de·ser* sunset
atletismo ⓜ *at·le·tees·mo* athletics
atmósfera ⓕ *at·mos·fe·ra* atmosphere
atrás *a·tras* back (position)
atraso ⓜ *a·tra·so* delay
audífono ⓜ *ow·dee·fo·no* hearing aid
autopista ⓕ *ow·to·pees·ta* highway
autor ⓜ *ow·tor* writer
auto servicio ⓜ *ow·to ser·vee·syo* self-service
avenida ⓕ *a·ve·nee·da* avenue
aventón ⓜ *a·ven·ton* ride
avergonzado/a ⓜ/ⓕ *a·ver·gon·sa·do/a*
  embarrassed
avión ⓜ *a·vyon* airplane
avispa ⓕ *a·vees·pa* wasp
ayer *a·yer* yesterday
ayuda ⓕ *a·yoo·da* help
ayudar *a·yoo·dar* help v
azúcar ⓜ *a·soo·kar* sugar
azul ⓜ&ⓕ *a·sool* blue

B

bailar *bai·lar* dance v
baile ⓜ *bai·le* dance
bajar ba·*khar* get off (bus, train)
bajo/a ⓜ/ⓕ *ba·kho/a* low · short (height)
balcón ⓜ *bal·kon* balcony
balde ⓜ *bal·de* bucket
balomano ba·lo·*ma·no* handball
banco ⓜ *ban·ko* bank
bandera ⓕ *ban·de·ra* flag
baño ⓜ *ba·nyo* bath · bathroom · toilet
  — público *poo·blee·ko* public toilet
bar ⓜ *bar* bar · pub
barato/a ⓜ/ⓕ *ba·ra·to/a* cheap
barbero ⓜ *bar·be·ro* barber
barco ⓜ *bar·ko* boat · ship
barra ⓕ *ba·ra* counter (at bar)
barro ⓜ *ba·ro* mud
básquetbol ⓜ *bas·ket·bol* basketball
basura ⓕ *ba·soo·ra* garbage
basurero ⓜ *ba·soo·re·ro* garbage can

batería ⓕ *ba·te·ree·a* battery · drums (kit)
bautismo ⓜ *bow·tees·mo* baptism
bebé ⓜ&ⓕ *be·be* baby
bebida ⓕ *be·bee·da* drink
béisbol ⓜ *bays·bol* baseball
bello/a ⓜ/ⓕ *be·yo/a* beautiful
besar be·*sar* kiss v
beso ⓜ *be·so* kiss
biblioteca ⓕ *bee·blee·o·te·ka* library
bibliotecario/a ⓜ/ⓕ *bee·blee·o·te·ka·ryo/a*
  librarian
bicho ⓜ *bee·cho* bug
bicicleta ⓕ *bee·see·kle·ta* bicycle
  — de carreras de *ka·re·ras* racing bike
  — montañera mon·ta·*nye·ra*
    mountain bike
bien *byen* fine · well
bienestar ⓜ *byen·es·tar* welfare
  — social so·*syal* social welfare
billete de banco ⓜ *bee·ye·te de ban·ko*
  banknote
binoculares ⓜ pl *bee·no·koo·la·res*
  binoculars
blanco y negro *blan·ko* ee *ne·gro*
  B&W (film) a
blanco/a ⓜ/ⓕ *blan·ko/a* white
bloqueado/a ⓜ/ⓕ *blo·ke·a·do/a* blocked
bloqueador ⓜ *blo·ke·a·dor* sunblock
boca ⓕ *bo·ka* mouth
boda ⓕ *bo·da* wedding
bola ⓕ *bo·la* ball (sport)
bolitas de algodón ⓕ pl
  bo·lee·tas de al·go·don cotton balls
bollo de pan ⓜ *bo·yo de pan* bread roll
bolsa ⓕ *bol·sa* bag
bolsillo ⓜ *bol·see·yo* pocket
bolso ⓜ *bol·so* handbag
bomba ⓕ *bom·ba* gas station · petrol station
bombillo ⓜ *bom·bee·yo* light bulb
bonito/a ⓜ/ⓕ *bo·nee·to/a* pretty
borde ⓜ *bor·de* ledge
borracho/a ⓜ/ⓕ *bo·ra·cho/a* drunk
bosque ⓜ *bos·ke* forest
  — lluvioso yoo·*vyo·so* rainforest
  — nuboso noo·*bo·so* cloud forest
botas ⓕ pl *bo·tas* boots
  — para caminata *pa·ra* ka·mee·*na·ta*
    hiking boots
botella ⓕ *bo·te·ya* bottle
  — de agua de *a·gwa* water bottle
botón ⓜ *bo·ton* button
boxeo ⓜ *bok·se·o* boxing
bóxer ⓜ *bok·ser* boxer shorts
bracier ⓜ *bra·syer* bra
brazo ⓜ *bra·so* arm (body)

brillo ⓜ *bree·yo lip balm*
bronceador ⓜ *bron·se·a·dor tanning lotion*
bronquitis ⓕ *bron·kee·tees bronchitis*
brújula ⓕ *broo·khoo·la compass*
buceo ⓜ *boo·se·o diving*
budista ⓜ&ⓕ *boo·dees·ta Buddhist* n&a
bueno/a ⓜ/ⓕ *bwe·no/a good · nice*
bufanda ⓕ *boo·fan·da scarf*
bulto ⓜ *bool·to lump*
bus ⓜ *boos bus · coach*
buscar *boos·kar look for*
buzón ⓜ *boo·son mailbox*

C

caballo ⓜ *ka·ba·yo horse*
cabeza ⓕ *ka·be·sa head*
cabra ⓕ *ka·bra goat*
cacao ⓜ *ka·kow cocoa*
cada ⓜ&ⓕ *ka·da each*
cadena ⓕ *ka·de·na chain · necklace*
 — **de bicicleta** *de bee·see·kle·ta bike chain*
caer *ka·er fall* v
café ⓜ *ka·fe café · coffee · brown*
 — **Internet** *een·ter·net Internet café*
caja ⓕ *ka·kha box · cash register*
 — **de cambios** *de kam·byos gearbox*
 — **fuerte** *fwer·te safe (for valuables)*
cajero/a ⓜ/ⓕ *ka·khe·ro/a cashier*
cajero automático ⓜ
 ka·khe·ro ow·to·ma·tee·ko ATM
calcetines ⓕ pl *kal·se·tee·nes stockings*
calculadora ⓕ *kal·koo·la·do·ra calculator*
calendario ⓜ *ka·len·da·ryo calendar*
calentado/a ⓜ/ⓕ *ka·len·ta·do/a heated*
calentador ⓜ *ka·len·ta·dor heater*
calentamiento ⓜ *ka·len·ta·myen·to heating*
calidad ⓕ *ka·lee·dad quality*
caliente ⓜ&ⓕ *ka·lyen·te hot*
callado/a ⓜ/ⓕ *ka·ya·do/a quiet*
calle ⓕ *ka·ye road · street*
 — **principal** *preen·se·pal main road*
calor ⓜ *ka·lor heat*
cama ⓕ *ka·ma bed*
 — **matrimonial** *ma·tree·mo·nyal double bed*
cámara ⓕ *ka·ma·ra camera*
 — **de video** *de vee·de·o video camera*
camas sencillas ⓕ pl *ka·mas sen·see·yas twin beds*
cambiar *kam·byar exchange (money)*
 — **un cheque** *oon che·ke cash a cheque*
cambio ⓜ *kam·byo change · exchange*

 — **de moneda** *de mo·ne·da currency exchange*
caminar *ka·mee·nar hike · walk*
caminata ⓕ *ka·mee·na·ta hiking*
camino ⓜ *ka·mee·no path · track · trail*
 — **de montaña** *de mon·ta·nya mountain path*
camión ⓜ *ka·myon truck*
 — **de todo-terreno** *de to·do·te·re·no all-terrain vehicle*
camisa ⓕ *ka·mee·sa shirt*
camiseta ⓕ *ka·mee·se·ta T-shirt*
campeonatos ⓜ pl *kam·pe·o·na·tos championships*
campo ⓜ *kam·po countryside · space (room)*
 — **de golf** *de golf golf course*
canasta ⓕ *ka·nas·ta basket*
cancelar *kan·se·lar cancel*
cáncer ⓜ *kan·ser cancer*
cancha de tenis ⓕ *kan·cha de te·nees tennis court*
canción ⓕ *kan·syon song*
candado ⓜ *kan·da·do lock · padlock*
 — **de bicicleta** *de bee·see·kle·ta bike lock*
canoa ⓕ *ka·no·a canoe*
cansado/a ⓜ/ⓕ *kan·sa·do/a tired*
cantante ⓜ&ⓕ *kan·tan·te singer*
cantar *kan·tar sing*
capa ⓕ *ka·pa raincoat*
 — **de ozono** *de o·so·no ozone layer*
cara ⓕ *ka·ra face*
caracol ⓜ *ka·ra·kol snail*
caravana ⓕ *ka·ra·va·na caravan*
cárcel ⓕ *kar·sel jail*
carne ⓕ *kar·ne meat*
carnicería ⓕ *kar·nee·se·ree·a butcher's shop*
carnicero ⓜ *kar·nee·se·ro butcher*
caro/a ⓜ/ⓕ *ka·ro/a expensive*
carpintero ⓜ *kar·peen·te·ro carpenter*
carrera ⓕ *ka·re·ra race (sport)*
carreras de caballo ⓕ pl
 ka·re·ras de ka·ba·yo horse racing
carro ⓜ *ka·ro car*
carta ⓕ *kar·ta letter (mail)*
cartera ⓕ *kar·te·ra purse*
cartón ⓜ *kar·ton carton*
casa ⓕ *ka·sa house*
casado/a ⓜ/ⓕ *ka·sa·do/a married*
casarse *ka·sar·se marry*
casco ⓜ *kas·ko helmet*
casetilla de teléfono ⓕ
 ka·se·tee·ya de te·le·fo·no phone box
casi *ka·see almost*
castellano *kas·te·ya·no Spanish (language)*
castillo ⓜ *kas·tee·yo castle*

catarata ① ka·ta·*ra*·ta *waterfall*
catedral ① ka·te·*dral* *cathedral*
católico/a ⑩/① ka·to·lee·ko/a *Catholic* n&a
caza ① *ka*·sa *hunting*
cédula de identificación ① se·doo·la de
  ee·den·tee·fee·ka·syon *identification card*
celebración ① se·le·bra·syon *celebration*
celoso/a ⑩/① se·lo·so/a *jealous*
cementerio ⑩ se·men·te·ryo *cemetery*
cena ① se·na *dinner*
cenicero ⑩ se·nee·se·ro *ashtray*
centavo ⑩ sen·*ta*·vo *cent*
centímetro ⑩ sen·*tee*·me·tro *centimetre*
central telefónica ① sen·*tral* te·le·fo·nee·ka
  telephone centre
centro ⑩ *sen*·tro *centre*
  — **comercial** ko·mer·*syal* *shopping centre*
  — **de la ciudad** de la syoo·*dad* *city centre*
cepillo ⑩ se·*pee*·yo *brush • hairbrush*
  — **de dientes** de *dyen*·tes *toothbrush*
cerámica ① se·*ra*·mee·ka *ceramics*
cerca ① *ser*·ka *fence*
cerca *ser*·ka *close • nearby*
cerdo ⑩ *ser*·do *pig • pork*
cerrado/a ⑩/① se·*ra*·do/a *closed • shut*
  — **con llave** kon *ya*·ve *locked*
cerrar se·*rar* *close* v
  — **con llave** kon *ya*·ve *lock* v
certificado ⑩ ser·tee·fee·*ka*·do *certificate*
  — **de nacimiento** de na·see·*myen*·to
  birth certificate
cerveza ① ser·*ve*·sa *beer*
chaleco salvavidas ⑩ cha·*le*·ko
  sal·va·*vee*·das *life jacket*
champaña ① cham·*pa*·nya *champagne*
champú ⑩ cham·poo *shampoo*
chancho ⑩ *chan*·cho *pig • pork*
chancletas ⑩ pl chan·*kle*·tas *sandals*
cheque ⑩ *che*·ke *check (banking) • cheque*
  — **de viajero** de vya·*khe*·ro
  travellers cheque
chequeo ⑩ che·*ke*·o *check-in (desk)*
chicle ⑩ *chee*·kle *chewing gum*
chica ① *chee*·ka *girl*
chico ⑩ *chee*·ko *boy*
chile ⑩ *chee*·le *chilli*
chineado/a ⑩/① chee·ne·*a*·do/a
  spoilt (person)
chiquito/a ⑩/① chee·*kee*·to/a *child*
chiste ⑩ *chees*·te *joke*
chivo ⑩ *chee*·vo *gig*
choque ⑩ *cho*·ke *crash*
chores ⑩ pl *cho*·res *shorts*
chupeta ① choo·*pe*·ta *dummy • pacifier*
ciclismo ⑩ see·*klees*·mo *cycling*

ciclista ⑩&① see·*klees*·ta *cyclist*
ciclo ⑩ see·*klo* *bike shop*
ciego/a ⑩/① *sye*·go/a *blind*
cielo ⑩ *sye*·lo *sky*
cien ⑩ syen *hundred*
ciencia ① *syen*·sya *science*
científico/a ⑩/① syen·*tee*·fee·ko/a *a scientist*
cigarrillo ⑩ see·ga·*ree*·yo *cigarette*
cigarro ⑩ see·*ga*·ro *cigar*
cilindro de gas ⑩ see·*leen*·dro de gas
  gas cartridge
cima ① *see*·ma *mountain peak*
cine ⑩ *see*·ne *cinema*
cinta de video ① *seen*·ta de vee·*de*·o
  video tape
cinturón ⑩ seen·too·*ron* *seatbelt*
circo ⑩ *seer*·ko *circus*
cistitis ① sees·*tee*·tees *cystitis*
cita ① *see*·ta *appointment*
ciudad ① syoo·*dad* *city*
ciudadanía ① syoo·da·da·nee·a *citizenship*
clarinete ⑩ kla·ree·*ne*·te *clarinet*
claro/a ⑩/① *kla*·ro/a *light (colour)*
clase ① *kla*·se *class (category)*
  — **económica** e·ko·no·*mee*·ka
  economy class
  — **ejecutiva** e·khe·koo·*tee*·va
  business class
clásico/a ⑩/① *kla*·see·ko/a *classical*
clavija ① kla·*vee*·kha *tent peg*
cliente ⑩&① klee·*en*·te *client*
closh ⑩ klosh *clutch (car)*
club nocturno ⑩ kloob nok·*toor*·no
  nightclub
cobija ① ko·*bee*·kha *blanket*
cocaína ① ko·ka·*ee*·na *cocaine*
coche ⑩ *ko*·che *stroller*
cocina ① ko·*see*·na *cooking • kitchen • stove*
cocinar ko·see·*nar* *cook* v
cocinero/a ⑩/① ko·see·*ne*·ro/a *cook*
coco ⑩ *ko*·ko *coconut*
coctel ⑩ kok·*tel* *cocktail*
código postal ⑩ *ko*·dee·go pos·*tal*
  postcode
cola ① *ko*·la *tail*
colchón ⑩ kol·*chon* *mattress*
colchoneta ① kol·cho·*ne*·ta *mat*
colector de tiquetes ⑩
  ko·lek·*tor* de tee·*ke*·tes *ticket collector*
colega ⑩&① ko·*le*·ga *colleague*
colegio ⑩ ko·le·*khyo* *high school*
color ⑩ ko·*lor* *colour*
comedia ① ko·me·*dya* *comedy*
comer ko·*mer* *eat*

comerciante ⓜ&ⓕ ko·mer·*syan*·te
tradesperson

comercio ⓜ ko·*mer*·syo *trade*

comida ⓕ ko·*mee*·da *food • meal*
— **de bebé** de be·*be* *baby food*

cómo *ko*·mo *how*

cómodo/a ⓜ/ⓕ *ko*·mo·do/a *comfortable*

compañero/a ⓜ/ⓕ kom·pa·*nye*·ro/a
companion

compañía ⓕ kom·pa·*nyee*·a *company (firm)*

compartir kom·*par*·teer *share* v

comprar kom·*prar* *buy*

compras ⓟ pl *kom*·pras *shopping*

comprometido/a ⓜ/ⓕ
kom·pro·me·*tee*·do/a *engaged (to marry)*

compromiso ⓜ kom·pro·*mee*·so
engagement (to marry)

computadora ⓕ kom·poo·ta·*do*·ra
computer

comunicación ⓕ ko·moo·nee·ka·*syon*
communications (profession)

comunión ⓕ ko·moo·*nyon* *communion*

comunista ⓜ&ⓕ ko·moo·*nees*·ta
communist n&a

con kon *with*
— **aire acondicionado**
ai·re a·kon·dee·syo·*na*·do *air-conditioned*

concierto ⓜ kon·*syer*·to *concert*

condición cardíaca ⓕ
kon·dee·*syon* kar·*dee*·a·ka *heart condition*

conducir kon·doo·*seer* *drive* v

conejo ⓜ ko·*ne*·kho *rabbit*

conexión ⓕ ko·nek·*syon* *connection*

conferencia ⓕ kon·fe·*ren*·sya
conference (small)

confesión ⓕ kon·fe·*syon*
confession (religious)

confiar kon·*fyar* *trust* v

confirmar kon·feer·*mar* *confirm (a booking)*

confite ⓜ kon·*fee*·te *candy*

congelado/a ⓜ/ⓕ kon·khe·*la*·do/a *frozen*

congelar kon·khe·*lar* *freeze*

congreso ⓜ kon·*gre*·so *conference (big)*

conmoción ⓕ kon·mo·*syon* *commission*

conocer ko·no·*ser* *know (someone)*

conocerse ko·no·*ser*·se *meet (first time)*

consejo ⓜ kon·*se*·kho *advice*

conservador(a) ⓜ/ⓕ kon·ser·va·*dor*/
kon·ser·va·*do*·ra *conservative* n&a

consigna ⓕ kon·*seeg*·na *left-luggage office*

constructor(a) ⓜ/ⓕ
kons·trook·*tor*/kons·trook·*to*·ra *builder*

construir kons·troo·*eer* *build*

consulado ⓜ kon·soo·*la*·do *consulate*

contaminación ⓕ kon·ta·mee·na·*syon*
pollution

contar kon·*tar* *count* v

contra agua *kon*·tra a·*gwa* *waterproof*

contratar kon·tra·*tar* *hire • rent* v

contrato ⓜ kon·*tra*·to *contract*

control remoto ⓜ kon·*trol* re·*mo*·to
remote control

contusión ⓕ kon·too·*syon* *concussion*

convento ⓜ kon·*ven*·to *convent*

corazón ⓜ ko·ra·*son* *heart*

cordillera ⓕ kor·dee·*ye*·ra *mountain range*

cordón de zapato ⓜ kor·*don* de sa·*pa*·to
shoelace

correcto/a ⓜ/ⓕ ko·*rek*·to/a *right (correct)*

correo ⓜ ko·*re*·o *mail • post office*

correr ko·*rer* *run* v

corriendo ⓜ ko·*ryen*·do *running*

corriente ⓕ ko·*ryen*·te *current (electricity)*

corrupción ⓕ ko·roop·*syon* *corruption*

corrupto/a ⓜ/ⓕ ko·*roop*·to/a *corrupt*

cortada ⓕ kor·*ta*·da *cut*

cortar kor·*tar* *cut* v

cortaúñas ⓜ kor·ta·oo·*nyas* *nail clippers*

corte ⓕ *kor*·te *court (legal)*

corte de pelo ⓜ *kor*·te de *pe*·lo *haircut*

coser ko·*ser* *sew*

costa ⓕ *kos*·ta *coast*

costar kos·*tar* *cost* v

costilla ⓕ kos·*tee*·ya *rib (body)*

costumbre ⓕ kos·*toom*·bre *custom*

cráneo ⓜ *kra*·ne·o *skull*

crecer kre·*ser* *grow*

crédito ⓜ *kre*·dee·to *credit*

crema ⓕ *kre*·ma *cream (food/lotion)*

cricket ⓜ *kree*·ket *cricket (sport)*

cristiano/a ⓜ/ⓕ krees·*tya*·no/a
Christian n&a

crudo/a ⓜ/ⓕ *kroo*·do/a *raw*

cruz ⓕ kroos *cross (religious)*

cuaderno ⓜ kwa·*der*·no *notebook*

cuadrapléjico/a ⓜ/ⓕ
kwa·dra·*ple*·khee·ko/a *quadriplegic*

cuál kwal *which*

cualidades ⓕ pl kwa·lee·*da*·des
qualifications

cualquier(a) ⓜ/ⓕ kwal·*kyer*/kwal·*kye*·ra *any*

cuándo *kwan*·do *when*

cuánto *kwan*·to *how much*

cuarentena ⓕ kwa·ren·*te*·na *quarantine*

cuarto ⓜ *kwar*·to *bedroom • quarter*
— **doble** *do*·ble *double room*

cubiertos ⓜ pl koo·*byer*·tos *cutlery*

cucaracha ⓕ koo·ka·*ra*·cha *cockroach*

cuchara ⓕ koo·*cha*·ra *spoon*

cucharita ① koo-cha-*ree*-ta *teaspoon*
cuchilla ① koo-*chee*-ya *pocketknife*
cuchillo ⑩ koo-*chee*-yo *knife*
cuello ⑩ *kwe*-yo *neck*
cuenta ① *kwen*-ta *account • bill • cheque*
— **bancaria** ban-*ka*-rya *bank account*
cuento ⑩ *kwen*-to *story*
cuerda ① *kwer*-da *rope*
cuero ⑩ *kwe*-ro *leather*
— **cabelludo** ka-be-*yoo*-do *scalp*
cuerpo ⑩ *kwer*-po *body*
cuesta abajo *kwes*-ta a-*ba*-kho *downhill*
cuesta arriba *kwes*-ta a-*ree*-ba *uphill*
cueva ① *kwe*-va *cave*
cuidar de kwee-*dar* de *look after*
culebra ① koo-*le*-bra *snake*
culpa ① *kool*-pa *(someone's) fault*
culpable ⑩&① kool-*pa*-ble *guilty*
cumpleaños ⑩ koom-ple-*a*-nyos *birthday*
cuna ① *koo*-na *crèche • child-minding centre*
cupón ⑩ koo-*pon* *coupon*
cura ⑩ *koo*-ra *priest*
curita ① koo-*ree*-ta *Band-Aid*
currículum ⑩ koo-*ree*-koo-loom *CV • résumé*

D

dar dar *give*
— **de comer** de ko-*mer* *feed* v
— **la bienvenida** la byen-ve-*nee*-da *welcome* v
— **vuelta** *vwel*-ta *turn* v
de de *from*
debajo de-*ba*-kho *below*
deber de-*ber* *owe*
débil ⑩&① *de*-beel *weak*
decidir de-see-*deer* *decide*
decir de-*seer* *say • tell*
dedo ⑩ *de*-do *finger*
— **del pie** del pye *toe*
defectuoso/a ⑩/① de-fek-*two*-so/a *faulty*
deforestación ① de-fo-res-ta-*syon* *deforestation*
delgado/a ⑩/① del-*ga*-do/a *thin*
demasiado de-ma-*sya*-do *too (much)*
democracia ① de-mo-*kra*-sya *democracy*
demostración ① de-mos-tra-*syon* *demonstration (display)*
dentista ⑩&① den-*tees*-ta *dentist*
dentro *den*-tro *inside*
— **de** de *within (time)*
deporte ⑩ de-*por*-te *sport*
deportista ⑩&① de-por-*tees*-ta *sportsperson*
depósito ⑩ de-*po*-see-to *deposit (bank)*

derecha ① de-*re*-cha *right (direction)*
derechista ⑩&① de-re-*chees*-ta *right-wing*
derecho ⑩ de-*re*-cho *law (profession)*
derechos civiles ⑩ pl
de-*re*-chos see-*vee*-les *civil rights*
derechos humanos ⑩ pl
de-*re*-chos oo-*ma*-nos *human rights*
derrame ⑩ de-*ra*-me *stroke (health)*
desayuno ⑩ de-sa-*yoo*-no *breakfast*
descansar des-kan-*sar* *rest* v
descendiente ⑩ de-sen-*dyen*-te *descendent*
descompuesto/a ⑩/① des-kom-*pwes*-to/a *broken down (car, etc)*
desconocido/a ⑩/① des-ko-no-*see*-do/a *stranger*
descuento ⑩ des-*kwen*-to *discount*
desde *des*-de *from • since*
desear de-se-*ar* *wish* v
desechos nucleares ⑩ pl
de-*se*-chos noo-kle-*a*-res *nuclear waste*
desecho tóxico ⑩ de-*se*-cho tok-*see*-ko *toxic waste*
desempleado/a ⑩/① de-sem-ple-*a*-do/a *unemployed*
desfase de horario ⑩ des-*fa*-se de o-*ra*-ryo *jet lag*
desierto ⑩ de-*syer*-to *desert*
desodorante ⑩ de-so-do-*ran*-te *deodorant*
despacio des-*pa*-syo *slowly*
despertar des-per-*tar* *wake (someone) up*
después des-*pwes* *after*
destino ⑩ des-*tee*-no *destination*
detallado/a ⑩/① de-ta-*ya*-do/a *itemised*
detalles ⑩ pl de-*ta*-yes *details*
detrás de-*tras* *behind*
día ⑩ *dee*-a *day*
diabetes ① dee-a-*be*-tes *diabetes*
diafragma ⑩ dya-*frag*-ma *diaphragm (contraceptive)*
diapositivas ① pl dya-po-see-*tee*-vas *slide (film)*
diarrea ① dee-a-*re*-a *diarrhoea*
diccionario ⑩ deek-syo-*na*-ryo *dictionary*
diciembre ⑩ dee-*syem*-bre *December*
diente ⑩ *dyen*-te *tooth*
dientes ⑩ pl *dyen*-tes *teeth*
dieta ① *dye*-ta *diet*
diferencia de hora ① dee-fe-*ren*-sya de o-ra *time difference*
diferente ⑩&① dee-fe-*ren*-te *different*
difícil ⑩&① dee-*fee*-seel *difficult*
digital ⑩&① dee-khee-*tal* *digital*
diminuto/a ⑩/① dee-mee-*noo*-to/a *tiny*
dinero ⑩ dee-*ne*-ro *money*
dios ⑩ *dee*-os *god*

dirección ⓕ dee·rek·syon *address • direction*
directo/a ⓜ/ⓕ dee·rek·to/a *direct • express*
director(a) ⓜ/ⓕ dee·rek·tor/dee·rek·to·ra
 director • manager (sport)
discapacitado/a ⓜ/ⓕ
 dees·ka·pa·see·ta·do/a *a disabled*
 — visual vee·swal *visually impaired*
discriminación ⓕ dees·kree·mee·na·syon
 discrimination
diseño ⓜ dee·se·nyo *design*
disfrutar dees·froo·tar *enjoy (oneself)*
disparar dees·pa·rar *shoot* v
disponible ⓜ&ⓕ dees·po·nee·ble
 free (available)
disquete ⓜ dees·ke·te *disk (floppy)*
DIU ⓜ de ee oo *IUD*
divertido/a ⓜ/ⓕ dee·ver·tee·do/a *a fun*
divertirse dee·ver·teer·se *have fun*
divorciado/a ⓜ/ⓕ dee·vor·sya·do/a
 divorced
doble ⓜ&ⓕ do·ble *double*
docena ⓕ do·se·na *dozen*
doctor(a) ⓜ/ⓕ dok·tor/dok·to·ra *doctor*
documental ⓜ do·koo·men·tal
 documentary
dólar ⓜ do·lar *dollar*
doler do·ler *hurt (be painful)*
dolor ⓜ do·lor *pain*
 — de cabeza de ka·be·sa *headache*
 — de diente de dyen·te *toothache*
 — de estómago de es·to·ma·go
 stomachache
dolores menstruales ⓜ pl
 do·lo·res mens·trwa·les *period pain*
doloroso/a ⓜ/ⓕ do·lo·ro·so/a *painful*
domingo ⓜ do·meen·go *Sunday*
dónde don·de *where*
dormir dor·meer *sleep* v
dos dos *two*
 — veces ve·ses *twice*
drama ⓜ dra·ma *drama*
droga ⓕ dro·ga *drug (illicit)*
drogadicción ⓕ dro·ga·deek·syon
 drug addiction
drogadicto/a ⓜ/ⓕ dro·ga·deek·to/a
 drug user
ducha ⓕ doo·cha *shower (bath)*
dueño/a ⓜ/ⓕ dwe·nyo/a
 landlord/lady • owner
dulce ⓜ&ⓕ dool·se *sweet* a
dulces ⓜ pl dool·ses *sweets* n
duro/a ⓜ/ⓕ doo·ro/a
 hard (not soft) • hard-boiled (egg) • loud

E

eczema ⓜ ek·se·ma *eczema*
edad ⓕ e·dad *age*
edificio ⓜ e·dee·fee·syo *building*
educación ⓕ e·doo·ka·syon *education*
efectivo ⓜ e·fek·tee·vo *cash*
egoísta ⓜ&ⓕ e·go·ees·ta *selfish*
ejemplo ⓜ e·khem·plo *example*
ejército ⓜ e·kher·see·to *military*
él ⓜ el *he • him*
elección ⓕ e·lek·syon *election*
electricidad ⓕ e·lek·tree·see·dad *electricity*
electricista ⓜ&ⓕ e·lek·tree·sees·ta
 electrician
ella e·ya *her • she*
ellos/as ⓜ/ⓕ pl e·yos/as *them • they*
embajada ⓕ em·ba·kha·da *embassy*
embajador(a) ⓜ/ⓕ em·ba·kha·dor/
 em·ba·kha·do·ra *ambassador*
embarazada ⓕ em·ba·ra·sa·da *pregnant*
emergencia ⓕ e·mer·khen·sya *emergency*
emocional ⓜ&ⓕ e·mo·syo·nal *emotional*
empezar em·pe·sar *start* v
empinado/a ⓜ/ⓕ em·pee·na·do/a *steep*
empleado/a ⓜ/ⓕ em·ple·a·do/a *employee*
empleador(a) ⓜ/ⓕ
 em·ple·a·dor/em·ple·a·do·ra *employer*
empujar em·poo·khar *push* v
en en *at • in*
 — frente de fren·te de *in front of • opposite*
enagua ⓕ e·na·gwa *skirt*
encantador(a) ⓜ/ⓕ
 en·kan·ta·dor/en·kan·ta·do·ra *charming*
encendedor ⓜ en·sen·de·dor
 cigarette lighter
encendido/a ⓜ/ⓕ en·sen·dee·do/a
 on (power)
enchufe ⓜ en·choo·fe *plug (electricity)*
encías ⓕ pl en·see·as *gums (mouth)*
encontrar en·kon·trar *find*
encontrarse en·kon·trar·se
 meet (get together)
energía nuclear ⓕ e·ner·khee·a noo·kle·ar
 nuclear energy
enero ⓜ e·ne·ro *January*
enfadado/a ⓜ/ⓕ en·fa·da·do/a *angry*
enfermedad ⓕ en·fer·me·dad *disease*
 — del viajero del vya·khe·ro
 travel sickness
 — venérea ve·ne·re·a *venereal disease*
enfermero/a ⓜ/ⓕ en·fer·me·ro/a *nurse*
enfermo/a ⓜ/ⓕ en·fer·mo/a *ill*
enorme ⓜ&ⓕ e·nor·me *huge*

ensalada ① en·sa·*la*·da *salad*
enseñar en·se·*nyar* *show* v · *teach*
entender en·ten·*der* *understand*
entrada ① en·*tra*·da *cover charge* · *entry*
entrar en·*trar* *enter*
entre *en*·tre *between*
entrenador(a) ⑩/①
en·tre·na·*dor*/en·tre·na·*do*·ra *coach*
entrenar en·tre·*nar* *coach* v
entrevista ① en·tre·*vees*·ta *interview*
enviar en·*vyar* *deliver* · *mail* · *send*
equipaje ⑩ e·kee·*pa*·khe *luggage*
equipo ⑩ e·*kee*·po *equipment* · *team*
— **de buceo** de boo·*se*·o
diving equipment
— **de sonido** de so·*nee*·do *stereo*
equitación ① e·kee·ta·*syon* *horse riding*
equivocado/a ⑩/① e·kee·vo·*ka*·do/a *wrong*
error ⑩ e·*ror* *mistake*
escalada ① es·ka·*la*·da *rock climbing*
escalar es·ka·*lar* *climb* v
escalas sociales ① es·*ka*·las so·*sya*·les
class system
escaleras ① pl es·ka·*le*·ras *stairway*
escape ① es·*ka*·pe *exhaust (car)*
escarcha ① es·*kar*·cha *frost*
escasez ① es·ka·*ses* *shortage*
escoger es·ko·*kher* *choose*
escribir es·kree·*beer* *write*
escuchar es·koo·*char* *listen*
escuela ① es·*kwe*·la *school*
escultura ① es·kool·*too*·ra *sculpture*
ese/a ⑩/① e·se/a *that* a
esgrima ① es·*gree*·ma *fencing (sport)*
esguince ⑩ es·*geen*·se *sprain*
esnorclear es·nor·kle·*ar* *snorkelling*
espacio disponible ⑩
es·*pa*·syo dees·po·*nee*·ble *vacancy*
espalda ① es·*pal*·da *back (body)*
España ① es·*pa*·nya *Spain*
español es·pa·*nyol* *Spanish (language)*
especial ⑩&① es·pe·*syal* *special*
especialista ⑩&① es·pe·sya·*lees*·ta
specialist n&a
espectáculo ⑩ es·pek·*ta*·koo·lo *show*
espejo ⑩ es·*pe*·kho *mirror*
esperar es·pe·*rar* *wait* v
espiral para mosquitos ①
es·pee·*ral pa*·ra mos·*kee*·tos *mosquito coil*
esposa ① es·*po*·sa *wife*
esposo ⑩&① es·*po*·so *husband*
espuma de afeitar ①
es·*poo*·ma de a·*fay*·tar *shaving cream*
esquí ⑩ es·*kee* *skiing*
— **acuático** a·*kwa*·tee·ko *water-skiing*

esquiar es·*kyar* *ski*
esquina ① es·*kee*·na *corner*
esta noche *es*·ta no·che *tonight*
estación ① es·ta·*syon* *station*
— **de bus** de boos *bus station*
— **de policía** de po·lee·*see*·a *police station*
— **de tren** de tren *railway station*
estadio ⑩ es·*ta*·dyo *stadium*
estado civil ⑩ es·*ta*·do see·*veel*
marital status
Estados Unidos ⑩ pl es·*ta*·dos oo·*nee*·dos
USA
estallar es·ta·*yar* *puncture*
estampilla ① es·tam·*pee*·ya *stamp (postage)*
estar es·*tar* *be (temporary)*
— **de acuerdo** de a·*kwer*·do *agree*
— **resfriado** res·*free*·a·do *have a cold*
estatua ① es·*ta*·twa *statue*
este/a ⑩/① *es*·te/a *this* a
este ⑩ *es*·te *east*
estilista ⑩&① es·tee·*lees*·ta *beautician*
estilo ⑩ es·*tee*·lo *style*
estómago ⑩ es·*to*·ma·go *stomach*
estrella ① es·*tre*·ya *star*
estreñimiento ⑩ es·tre·nyee·*myen*·to
constipation
estuario ⑩ es·*twa*·ryo *estuary*
estudiante ⑩&① es·too·*dyan*·te *student*
estudio ⑩ es·*too*·dyo *studio*
estúpido/a ⑩/① es·*too*·pee·do/a *stupid*
etiqueta del equipaje ①
e·tee·*ke*·ta del e·kee·*pa*·khe *luggage tag*
eutanasia ① e·oo·ta·*na*·sya *euthanasia*
exactamente ek·sak·ta·*men*·te *exactly*
excelente ⑩&① ek·se·*len*·te *excellent*
exceso de equipaje ⑩
ek·*se*·so de e·kee·*pa*·khe *excess baggage*
excluido/a ⑩/① eks·kloo·ee·do/a *excluded*
exhibición ① ek·see·bee·*syon* *exhibition*
experiencia ① eks·pe·*ryen*·sya *experience*
— **laboral** la·bo·*ral* *work experience*
explotación ① eks·plo·ta·*syon* *exploitation*
éxtasis ⑩ eks·ta·sees *ecstasy (drug)*
extensión ① eks·ten·*syon* *extension (visa)*
extranjero/a ⑩/① eks·tran·*khe*·ro/a *foreign*
extrañar eks·tra·*nyar* *miss (feel absence of)*

F

fábrica ① *fa*·bree·ka *factory*
fácil ⑩&① *fa*·seel *easy*
faja del abanico ① *fa*·kha del a·ba·*nee*·ko
fanbelt
familia ① fa·*mee*·lya *family*
famoso/a ⑩/① fa·*mo*·so/a *famous*

fantástico fan·tas·tee·ko *great • fantastic*
farmacéutico/a ⓜ/① far·ma·se·oo·tee·ko/a *chemist • pharmacist*
farmacia ① far·ma·sya *pharmacy*
faul ⓜ *fa·ool foul (soccer)*
fax ⓜ faks *fax machine*
febrero ⓜ fe·bre·ro *February*
fecha ① fe·cha *date (day)*
— **de nacimiento** de na·see·myen·to *date of birth*
felicidades fe·lee·see·da·des *congratulations*
feliz ⓜ&① fe·lees *happy*
feriado ⓜ fe·ree·a·do *holiday*
ferretería ① fe·re·te·ree·a *hardware store*
ficción ① feek·syon *fiction*
fiebre ① fye·bre *fever*
— **del heno** del e·no *hay fever*
fiesta ① fyes·ta *festival • party (night out)*
fila ① fee·la *queue*
filtrado/a ⓜ/① feel·tra·do/a *filtered*
fin ⓜ feen *end*
— **de semana** de se·ma·na *weekend*
finca ① feen·ka *farm*
finquero/a ⓜ/① feen·ke·ro/a *farmer*
firma ① feer·ma *signature*
firmar feer·mar *sign (one's name)*
flash ⓜ flash *flash (camera)*
flauta ① fla·oo·ta *flute*
flojo/a ⓜ/① flo·kho/a *loose*
flor ① flor *flower*
flora y fauna ① flo·ra ee fow·na *wildlife*
floristería ① flo·rees·te·ree·a *florist (shop)*
foco ⓜ fo·ko *flashlight • torch*
focos ⓜ pl fo·kos *headlights*
fondo ⓜ fon·do *bottom (position)*
forma ① for·ma *shape • manner*
fósforos ⓜ pl fos·fo·ros *matches (lighting)*
foto ① fo·to *photo*
fotografía ① fo·to·gra·fee·a *photography*
fotografiar fo·to·gra·fyar *photograph*
fotógrafo/a ⓜ/① fo·to·gra·fo/a *photographer*
frágil ⓜ&① fra·kheel *fragile*
francés fran·ses *French (language)*
franela ① fra·ne·la *flannel (face cloth)*
franqueo ⓜ fran·ke·o *postage*
frasco ⓜ fras·ko *jar*
freír fre·eer *fry*
frenos ⓜ pl fre·nos *brakes*
fresco/a ⓜ/① fres·ko/a *cool • fresh*
frío/a ⓜ/① free·o/a *cold*
frito/a ⓜ/① free·to/a *fried*
frontera ① fron·te·ra *border (geographic)*
fruta ① froo·ta *fruit*
frutas secas ① pl froo·tas se·kas *dried fruit*

fuego ⓜ fwe·go *fire*
fuera de servicio fwe·ra de ser·vee·syo *out of order*
fuerte ⓜ&① fwer·te *strong*
fumar foo·mar *smoke* v
funcionar foon·syo·nar *work (function)*
funda ① foon·da *pillowcase*
funeral ⓜ foo·ne·ral *funeral*
fútbol ⓜ foot·bol *football • soccer*
futuro ⓜ foo·too·ro *future*

G

galería ① ga·le·ree·a *gallery*
galleta ① ga·ye·ta *biscuit (sweet) • cookie*
— **salada** sa·la·da *cracker*
ganador(a) ⓜ/① ga·na·dor/ga·na·do·ra *winner*
ganar ga·nar *earn • win*
garaje ⓜ ga·ra·khe *garage*
garantizado/a ⓜ/① ga·ran·tee·sa·do/a *guaranteed*
garganta ① gar·gan·ta *throat*
gas ⓜ gas *(cooking)*
gasa ① ga·sa *gauze*
gasolina ① ga·so·lee·na *gas • petrol*
gastritis ⓜ gas·tree·tees *gastroenteritis*
gato/a ⓜ/① ga·to/a *cat*
gay ⓜ&① gay *gay* n&a
gemelos/as ⓜ/① pl khe·me·los/as *twins*
gente ① khen·te *people*
gerente ⓜ&① khe·ren·te *manager (business)*
gimnasia ① kheem·na·sya *gymnastics*
gimnasio ⓜ kheem·na·syo *gym (place)*
ginebra ① khee·ne·bra *gin*
ginecólogo/a ⓜ/① khee·ne·ko·lo·go/a *gynaecologist*
gobierno ⓜ go·byer·no *government*
gol ⓜ gol *goal (sport)*
golpe ⓜ gol·pe *strike (hit)*
gordo/a ⓜ/① gor·do/a *fat*
gotas para los ojos ① pl go·tas pa·ra los o·khos *eye drops*
grabación ① gra·ba·syon *recording*
grabar gra·bar *record* v
grada ① gra·da *step*
gradas ① pl gra·das *escalator*
grados ⓜ pl gra·dos *degrees (temperature)*
gramo ⓜ gra·mo *gram*
grande ⓜ&① gran·de *big*
granola ① gra·no·la *muesli*
gratis ⓜ&① gra·tees *complimentary (free)*
gripe ① gree·pe *influenza*
gris ⓜ&① grees *grey*

gritar gree-*tar* shout
grueso/a ⓜ/ⓕ grwe-*so*/a thick
grupo ⓜ *groo*-po group
— **de rock** de rok rock group
— **musical** moo-see-*kal* band (music)
— **sanguíneo** san-gee-ne-o blood group
guantes ⓜ pl gwan-tes gloves
guapo/a ⓜ/ⓕ *gwa*-po/a handsome
guardaropa ⓜ gwar-da-ro-pa cloakroom
guarda rural ⓜ&ⓕ *gwar*-da roo-*ral*
police officer (country)
guerra ⓕ *ge*-ra war
guía ⓕ *gee*-a audio guide
— **de entretenimiento**
de en-tre-te-nee-*myen*-to
entertainment guide
— **telefónica** te-le-fo-nee-ka phone book
— **turística** too-*rees*-tee-ka guidebook
guía ⓜ&ⓕ *gee*-a guide (person)
guitarra ⓕ gee-*ta*-ra guitar
gustar goos-*tar* like v

H

habitación ⓕ a-bee-ta-*syon* room
— **sencilla** sen-*see*-ya single room
hablar ab-*lar* speak • talk
hace (tres días) a-se (tres *dee*-as)
(three days) ago
hacer a-*ser* do • make
hachís ⓜ a-*chees* hashish
hacia a-see-a towards
halal ⓜ&ⓕ a-*lal* halal
halar a-*lar* pull
hamaca ⓕ a-*ma*-ka hammock
hambriento/a ⓜ/ⓕ am-bree-*yen*-to/a
hungry
hasta as-ta until
hecho/a a mano ⓜ/ⓕ e-cho/a a *ma*-no
handmade
heladería ⓕ e-la-de-*ree*-a ice-cream parlour
helado ⓜ e-*la*-do ice cream
hembra ⓕ em-bra female
hepatitis ⓕ e-pa-*tee*-tees hepatitis
herida ⓕ e-*ree*-da injury
hermana ⓕ er-*ma*-na sister
hermano ⓜ er-*ma*-no brother
heroína ⓕ e-ro-*ee*-na heroin
herpes ⓜ er-pes shingles (illness)
hervido/a ⓜ/ⓕ er-*vee*-do/a boiled
hielo ⓜ *ye*-lo ice
hierba ⓕ *yer*-ba dope (drugs) • herb
hierbero/a ⓜ/ⓕ yer-be-ro/a herbalist
hija ⓕ ee-*kha* daughter
hijo ⓜ *ee*-kho son

hilo ⓜ *ee*-lo string • thread
— **dental** den-*tal* dental floss
hinchazón ⓕ een-cha-*son* swelling
hindú ⓜ&ⓕ een-*doo* Hindu n&a
historia ⓕ ees-*to*-rya history
histórico/a ⓜ/ⓕ ees-to-ree-ko/a historical
hogar ⓜ o-*gar* home
hoja ⓕ o-*kha* leaf
hombre ⓜ om-bre man
— **de negocios** de ne-*go*-syos
businessman
hombro ⓜ om-bro shoulder
homeopatía ⓕ o-me-o-pa-*tee*-a
homeopathy
homosexual ⓜ&ⓕ o-mo-sek-*swal*
homosexual n&a
hondo/a ⓜ/ⓕ on-do/a deep
hora ⓕ o-ra hour
horario ⓜ o-*ra*-ryo opening hours
hormiga ⓕ or-*mee*-ga ant
horno ⓜ or-no oven
— **microondas** mee-kro-on-das
microwave oven
horóscopo ⓜ o-*ros*-ko-po horoscope
horrible ⓜ&ⓕ o-*ree*-ble awful
hospital ⓜ os-pee-*tal* hospital
hospitalidad ⓕ os-pee-ta-lee-*dad* hospitality
hotel ⓜ o-*tel* hotel
hoy oy today
huelga ⓕ *wel*-ga strike (stoppage)
hueso ⓜ we-so bone
huevo ⓜ *we*-vo egg
humanidades ⓕ pl oo-ma-nee-*da*-des
humanities
humectante ⓜ oo-mek-*tan*-te moisturiser

I

identificación ⓕ ee-den-tee-fee-ka-*syon*
identification
idioma ⓜ ee-*dyo*-ma language
idiota ⓜ&ⓕ ee-*dyo*-ta idiot
iglesia ⓕ ee-*gle*-sya church
igualdad ⓕ ee-gwal-*dad* equality
— **de oportunidades**
de o-por-too-nee-*da*-des equal opportunity
importante ⓜ&ⓕ eem-por-*tan*-te
important
imposible ⓜ&ⓕ eem-po-*see*-ble impossible
impresora ⓕ eem-pre-*so*-ra
printer (computer)
impuesto ⓜ eem-*pwes*-to tax
— **de salida** de sa-*lee*-da airport tax
— **de ventas** de *ven*-tas sales tax
incluido/a ⓜ/ⓕ een-kloo-*ee*-do/a included

incómodo/a ⓜ/ⓕ een·ko·mo·do/a
uncomfortable
indicador ⓜ een·dee·ka·dor *indicator*
indigente ⓜ&ⓕ een·dee·khen·te
homeless n&a
indigestión ⓕ een·dee·khes·tyon
indigestion
industria ⓕ een·doos·tree·a *industry*
infección ⓕ een·fek·syon *infection*
— **urinaria** oo·ree·na·rya *urinary infection*
inflamación ⓕ een·fla·ma·syon
inflammation
información ⓕ een·for·ma·syon *information*
informática ⓕ een·for·ma·tee·ka *IT*
ingeniería ⓕ een·khe·nye·ree·a *engineering*
ingeniero/a ⓜ/ⓕ een·khe·nye·ro/a *engineer*
Inglaterra ⓕ een·gla·te·ra *England*
inglés een·gles *English (language)*
ingrediente ⓜ een·gre·dyen·te *ingredient*
inicio ⓜ ee·nee·syo *start*
injusto/a ⓜ/ⓕ een·khoos·to/a *unfair*
inocente ⓜ&ⓕ e·no·sen·te *innocent*
insecto ⓜ een·sek·to *insect*
inseguro/a ⓜ/ⓕ een·se·goo·ro/a *unsafe*
insolación ⓕ een·so·la·syon *sunstroke*
instructor(a) ⓜ/ⓕ
eens·trook·tor/eens·trook·to·ra *instructor*
interesante ⓜ&ⓕ een·te·re·san·te
interesting
intermedio ⓜ een·ter·me·dyo *intermission*
internacional ⓜ&ⓕ een·ter·na·syo·nal
international
intérprete ⓜ&ⓕ een·ter·pre·te *interpreter*
inundación ⓕ ee·noon·da·syon *flood*
invierno ⓜ een·vyer·no *winter*
invitar een·vee·tar *invite* v
inyección ⓕ een·yek·syon *injection*
inyectar een·yek·tar *inject*
ir eer *go*
— **de compras** de kom·pras *go shopping*
isla ⓕ ees·la *island*
itinerario ⓜ ee·tee·ne·ra·ryo *timetable*
izquierda ⓕ ees·kyer·da *left (direction)*
izquierdista ⓜ&ⓕ ees·kyer·dees·ta
left-wing

J

jabón ⓜ kha·bon *soap*
jarabe para la tos ⓜ kha·ra·be pa·ra la tos
cough medicine
jardín ⓜ khar·deen *garden*
— **botánico** bo·ta·nee·ko *botanic garden*
jardinería ⓕ khar·dee·ne·ree·a *gardening*
jardinero/a ⓜ/ⓕ khar·dee·ne·ro/a *gardener*

jardines públicos ⓜ pl
khar·dee·nes poo·blee·kos *public gardens*
jeringa ⓕ khe·reen·ga *syringe*
joven ⓜ&ⓕ kho·ven *young*
joyas ⓕ pl kho·yas *jewellery*
judío/a ⓜ/ⓕ khoo·dee·o/a *Jewish*
juego de computadora ⓜ khwe·go de
kom·poo·ta·do·ra *computer game*
Juegos Olímpicos ⓜ pl
khwe·gos o·leem·pee·kos *Olympic Games*
jueves ⓜ khwe·ves *Thursday*
juez(a) ⓜ/ⓕ khwes/khwe·sa *judge*
jugar khoo·gar *play (cards, etc)*
jugo ⓜ khoo·go *juice*
juguetería ⓕ khoo·ge·te·ree·a *toy shop*
julio ⓜ khoo·lyo *July*
junio ⓜ khoo·nyo *June*
junto a khoon·to a *beside • next to*
juntos/as ⓜ/ⓕ pl khoon·tos/as *together*

K

kilogramo ⓜ kee·lo·gra·mo *kilogram*
kilómetro ⓜ kee·lo·me·tro *kilometre*
kínder ⓜ keen·der *kindergarten*
klínex ⓜ klee·neks *tissues*
kosher ⓜ&ⓕ ko·sher *kosher*

L

labios ⓜ pl la·byos *lips*
lado ⓜ la·do *side*
ladrón(a) ⓜ/ⓕ la·dron/la·dro·na *thief*
lagartija ⓕ la·gar·tee·kha *lizard*
lago ⓜ la·go *lake*
lana ⓕ la·na *wool*
lancha ⓕ lan·cha *motorboat*
lapicero ⓜ la·pee·se·ro *ballpoint pen*
lápiz ⓜ la·pees *pencil*
largo/a ⓜ/ⓕ lar·go/a *long*
lastimado/a ⓜ/ⓕ las·tee·ma·do/a *injured*
lastimar las·tee·mar *hurt (cause pain)*
lata ⓕ la·ta *can • tin*
lavadora ⓕ la·va·do·ra *washing machine*
lavandería ⓕ la·van·de·ree·a
launderette • laundry (place)
lavar la·var *wash (something)*
lavarse la·var·se *wash (oneself)*
laxante ⓜ lak·san·te *laxative*
leche ⓕ le·che *milk*
lectura ⓕ lek·too·ra *reading*
leer le·er *read*
legal ⓜ&ⓕ le·gal *legal*
legislación ⓕ le·khees·la·syon *legislation*

lejos *le·*khos *far (away)*
lentes de contacto ⓜ pl
 *len·*tes de kon·*tak·*to *contact lenses*
lente zoom ⓜ *len·*te soom *zoom lens*
lento/a ⓜ/ⓕ *len·*to/a *slow*
leña ⓕ *le·*nya *firewood*
lesbiana ⓕ les·*bya·*na *lesbian* n&a
ley ⓕ lay *law (legislation)*
libra ⓕ *lee·*bra *pound (currency/weight)*
libre ⓜ&ⓕ *lee·*bre *free (not bound)*
librería ⓕ lee·bre·*ree·*a *book shop • stationer*
libro ⓜ *lee·*bro *book*
 — de frases de *fra·*ses *phrasebook*
 — de oraciones de o·ra·*syo·*nes
 prayer book
licencia ⓕ lee·*sen·*sya *licence*
 — de conductor de kon·*dook·*tor
 driving licence
licorera ⓕ lee·ko·*re·*ra
 bottle shop • liquor store
líder ⓜ *lee·*der *leader*
ligar lee·*gar chat up (flirt)*
límite de equipaje ⓜ *lee·*mee·te de
 e·kee·*pa·*khe *baggage allowance*
límite de velocidad ⓜ
 *lee·*mee·te de ve·lo·see·*dad speed limit*
limonada ⓕ lee·mo·*na·*da *lemonade*
limpiar leem·*pyar clean* v
limpieza ⓕ leem·*pye·*sa *cleaning*
limpio/a ⓜ/ⓕ *leem·*pyo/a *clean*
lino ⓜ *lee·*no *linen (material)*
listo/a ⓜ/ⓕ *lees·*to/a *ready*
litera ⓕ lee·*te·*ra *sleeping berth*
liviano/a ⓜ/ⓕ lee·*vya·*no/a *a light (weight)*
llamada a cobrar ⓕ ya·*ma·*da a ko·*brar
 collect call
llamar ya·*mar call* v • *telephone* v
llanta ⓕ *yan·*ta *tire • tyre*
llanuras ⓕ pl ya·*noo·*ras *tropical plains*
llave ⓕ *ya·*ve *key (door etc)*
llegadas ⓕ pl ye·*ga·*das *arrivals (airport)*
llegar ye·*gar arrive*
llenar ye·*nar fill*
lleno/a ⓜ/ⓕ *ye·*no/a *full*
 — de gente de khen·te *crowded*
llevar ye·*var carry • take*
lluvia ⓕ *yoo·*vya *rain*
local ⓜ&ⓕ lo·*kal local*
loco/a ⓜ/ⓕ *lo·*ko/a *crazy*
loma ⓕ *lo·*ma *hill*
lombrices ⓕ pl lom·*bree·*ses
 intestinal worms
loro/a ⓜ/ⓕ *lo·*ro/a *parrot*
lubricante ⓜ loo·bree·*kan·*te *lubricant*
lucrar loo·*krar profit* v

lugar ⓜ loo·*gar place • venue*
 — de nacimiento de na·see·*myen·*to
 place of birth
lujoso/a ⓜ/ⓕ loo·*kho·*so/a *luxury*
luna ⓕ *loo·*na *moon*
 — de miel de myel *honeymoon*
lunes ⓜ *loo·*nes *Monday*
luz ⓕ lus *light*

M

macrobiótica ⓕ ma·kro·*byo·*tee·ka
 health-food store
madera ⓕ ma·*de·*ra *wood*
madre ⓕ *ma·*dre *mother*
maestro/a ⓜ/ⓕ ma·*es·*tro/a *teacher*
malaria ⓕ ma·*la·*rya *malaria*
maleta ⓕ ma·*le·*ta *suitcase*
malo/a ⓜ/ⓕ *ma·*lo/a *bad • off (spoilt)*
mamografía ⓕ ma·mo·gra·*fee·*a
 mammogram
mandar man·*dar send*
mandíbula ⓕ man·*dee·*boo·la *jaw*
manglar ⓜ man·*glar mangrove*
manifestación ⓕ ma·nee·fes·ta·*syon*
 demonstration (rally)
manillar ⓜ ma·nee·*yar handlebars*
mano ⓕ *ma·*no *hand*
mantel ⓜ man·*tel tablecloth*
mañana ⓕ ma·*nya·*na *morning*
mañana ma·*nya·*na *tomorrow*
mapa ⓜ *ma·*pa *map*
 — de calles de *ka·*yes *road map*
maquillaje ⓜ ma·kee·*ya·*khe *make-up*
máquina ⓕ *ma·*kee·na *machine*
 — de tiquetes de tee·*ke·*tes
 ticket machine
mar ⓜ mar *sea*
maravilloso/a ⓜ/ⓕ ma·ra·vee·*yo·*so/a
 wonderful
marcación directa ⓕ mar·ka·*syon*
 dee·*rek·*ta *direct-dial*
marcador ⓜ mar·ka·*dor scoreboard*
marcapasos ⓜ mar·ka·*pa·*sos *pacemaker*
Mar Caribe ⓜ mar ka·*ree·*be *Caribbean Sea*
marea ⓕ ma·*re·*a *tide*
mareado/a ⓜ/ⓕ ma·re·*a·*do/a
 dizzy • seasick
margarina ⓕ mar·ga·*ree·*na *margarine*
marihuana ⓕ ma·ree·*wa·*na *marijuana*
mariposa ⓕ ma·ree·*po·*sa *butterfly*
martes ⓜ *mar·*tes *Tuesday*
martillo ⓜ mar·*tee·*yo *hammer*
marzo ⓜ *mar·*so *March*

más mas *more*
— **cerca** *ser*·ka *closer*
— **grande** ⓜ&ⓕ *gran*·de *bigger*
— **pequeño/a** ⓜ/ⓕ pe·ke·nyo/a *smaller*
— **tarde** *tar*·de *later*
masaje ⓜ ma·*sa*·khe *massage*
masajeador ⓜ ma·sa·khe·a·*dor* *masseur*
masajeadora ⓕ ma·sa·khe·a·*do*·ra *masseuse*
mascara ⓕ mas·*ka*·ra *goggles (diving)*
mascarilla ⓕ mas·ka·*ree*·ya *goggles (swimming)*
mata ⓕ *ma*·ta *plant*
matrimonio ⓜ ma·tree·*mo*·nyo *marriage*
mayo ⓜ *ma*·yo *May*
mecánico/a ⓜ/ⓕ me·*ka*·nee·ko/a *mechanic*
medianoche ⓕ me·dya·no·che *midnight*
medias ⓕ pl *me*·dyas *socks*
medicamento ⓜ me·dee·ka·*men*·to *medication*
medicina ⓕ me·dee·*see*·na *medicine (profession)*
medidor de luz ⓜ me·dee·*dor* de lus *light meter*
medio ⓜ *me*·dyo *half*
— **ambiente** am·*byen*·te *environment*
mediodía ⓜ me·dyo·*dee*·a *midday • noon*
medios ⓜ pl *me*·dyos *media*
meditación ⓕ me·dee·ta·*syon* *meditation*
mejor me·*khor* *better*
melodía ⓕ me·lo·*dee*·a *tune*
mendigo/a ⓜ/ⓕ men·*dee*·go/a *beggar*
menos *me*·nos *less*
mensaje ⓜ men·*sa*·khe *message*
mentir men·*teer* *lie (not tell the truth)*
mentiroso/a ⓜ/ⓕ men·tee·ro·so/a *liar*
menú ⓜ me·*noo* *menu*
menudo ⓜ me·*noo*·do *loose change*
mercado ⓜ mer·*ka*·do *market*
— **callejero** ka·ye·*khe*·ro *street market*
— **de pulgas** de *pool*·gas *fleamarket*
— **negro** *ne*·gro *black market*
merienda ⓕ me·*ryen*·da *snack*
mes ⓜ mes *month*
mesa ⓕ *me*·sa *table*
mesero/a ⓜ/ⓕ me·*se*·ro/a *waiter*
meseta ⓕ me·*se*·ta *plateau*
meta ⓕ *me*·ta *finish*
metal ⓜ me·*tal* *metal*
metro ⓜ *me*·tro *metre*
mezclar mes·*klar* *mix*
mezquita ⓕ mes·*kee*·ta *mosque*
mi mee *my*
mí mee *me*
miembro/a ⓜ/ⓕ *myem*·bro/a *member*
miércoles ⓜ *myer*·ko·les *Wednesday*

migración ⓕ mee·gra·*syon* *immigration*
migraña ⓕ mee·*gra*·nya *migraine*
milímetro ⓜ mee·*lee*·me·tro *millimetre*
millón ⓜ mee·*yon* *million*
minuto ⓜ mee·*noo*·to *minute*
mirador ⓜ mee·ra·*dor* *lookout*
misa ⓕ *mee*·sa *mass (Catholic)*
mismo/a ⓜ/ⓕ *mees*·mo/a *same*
mitad ⓕ mee·*tad* *half*
mochila ⓕ mo·*chee*·la *backpack*
moda ⓕ *mo*·da *fashion*
módem ⓜ *mo*·dem *modem*
moderno/a ⓜ/ⓕ mo·der·no/a *modern*
mojado/a ⓜ/ⓕ mo·*kha*·do/a *wet*
monasterio ⓜ mo·nas·*te*·ryo *monastery*
monedas ⓕ pl mo·*ne*·das *coins*
monja ⓕ *mon*·kha *nun*
monje ⓜ *mon*·khe *monk*
mono ⓜ *mo*·no *monkey*
mononucleosis ⓕ mo·no·noo·kle·*o*·sees *glandular fever*
montaña ⓕ mon·*ta*·nya *mountain*
montañismo ⓜ mon·ta·*nyees*·mo *mountaineering*
montura ⓕ mon·*too*·ra *saddle*
monumento ⓜ mo·noo·*men*·to *monument*
moquera ⓕ mo·*ke*·ra *runny nose*
morado/a ⓜ/ⓕ mo·*ra*·do/a *purple*
mordida ⓕ mor·*dee*·da *bite (dog)*
moretón ⓜ mo·re·*ton* *bruise*
morir mo·*reer* *die*
mosca ⓕ *mos*·ka *fly*
mosquitero ⓜ mos·kee·*te*·ro *mosquito net*
mota ⓕ *mo*·ta *dope (drugs)*
motel ⓜ mo·*tel* *motel*
moto ⓕ *mo*·to *motorbike*
motor ⓜ mo·*tor* *engine*
mucho/a ⓜ/ⓕ *moo*·cho/a *(a) lot • much*
muchos/as ⓜ/ⓕ pl *moo*·chos/as *many*
mudo/a ⓜ/ⓕ *moo*·do/a *mute*
muebles ⓜ pl *mwe*·bles *furniture*
muerto/a ⓜ/ⓕ *mwer*·to/a *dead*
mujer ⓕ moo·*kher* *woman*
— **de negocios** de ne·*go*·syos *businesswoman*
multa ⓕ *mool*·ta *fine (payment)*
Mundial ⓜ moon·*dyal* *World Cup*
mundo ⓜ *moon*·do *world*
muñeca ⓕ moo·*nye*·ka *doll • wrist*
músculo ⓜ *moos*·koo·lo *muscle*
museo ⓜ moo·*se*·o *museum*
música ⓕ *moo*·see·ka *music*
músico/a ⓜ/ⓕ *moo*·see·ko/a *musician*

musulmán/musulmana ⓜ/ⓕ
moo·sool·*man*/moo·sool·*ma*·na
Muslim n&a
muy mooy *very*

N

nacionalidad ⓕ na·syo·na·lee·*dad*
nationality
nada *na*·da *nothing*
nadar na·*dar* *swim*
nado ⓜ *na*·do *swimming*
naipes ⓜ pl *nai*·pes *cards (playing)*
narcotraficante ⓜ&ⓕ nar·ko·tra·fee·*kan*·te
drug dealer
narcotráfico ⓜ nar·ko·*tra*·fee·ko
drug trafficking
nariz ⓕ na·*rees* *nose*
naturaleza ⓕ na·too·ra·*le*·sa *nature*
náuseas ⓕ pl *now*·se·as *nausea*
navaja ⓕ na·*va*·kha *penknife*
navajilla ⓕ na·va·*khee*·ya *razor blade*
Navidad ⓕ na·vee·*dad* *Christmas*
necesario/a ⓜ/ⓕ ne·se·*sa*·ryo/a *necessary*
necesitar ne·se·see·*tar* *need* v
negar ne·*gar* *refuse* v
negativo/a ⓜ/ⓕ ne·ga·*tee*·vo/a *negative*
negativos ⓜ pl ne·ga·*tee*·vos
negatives (photos)
negocio ⓜ ne·*go*·syo *business*
negro/a ⓜ/ⓕ *ne*·gro/a *black*
neumático ⓜ ne·oo·*ma*·tee·ko *tube (tyre)*
neuropatía ⓕ ne·oo·ro·pa·*tee*·a *naturopathy*
nieto/a ⓜ/ⓕ *nye*·to/a *grandchild*
nieve ⓕ *nye*·ve *snow*
ninguno/a ⓜ/ⓕ neen·*goo*·no/a
neither · none
niñera ⓕ nee·*nye*·ra *babysitter*
niño/a ⓜ/ⓕ *nee*·nyo/a *child*
niños/as ⓜ/ⓕ pl *nee*·nyos/as *children*
no no *no · not*
— **fumado** foo·*ma*·do *nonsmoking*
noche ⓕ *no*·che *evening · night*
nombre ⓜ *nom*·bre *name*
— **cristiano** krees·*tya*·no *given name*
norte ⓜ *nor*·te *north*
nosotros/as ⓜ/ⓕ pl no·*so*·tros/as *we*
nostálgico/a ⓜ/ⓕ nos·*tal*·khee·ko/a
homesick
noticias ⓕ pl no·*tee*·syas *news*
novela ⓕ no·*ve*·la *soap opera*
novia ⓕ *no*·vya *girlfriend*
noviembre ⓜ no·*vyem*·bre *November*
novio ⓜ *no*·vyo *boyfriend*
nube ⓕ *noo*·be *cloud*

nublado/a ⓜ/ⓕ noo·*bla*·do/a *cloudy*
nuestro/a ⓜ/ⓕ *nwes*·tro/a *our*
nuevo/a ⓜ/ⓕ *nwe*·vo/a *new*
número ⓜ *noo*·me·ro *number*
— **de habitación** de a·bee·ta·*syon*
room number
— **de pasaporte** de pa·sa·*por*·te
passport number
— **de placa** de *pla*·ka *license plate number*
nunca *noon*·ka *never*

O

o o *or*
objetivo ⓜ ob·khe·*tee*·vo *lens (camera)*
obra de teatro ⓕ *o*·bra de te·*a*·tro
play (theatre)
observar ob·ser·*var* *watch* v
obtener ob·te·*ner* *get*
océano ⓜ o·*se*·a·no *ocean*
Océano Atlántico ⓜ o·se·*a*·no at·*lan*·tee·ko
Atlantic Ocean
Océano Pacífico ⓜ o·se·*a*·no pa·*see*·fee·ko
Pacific Ocean
octubre ⓜ ok·*too*·bre *October*
ocupado/a ⓜ/ⓕ o·koo·*pa*·do/a
busy · engaged (phone)
oeste ⓜ o·*es*·te *west*
oficina ⓕ o·fee·*see*·na *office*
— **de objetos perdidos** de ob·*khe*·tos
per·*dee*·dos *lost-property office*
— **de turismo** de too·*rees*·mo *tourist office*
oír o·*eer* *hear*
ojos ⓜ pl *o*·khos *eyes*
ola ⓕ *o*·la *wave (beach)*
olla ⓕ *o*·ya *pot · saucepan*
olor ⓜ o·*lor* *smell*
olvidar ol·vee·*dar* *forget*
operación ⓕ o·pe·ra·*syon*
operation (medical)
operador/a ⓜ/ⓕ o·pe·ra·*dor*/o·pe·ra·*do*·ra
telephone operator
opinión ⓕ o·pee·*nyon* *opinion*
oportunidad ⓕ o·por·too·nee·*dad* *chance*
optometrista ⓜ&ⓕ op·to·me·*trees*·ta
optometrist
opuesto o·*pwes*·to *opposite*
oración ⓕ o·ra·*syon* *prayer*
orden ⓕ *or*·den *command · order*
ordenar or·de·*nar* *order* v
ordinario/a ⓜ/ⓕ or·dee·*na*·ryo/a *ordinary*
oreja ⓕ o·*re*·kha *ear*
orgasmo ⓜ or·*gas*·mo *orgasm*
original ⓜ&ⓕ o·ree·khee·*nal* *original*
oro ⓜ *o*·ro *gold*

orquesta ① or·kes·ta orchestra
oscuro/a ⑩/① os·koo·ro/a
  dark (colour/night)
otoño ⑩ o·to·nyo autumn · fall
otra vez o·tra ves again
otro/a ⑩/① o·tro/a another · other
ovario ⑩ o·va·ryo ovary
oveja ① o·ve·kha sheep
oxígeno ⑩ ok·see·khe·no oxygen

P

padre ⑩ pa·dre father
pagar pa·gar pay
página ① pa·khee·na page
pago ⑩ pa·go payment
país ⑩ pa·ees country
pájaro ⑩ pa·kha·ro bird
palabra ① pa·la·bra word
palacio ⑩ pa·la·syo palace
palillo de dientes ⑩ pa·lee·yo de dyen·tes
  toothpick
palillos chinos ⑩ pl pa·lee·yos chee·nos
  chopsticks
pan ⑩ pan bread
panadería ① pa·na·de·ree·a bakery
pancito ⑩ pan·see·to biscuit (savoury)
panfleto ⑩ pan·fle·to brochure
pantalones ⑩ pl pan·ta·lo·nes trousers
pañal ⑩ pa·nyal diaper · nappy
paño ⑩ pa·nyo towel
  — para la cara pa·ra la ka·ra face cloth
pañuelo ⑩ pa·nywe·lo handkerchief
papá ⑩ pa·pa dad
papanicolau ⑩ pa·pa·nee·ko·low pap smear
papás ⑩ pl pa·pas parents
papel ⑩ pa·pel paper
  — higiénico ee·khye·nee·ko toilet paper
papeleo ⑩ pa·pe·le·o paperwork
paperas ① pl pa·pe·ras mumps
paquete ⑩ pa·ke·te package · packet
para pa·ra for
  — siempre syem·pre forever
parabrisas ⑩ pa·ra·bree·sas windscreen
parada ① pa·ra·da stop (bus, tram)
  — de bus de boos bus stop
  — de taxis de tak·sees taxi stand
parapléjico/a ⑩/① pa·ra·ple·khee·ko/a
  paraplegic
parar pa·rar stop (cease)
parcela ① par·se·la parcel
pared ① pa·red wall
pareja ① pa·re·kha couple · pair
parlamento ⑩ par·la·men·to parliament
parque ⑩ par·ke park
  — nacional na·syo·nal national park

parquear par·ke·ar park (vehicle) v
parqueo ⑩ par·ke·o car park
parte ① par·te part (component)
partidario/a ⑩/① par·tee·da·ryo/a
  supporter (politics)
partido ⑩ par·tee·do
  game (sport) · match · party (politics)
partir ⑩ par·teer depart
pasado ⑩ pa·sa·do past
  — mañana ma·nya·na day after tomorrow
pasado/a ⑩/① pa·sa·do/a last (previous)
pasajero/a ⑩/① pa·sa·khe·ro/a a passenger
pasaporte ⑩ pa·sa·por·te passport
pasar pa·sar pass v
Pascua ① pas·kwa Easter
pasillo ⑩ pa·see·yo aisle (on plane)
pasta de dientes ① pas·ta de dyen·tes
  toothpaste
pastel ⑩ pas·tel pastry · pie
pastelería ① pas·te·le·ree·a cake shop
pastilla ① pas·tee·ya pill
  — anticonceptiva an·tee·kon·sep·tee·va
  the pill (contraceptive)
  — para el dolor pa·ra el do·lor painkiller
pastillas para dormir ① pl
  pas·tee·yas pa·ra dor·meer sleeping pills
patear pa·te·ar kick v
patinar pa·tee·nar skate v
paz ① pas peace
peatón ⑩ pe·a·ton pedestrian
pecho ⑩ pe·cho breast · chest
pedal ⑩ pe·dal pedal
pedazo ⑩ pe·da·so piece
pedido ⑩ pe·dee·do order (food)
pedir pe·deer ask (for something)
  — prestado pres·ta·do borrow
  — un aventón oon a·ven·ton hitchhike
pegamento ⑩ pe·ga·men·to glue
peine ⑩ pay·ne comb
pelea ① pe·le·a fight
película ① pe·lee·koo·la film (cinema)
peligroso/a ⑩/① pe·lee·gro·so/a dangerous
pelo ⑩ pe·lo hair
peluquero/a ⑩/① pe·loo·ke·ro/a hairdresser
pene ⑩ pe·ne penis
pensar pen·sar think
pensión ① pen·syon guesthouse
pensionado/a ⑩/① pen·syo·na·do/a
  pensioner
pequeño/a ⑩/① pe·ke·nyo/a small
perder per·der lose · miss
perdido/a ⑩/① per·dee·do/a lost
perdonar per·do·nar forgive
perezoso/a ⑩/① pe·re·so·so/a lazy
perfecto/a ⑩/① per·fek·to/a perfect

perfume m per·*foo*·me *perfume*
periódico m pe·*ryo*·dee·a *newspaper*
periodista m&f pe·ree·o·dees·ta *journalist*
permiso m per·*mee*·so *permission • permit*
— **de trabajo** de tra·ba·kho *work permit*
pero *pe*·ro *but*
perro/a m pe·ro/a *dog*
— **guía** *gee*·a *guide dog*
persona f per·*so*·na *person*
pesado/a m/f pe·*sa*·do/a *heavy*
pesar pe·*sar* *weigh*
pesas f pl *pe*·sas *weights*
pesca f *pes*·ka *fishing*
pescado m pes·*ka*·do *fish (meat)*
peso m *pe*·so *weight*
petición f pe·tee·*syon* *petition*
petróleo m pe·*tro*·le·o *oil (petrol)*
pez m pes *fish (animal)*
picada f pee·*ka*·da *bite (insect)*
picadillo m pee·ka·*dee*·yo *mince*
picazón f pee·ka·*son* *itch*
pico m *pee*·ko *pickaxe*
pie m pye *foot*
piedra f *pye*·dra *rock • stone*
piel f pyel *skin*
pierna f *pyer*·na *leg (body)*
pijiado/a m/f pee·*khya*·do/a *stoned (drugged)*
pimienta f pee·*myen*·ta *pepper (spice)*
pintor(a) m/f peen·*tor*/peen·*to*·ra *painter*
pintura f peen·*too*·ra *painting*
— **de labios** de *la*·byos *lipstick*
pinzas f pl *peen*·sas *tweezers*
piojos m pl *pyo*·khos *lice*
piscina f pee·*see*·na *swimming pool*
piso m *pee*·so *floor (storey)*
pista f *pees*·ta *racetrack*
pistola f pees·*to*·la *gun*
placa f *pla*·ka *numberplate*
plancha f *plan*·cha *iron (for clothes)*
planeta m pla·*ne*·ta *planet*
plano/a m/f *pla*·no/a *flat*
plástico m *plas*·tee·ko *plastic*
plata f *pla*·ta *silver*
plataforma f pla·ta·*for*·ma *platform*
plato m *pla*·to *dish (food) • plate*
— **hondo** *on*·do *bowl*
playa f *pla*·ya *beach*
plaza f *pla*·sa *square (town)*
plomero m plo·*me*·ro *plumber*
pobre m&f *po*·bre *poor*
pobreza f po·*bre*·sa *poverty*
poco/a m/f *po*·ko/a *few • little (quantity)*
poder m po·*der* *power*
poder po·*der* *can (be able/have permission)*

podrido/a m/f po·*dree*·do/a *spoilt (food)*
poesía f po·e·*see*·a *poetry*
polen m *po*·len *pollen*
policía f po·lee·*see*·a *police*
policía m&f po·lee·*see*·a *police officer (city)*
política f po·*lee*·tee·ka *policy • politics*
político m po·*lee*·tee·ko *politician*
político/a m/f po·*lee*·tee·ko/a *political*
polvo m *pol*·vo *powder*
poner po·*ner* *put*
ponerse po·*ner*·se *wear*
popular m&f po·poo·*lar* *popular*
por por *for*
— **a noche** a *no*·che *overnight*
— **qué** ke *why*
porcentaje m por·sen·*ta*·khe *per cent*
porque *por*·ke *because*
portero m por·*te*·ro *goalkeeper*
posible m&f po·*see*·ble *possible*
positivo/a m/f po·see·*tee*·vo/a *positive*
postal f pos·*tal* *postcard*
póster m *pos*·ter *poster*
postre m *pos*·tre *dessert*
precio m *pre*·syo *price*
precipicio m pre·see·*pee*·syo *cliff*
preferir pre·fe·*reer* *prefer*
pregunta f pre·*goon*·ta *question*
preguntar pre·goon·*tar* *ask (a question)*
preocupado/a m/f pre·o·koo·*pa*·do/a *worried*
preparar pre·pa·*rar* *prepare*
presentación f pre·sen·ta·*syon* *performance*
presente m pre·*sen*·te *present (time)*
preservativo m pre·ser·va·*tee*·vo *condom*
presidente m&f pre·see·*den*·te *president*
presión f pre·*syon* *pressure (tyre)*
— **sanguínea** san·*gee*·ne·a *blood pressure*
presupuesto m pre·soo·*pwes*·to *budget*
prevenir pre·ve·*neer* *stop (prevent)*
primavera f pree·ma·*ve*·ra *spring (season)*
primera clase f pree·*me*·ra *kla*·se *first class*
primer(a) ministro/a m/f pree·*mer*
mee·*nees*·tro/pree·*me*·ra mee·*nees*·tra
prime minister
primero/a m/f pree·*me*·ro/a *first*
primeros auxilios m pl
pree·*me*·ros owk·*see*·lyos *first-aid kit*
principal m&f preen·see·*pal* *main*
privado/a m/f pree·va·do/a *private*
producir pro·doo·*seer* *produce* v
programa m pro·*gra*·ma *program* v
prometer pro·me·*ter* *promise*
prometido/a m/f pro·me·*tee*·do/a *fiancé/fiancée*

promoción ① pro·mo·*syon* sale
pronto ⓜ *pron*·to soon
propina ① pro·*pee*·na tip (gratuity)
prostituto/a ⓜ/① pros·tee·*too*·to/a
  prostitute
protectores ⓜ pl pro·tek·*to*·res panty liners
proteger pro·te·*kher* protect
protegido/a ⓜ/① pro·te·*khee*·do/a
  protected
protesta ① pro·*tes*·ta protest
protestar pro·tes·*tar* protest v
provisiones ① pl pro·vee·*syo*·nes provisions
próximo/a ⓜ/① *prok*·see·mo/a
  following · next
proyector ⓜ pro·yek·*tor* projector
prueba ① *prwe*·ba test
  — de embarazo de em·ba·*ra*·so
    pregnancy test kit
  — de sangre de *san*·gre blood test
pruebas nucleares ① pl
  prwe·bas noo·kle·*a*·res nuclear testing
pueblo ⓜ *pwe*·blo village
puente ⓜ *pwen*·te bridge (structure)
puerta ① *pwer*·ta door · gate (airport, etc)
  — de salida de sa·*lee*·da departure gate
puerto ⓜ *pwer*·to harbour · port
pulga ① *pool*·ga flea
pulmón ⓜ pool·*mon* lung
punto de control ⓜ *poon*·to de kon·*trol*
  checkpoint (border)
puro/a ⓜ/① *poo*·ro/a pure

Q

qiropráctico ⓜ kee·ro·*prak*·tee·ko
  chiropractor
qué ke what
quebrado/a ⓜ/① ke·*bra*·do/a broken
quebrar ke·*brar* break (in general) v
quedarse ke·*dar*·se stay
  — varado va·*ra*·do break down (car)
queja ① *ke*·kha complaint
quejarse ke·*khar*·se complain
quemado/a ⓜ/① ke·*ma*·do/a burnt
quemadura ① ke·ma·*doo*·ra burn
  — de sol de sol sunburn
queque ⓜ *ke*·ke cake
querer ke·*rer* want
quién kyen who
quincena ① keen·*se*·na fortnight
quiosco ⓜ *kyos*·ko kiosk
quiste en los ovarios ⓜ
  kees·te en los o·*va*·ryos ovarian cyst

R

rabia ① *ra*·bya rabies
racismo ⓜ ra·*sees*·mo racism
radiador ⓜ ra·dya·*dor* radiator
radio ⓜ *ra*·dyo spoke (wheel)
radio ① *ra*·dyo radio
rancio/a ⓜ/① *ran*·syo/a stale
rápido/a ⓜ/① *ra*·pee·do/a fast
raqueta ① ra·*ke*·ta racquet
raro/a ⓜ/① *ra*·ro/a rare · strange · unusual
rasuradora ① ra·soo·ra·*do*·ra razor
rasurar ra·soo·*rar* shave v
rata ① *ra*·ta rat
ratón ⓜ ra·*ton* mouse (animal)
razón ① ra·*son* reason
realista ⓜ&① re·a·*lees*·ta realistic
receta ① re·*se*·ta prescription (medical)
recibo ⓜ re·*see*·bo receipt
reciclable ⓜ&① re·see·*kla*·ble recyclable
reciclar re·see·*klar* recycle
recientemente re·syen·te·*men*·te recently
reclamo de equipaje ⓜ
  re·*kla*·mo de e·kee·*pa*·khe baggage claim
recomendar re·ko·men·*dar* recommend
recto/a ⓜ/① *rek*·to/a straight
recuerdo ⓜ re·*kwer*·do souvenir
recursos humanos ⓜ pl
  re·*koor*·sos oo·*ma*·nos human resources
red ① red net · network (phone/Internet)
redondo/a ⓜ/① re·*don*·do/a round
referencia ① re·fe·*ren*·sya reference
reflexología ① re·flek·so·lo·*khee*·a
  reflexology
refresco ⓜ re·*fres*·ko soft drink
refri ⓜ *re*·free refrigerator
refugiado/a ⓜ/① re·foo·*khya*·do/a refugee
regalo ⓜ re·*ga*·lo gift
  — de bodas de *bo*·das wedding present
regional ⓜ&① re·khyo·*nal* regional
registro del carro ⓜ re·*khees*·tro del *ka*·ro
  car registration
regla ① *re*·gla menstruation · rule
reina ① *ray*·na queen
reintegro ⓜ re·een·te·*gro* refund
reír re·*eer* laugh v
relación ① re·la·*syon* relationship
relaciones públicas ① pl
  re·la·*syo*·nes *poo*·blee·kas public relations
relajarse re·la·*khar*·se relax
religión ① re·lee·*khyon* religion
religioso/a ⓜ/① re·lee·*khyo*·so/a religious
reliquia ① re·*lee*·kya relic
reloj ⓜ re·*lokh* clock · watch
  — despertador des·per·ta·*dor* alarm clock

remo ⓜ *re·*mo *rowing*
remoto/a ⓜ/ⓕ *re·*mo·to/a *remote*
reo/a ⓜ/ⓕ *re·*o/a *prisoner*
reparar re·pa·rar *repair*
repelente ⓜ re·pe·len·te *insect repellent*
repisa ⓕ re·pee·sa *shelf*
república ⓕ re·poo·blee·ka *republic*
reservación ⓕ re·ser·va·syon *reservation (booking)*
reservar re·ser·var *book (make a booking)*
resorte ⓜ re·sor·te *spring (coil)*
responder res·pon·der *answer* ⓥ
respuesta ⓕ res·pwes·ta *answer*
restaurante ⓜ res·tow·ran·te *restaurant*
retirado/a ⓜ/ⓕ re·tee·ra·do/a *retired*
revisar re·vee·sar *check* ⓥ
revisión ⓕ re·vee·syon *review*
revista ⓕ re·vees·ta *magazine*
revuelto/a ⓜ/ⓕ re·vwel·to/a *scrambled (eggs)*
rey ⓜ ray *king*
rico/a ⓜ/ⓕ ree·ko/a *rich • tasty • wealthy*
riesgo ⓜ ryes·go *risk*
riñón ⓜ ree·nyon *kidney*
río ⓜ ree·o *river*
ritmo ⓜ reet·mo *rhythm*
robado/a ⓜ/ⓕ ro·ba·do/a *stolen*
robar ro·bar *steal*
robo ⓜ ro·bo *rip-off*
rodilla ⓕ ro·dee·ya *knee*
rojo/a ⓜ/ⓕ ro·kho/a *red*
rollo ⓜ ro·yo *film (for camera)*
romántico/a ⓜ/ⓕ ro·man·tee·ko/a *romantic* n&a
romper rom·per *break (smash)*
ron ⓜ ron *rum*
ronda ⓕ ron·da *round (drinks)*
ropa ⓕ ro·pa *clothing • laundry*
— **de cama** de ka·ma *bedding*
— **interior** een·te·ryor *underwear*
rosado/a ⓜ/ⓕ ro·sa·do/a *pink*
rotonda ⓕ ro·ton·da *roundabout*
rubéola ⓕ roo·be·o·la *rubella*
rueda ⓕ rwe·da *wheel*
ruidoso/a ⓜ/ⓕ rwee·do·so/a *noisy*
ruinas ⓕ pl rwee·nas *ruins*
ruta ⓕ roo·ta *route*

S

sábado ⓜ sa·ba·do *Saturday*
sábana ⓕ sa·ba·na *sheet (bed)*
sábanas ⓕ pl sa·ba·nas *linen (sheets)*
saber sa·ber *know (something)*
sacacorchos ⓜ sa·ka·kor·chos *corkscrew*

saco de dormir ⓜ sa·ko de dor·meer *sleeping bag*
sal ⓕ sal *salt*
sala de espera ⓕ sa·la de es·pe·ra *waiting room*
salario ⓜ sa·la·ryo *salary*
saldo ⓜ sal·do *balance (account)*
salida ⓕ sa·lee·da *departure • exit*
— **de noche** de no·che *night out*
salir sa·leer *go out*
— **con** kon *go out with (date)*
salón de belleza ⓜ sa·lon de be·ye·sa *beauty salon*
salpullido ⓜ sal·poo·yee·do *nappy rash*
salsa ⓕ sal·sa *sauce*
saltar sal·tar *jump* ⓥ
salud ⓕ sa·lood *health*
sangre ⓕ san·gre *blood*
santo/a ⓜ/ⓕ san·to/a *saint*
santuario ⓜ san·too·a·ryo *shrine*
sarampión ⓜ sa·ram·pyon *measles*
sartén ⓜ sar·ten *frying pan*
sastre ⓜ sas·tre *tailor*
secar se·kar *dry (clothes, etc)* ⓥ
secarse se·kar·se *dry (oneself)* ⓥ
seco/a ⓜ/ⓕ se·ko/a *dried • dry*
secretario/a ⓜ/ⓕ se·kre·ta·ryo/a *secretary*
seda ⓕ se·da *silk*
seguir se·geer *follow*
segunda clase ⓕ se·goon·da kla·se *second class*
segundo ⓜ se·goon·do *second (time unit)*
segundo/a ⓜ/ⓕ se·goon·do/a *second (number)*
seguro ⓜ se·goo·ro *insurance*
seguro/a ⓜ/ⓕ se·goo·ro/a *safe*
semáforo ⓜ se·ma·fo·ro *traffic light*
semana ⓕ se·ma·na *week*
sencillo/a ⓜ/ⓕ sen·see·yo/a *simple*
sendero ⓜ sen·de·ro *footpath • hiking route*
— **de bicicleta** de bee·see·kle·ta *bike trail*
senos ⓜ pl se·nos *breasts (body)*
sensible ⓜ&ⓕ sen·see·ble *sensible*
sensual ⓜ&ⓕ sen·swal *sensual*
sentarse sen·tar·se *sit*
sentimientos ⓜ pl seen·tee·myen·tos *feelings*
sentir sen·teer *feel (emotions)*
señal ⓕ se·nyal *sign*
señalar se·nya·lar *point* ⓥ
separado/a ⓜ/ⓕ se·pa·ra·do/a *separate*
septiembre ⓜ sep·tyem·bre *September*
ser ser *be (permanent)*
serio/a ⓜ/ⓕ se·ryo/a *serious*
servicio ⓜ ser·vee·syo *service • service charge*
— **militar** mee·lee·tar *military service*

servilleta ① ser·vee·ye·ta *serviette*
sesión de ejercicios ①
se·*syon* de e·kher·*see*·syos *workout*
sexismo ⑩ sek·*sees*·mo *sexism*
sexo ⑩ *sek*·so *sex*
— **seguro** se·*goo*·ro *safe sex*
si see *if*
sí see *yes*
SIDA ⑩ *see*·da *AIDS*
siempre *syem*·pre *always*
silla ① *see*·ya *chair*
— **de comer para niños**
de ko·*mer* pa·ra *nee*·nyos *highchair*
— **de ruedas** de *rwe*·da *wheelchair*
— **para niños** pa·ra *nee*·nyos *child seat*
similar ⑩&① see·mee·*lar similar*
sin seen *without*
— **espacio** es·*pa*·syo *booked out*
— **plomo** *plo*·mo *unleaded (petrol)*
sinagoga ① see·na·*go*·ga *synagogue*
sintético/a ⑩/① seen·*te*·tee·ko/a *synthetic*
sobornar so·bor·*nar bribe* v
soborno ⑩ so·*bor*·no *bribe*
sobre *so*·bre *about* • *above* • *on*
sobre ⑩ *so*·bre *envelope*
sobredosis ① so·bre·*do*·sees *overdose*
socado/a ⑩/① so·*ka*·do/a *tight*
socialista ⑩&① so·sya·*lees*·ta *socialist* n&a
sol ⑩ sol *sun*
solamente so·la·*men*·te *only*
soldado ⑩ sol·*da*·do *soldier*
soleado/a ⑩/① so·le·*a*·do/a *sunny*
sólo *so*·lo *only*
solo/a ⑩/① *so*·lo/a *alone*
soltero/a ⑩/① sol·*te*·ro/a *single (person)*
sombra ① *som*·bra *shade* • *shadow*
sombrero ⑩ som·*bre*·ro *hat*
sombrilla ① som·*bree*·ya *umbrella*
sonreír son·re·*eer smile* v
sopa ① *so*·pa *soup*
sordo/a ⑩/① *sor*·do/a *deaf*
sorpresa ① sor·*pre*·sa *surprise*
su soo *her* • *his* • *their* • *your* sg pol&pl
subtítulos ⑩ pl soob·*tee*·too·los *subtitles*
suburbio ⑩ soo·*boor*·byo *suburb*
sucio/a ⑩/① *soo*·syo/a *dirty*
suegra ① *swe*·gra *mother-in-law*
suegro ⑩ *swe*·gro *father-in-law*
suelo ⑩ *swe*·lo *floor (ground)*
sueño ⑩ *swe*·nyo *dream* • *sleep*
suerte ① *swer*·te *luck*
suéter ⑩ *swe*·ter *jumper* • *sweater*
suficiente soo·fee·*syen*·te *enough*
súper ⑩ *soo*·per *convenience store*
supermercado ⑩ soo·per·mer·*ka*·do
supermarket

superstición ① soo·per·stee·*syon*
superstition
sur ⑩ soor *south*
surf ⑩ soorf *surfing*
surfear soor·fe·*ar surf* v

T

tabaco ⑩ ta·*ba*·ko *tobacco*
tabaquería ① ta·ba·ke·*ree*·a *tobacconist*
tabla de surf ① *ta*·bla de soorf *surfboard*
tabla para picar ① *ta*·bla pa·ra pee·*kar*
chopping board
tajada ① ta·*kha*·da *slice*
talcos ⑩ pl *tal*·kos *baby powder*
taller ⑩ ta·*yer workshop*
tal vez tal ves *maybe*
tamaño ⑩ ta·*ma*·nyo *size (general)*
también tam·*byen also* • *too*
tambor ⑩ tam·*bor drum (instrument)*
tampón ⑩ tam·*pon tampon*
tapón ⑩ ta·*pon plug (bath)*
tapones para los oídos ⑩ pl
ta·*po*·nes pa·ra los o·*ee*·dos *earplugs*
tarde ① *tar*·de *afternoon*
tarde *tar*·de *late* adv
tarifa ① ta·*ree*·fa *fare*
tarjeta ① tar·*khe*·ta *card*
— **de crédito** de *kre*·dee·to *credit card*
— **de memoria** de me·*mo*·rya
memory card
— **de teléfono** de te·*le*·fo·no *phone card*
— **SIM** seem *SIM card*
taxi ⑩ *tak*·see *taxi*
taza ① *ta*·sa *cup*
té ⑩ te *tea*
teatro ⑩ te·*a*·tro *theatre*
teclado ⑩ te·*kla*·do *keyboard*
técnica ① *tek*·nee·ka *technique*
tela ① *te*·la *fabric*
teleférico ⑩ te·le·*fe*·ree·ko *cable car*
teléfono ⑩ te·*le*·fo·no *telephone*
— **celular** se·loo·*lar* cell/*mobile phone*
— **público** *poo*·blee·ko *public phone*
telegrama ⑩ te·le·*gra*·ma *telegram*
telescopio ⑩ te·les·*ko*·pyo *telescope*
televisión ① te·le·vee·*syon television*
televisor ⑩ te·le·vee·*sor* TV
temperatura ① tem·pe·ra·*too*·ra
temperature (weather)
templo ⑩ *tem*·plo *temple (building)*
temporada ① tem·po·*ra*·da *season*
temprano tem·*pra*·no *early* adv
tendedero ⑩ ten·de·*de*·ro *clothesline*
tenedor ⑩ te·ne·*dor fork*
tener te·*ner have*
— **sed** sed *be thirsty*
— **sueño** *swe*·nyo *be sleepy*

tenis ⓜ *te·*nees *tennis*
— **de mesa** de *me·*sa *table tennis*
tensión premenstrual ⓕ ten·*syon* pre·mens·*trwal premenstrual tension*
tercero/a ⓜ/ⓕ ter·se·ro/a *third*
terco/a ⓜ/ⓕ *ter·*ko/a *stubborn*
terminar ter·mee·*nar finish* v
termo ⓜ *ter·*mo *hot water bottle*
ternera ⓕ ter·*ne·*ra *veal*
terremoto ⓜ te·re·*mo·*to *earthquake*
terrible ⓜ&ⓕ te·*ree·*ble *terrible*
terrorismo ⓜ te·ro·*rees·*mo *terrorism*
ti tee *you* sg inf
tía ⓕ *tee·*a *aunt*
tibio/a ⓜ/ⓕ *tee·*byo/a *warm*
tiempo ⓜ *tyem·*po *time • weather*
— **completo** kom·*ple·*to *full-time*
— **parcial** par·*syal part-time*
tienda ⓕ *tyen·*da *shop*
— **de artículos usados** de ar·*tee·*koo·los oo·*sa·*dos *secondhand shop*
— **de cámaras** de *ka·*ma·ras *camera shop*
— **de campaña** de kam·*pa·*nya *tent*
— **de electrónicos** de e·lek·*tro·*nee·kos *electrical store*
— **de música** de *moo·*see·ka *music shop*
— **de recuerdos** de re·*kwer·*dos *souvenir shop*
— **de ropa** de *ro·*pa *clothing store*
— **deportiva** de·por·*tee·*va *sports store*
— **por departamentos** por de·par·ta·*men·*tos *department store*
tierno/a ⓜ/ⓕ *tyer·*no/a *soft-boiled (eggs)*
tierra ⓕ *tye·*ra *Earth • land*
tifoidea ⓕ tee·foy·*de·*a *typhoid*
tijeras ⓕ pl tee·*khe·*ras *scissors*
timbre ⓜ *teem·*bre *ring (phone)*
tímido/a ⓜ/ⓕ *tee·*mee·do/a *shy*
tío ⓜ *tee·*o *uncle*
típico/a ⓜ/ⓕ *tee·*pee·ko/a *typical*
tipo ⓜ *tee·*po *type*
— **de cambio** de *kam·*byo *exchange rate*
tiquete ⓜ tee·*ke·*te *ticket*
— **de abordaje** de a·bor·*da·*khe *boarding pass*
— **de ida** de *ee·*da *one-way ticket*
— **de ida y vuelta** de *ee·*da ee *vwel·*ta *return ticket*
— **de stand-by** de stan·*bai stand-by ticket*
título de propiedad ⓜ *tee·*too·lo de pro·pye·*dad car owner's title*
toalla sanitaria ⓕ to·*a·*ya sa·nee·*ta·*rya *sanitary napkin*
toallita ⓕ to·a·*yee·*ta *wash cloth (flannel)*
tobillo ⓜ to·*bee·*yo *ankle*
tocar to·*kar touch • play (instrument)*

todavía (no) to·da·*vee·*a (no) *(not) yet*
todo *to·*do *everything*
todo/a ⓜ/ⓕ *to·*do/a *all • every*
todos/as ⓜ/ⓕ pl *to·*dos/as *everyone*
todos los días *to·*dos los *dee·*as *every day*
tomar to·*mar take • drink*
— **una foto** *oo·*na *fo·*to *take a photo*
tono ⓜ *to·*no *dial tone*
tormenta ⓕ tor·*men·*ta *storm*
— **eléctrica** e·*lek·*tree·ka *thunderstorm*
torre ⓕ *to·*re *tower*
tos ⓕ tos *cough*
toser to·*ser cough* v
tostada ⓕ tos·*ta·*da *toast (food)*
tostador ⓜ tos·ta·*dor toaster*
tour ⓜ toor *tour*
— **con guía** kon *gee·*a *guided tour*
trabajador(a) ⓜ/ⓕ tra·ba·kha·*dor/* tra·ba·kha·*do·*ra *labourer • worker*
trabajar tra·ba·*khar work* v
trabajo ⓜ tra·*ba·*kho *work*
— **temporal** tem·po·*ral casual work*
traducir tra·doo·*seer translate*
traductor(a) ⓜ/ⓕ tra·dook·*tor/*tra·dook·*to·*ra *translator*
traer tra·*er bring*
trago ⓜ *tra·*go *alcoholic drink*
tramposo/a ⓜ/ⓕ tram·po·*so/*a *cheat*
tránsito ⓜ *tran·*see·to *traffic*
transporte ⓜ trans·*por·*te *transport*
tranvía ⓜ tran·*vee·*a *tram*
trasero ⓜ tra·*se·*ro *bottom (body)*
tratar tra·*tar try (attempt)*
tren ⓜ tren *train*
triste ⓜ&ⓕ *trees·*te *sad*
trompeta ⓕ trom·*pe·*ta *trumpet*
trotar ⓜ tro·*tar jogging*
tu too *your* sg inf
tú too *you* sg inf
tubo ⓜ *too·*bo *faucet • tap*
— **interno** een·*ter·*no *inner tube (tyre)*
tumba ⓕ *toom·*ba *grave*
tumor ⓜ too·*mor tumour*
turista ⓜ&ⓕ too·*rees·*ta *tourist*

U

último/a ⓜ/ⓕ *ool·*tee·mo/a *last (final)*
ultrasonido ⓜ ool·tra·so·*nee·*do *ultrasound*
una vez *oo·*na ves *once*
uniforme ⓜ oo·nee·*for·*me *uniform*
universidad ⓕ oo·nee·ver·see·*dad university*
universo ⓜ oo·nee·*ver·*so *universe*
uno/a ⓜ/ⓕ *oo·*no/a *one* n&a
urgente ⓜ&ⓕ oor·*khen·*te *urgent*

usado/a ⓜ/ⓕ oo-*sa*-do/a *secondhand*
usted oos-*ted* *you* sg pol
ustedes oos-*te*-des *you* pl
útil ⓜ&ⓕ *oo*-teel *useful*

V

vaca ⓕ *va*-ka *cow*
vacación ⓕ va-ka-*syon* *holidays • vacation*
vacilón/vacilona ⓜ/ⓕ
  va-see-*lon*/va-see-*lo*-na *funny*
vacío/a ⓜ/ⓕ va-*see*-o/a *empty*
vacunación ⓕ va-koo-na-*syon* *vaccination*
vagina ⓕ va-*khee*-na *vagina*
validar va-lee-*dar* *validate*
valiente ⓜ&ⓕ va-*lyen*-te *brave*
valija ⓕ va-*lee*-kha *briefcase*
valioso/a ⓜ/ⓕ va-*lyo*-so/a *valuable*
valle ⓜ *va*-ye *valley*
valor ⓜ va-*lor* *value (price)*
van ⓜ van *van*
varicela ⓕ va-ree-*se*-la *chicken pox*
varios/as ⓜ/ⓕ pl *va*-ryos/as *several*
vasija ⓕ va-*see*-kha *pot (ceramics)*
vaso ⓜ *va*-so *glass (drinking)*
vegetal ⓜ ve-khe-*tal* *vegetable*
vegetariano/a ⓜ/ⓕ ve-khe-ta-*rya*-no/a
  vegetarian n&a
vejiga ⓕ ve-*khee*-ga *bladder*
vela ⓕ *ve*-la *candle*
velocidad ⓕ ve-lo-see-*dad* *speed (travel)*
velocímetro ⓜ ve-lo-*see*-me-tro
  speedometer
vena ⓕ *ve*-na *vein*
vendaje ⓜ ven-*da*-khe *bandage*
vendedor de pescado ⓜ
  ven-de-*dor* de pes-*ka*-do *fishmonger*
vender ven-*der* *sell*
venenoso/a ⓜ/ⓕ ve-ne-*no*-so/a *poisonous*
venir ve-*neer* *come*
venta de periódicos ⓕ
  ven-ta de pe-*ryo*-dee-kos *newsstand*
ventana ⓕ ven-*ta*-na *window*
ventanilla ⓕ ven-ta-*nee*-ya *ticket office*
ventilador ⓜ ven-tee-la-*dor* *fan (machine)*
ver ver *look • see*
verano ⓜ ve-*ra*-no *summer*
verde ⓜ&ⓕ *ver*-de *green*
verdurería ⓕ ver-doo-re-*ree*-a *greengrocer*
vestíbulo ⓜ ves-*tee*-boo-lo *foyer*
vestido ⓜ ves-*tee*-do *dress*
  — de baño de *ba*-nyo *bathing suit*

vestidores ⓜ pl ves-tee-*do*-res
  changing room
viajar vya-*khar* *travel*
viaje ⓜ *vya*-khe *journey*
vid ⓕ veed *vine*
vida ⓕ *vee*-da *life*
viejo/a ⓜ/ⓕ *vye*-kho/a *old (age)*
viento ⓜ *vyen*-to *wind*
viernes ⓜ *vyer*-nes *Friday*
VIH ⓜ la ee *a*-che *HIV*
vinagre ⓜ vee-*na*-gre *vinegar*
vino ⓜ *vee*-no *wine*
viñedo ⓜ vee-*nye*-do *vineyard*
violación ⓕ vyo-la-*syon* *rape*
violar vyo-*lar* *rape* v
violín ⓜ vee-o-*leen* *violin*
virus ⓜ *vee*-roos *virus*
visa ⓕ *vee*-sa *visa*
visita ⓕ vee-*see*-ta *visit*
vista ⓕ *vees*-ta *view*
vitaminas ⓕ pl vee-ta-*mee*-nas *vitamins*
vivir vee-*veer* *live*
volar vo-*lar* *fly* v
volcán ⓜ vol-*kan* *volcano*
volibol ⓜ vo-lee-*bol* *volleyball*
  — de playa de *pla*-ya *beach volleyball*
volumen ⓜ vo-*loo*-men *volume*
volver vol-*ver* *return*
vos vos *you* sg inf
votar vo-*tar* *vote* v
voz ⓕ vos *voice*
vuelo ⓜ *vwe*-lo *flight*
vuelto ⓜ *vwel*-to *change (coins)*

Y

y ee *and*
ya ya *already*
yo yo *I*

Z

zacate ⓜ sa-*ka*-te *grass (lawn)*
zancudo ⓜ san-*koo*-do *mosquito*
zapatería ⓕ sa-pa-te-*ree*-a *shoe shop*
zapato ⓜ sa-*pa*-to *shoe*
zodíaco ⓜ so-*dee*-a-ko *zodiac*
zoológico ⓜ so-o-*lo*-khee-ko *zoo*
zorzal ⓜ sor-*sal* *thrush (health)*

FINDER

The topics covered in this book are listed below in Spanish. Show this page to your Costa Rican friends if you're having trouble understanding them.

FINDER

253

don't just stand there, say something!

What kind of traveller are you?

A. You're eating chicken for dinner *again* because it's the only word you know.

B. When no one understands what you say, you step closer and shout louder.

C. When the barman doesn't understand your order, you point frantically at the beer.

D. You're surrounded by locals, swapping jokes, email addresses and experiences – other travellers want to borrow your phrasebook.

If you answered A, B, or C, you NEED Lonely Planet's phrasebooks.

- **Talk to everyone everywhere**
  Over 120 languages, more than any other publisher

- **The right words at the right time**
  Quick-reference colour sections, two-way dictionary, easy pronunciation, every possible subject

- **Lonely Planet Fast Talk** – essential language for short trips and weekends away

- **Lonely Planet Phrasebooks** – for every phrase you need in every language you want

'Best for curious and independent travellers' – *Wall Street Journal*

Lonely Planet Offices

Australia
90 Maribyrnong St, Footscray,
Victoria 3011
☎ 03 8379 8000
fax 03 8379 8111
✉ talk2us@lonelyplanet.com.au

USA
150 Linden St, Oakland,
CA 94607
☎ 510 893 8555
fax 510 893 8572
✉ info@lonelyplanet.com

UK
72-82 Rosebery Ave,
London EC1R 4RW
☎ 020 7841 9000
fax 020 7841 9001
✉ go@lonelyplanet.co.uk

www.lonelyplanet.com